LIS Career
Sourcebook

LIS Career Sourcebook

Managing and Maximizing
Every Step of Your Career

G. KIM DORITY

LIBRARIES UNLIMITED

AN IMPRINT OF ABC-CLIO, LLC
Santa Barbara, California • Denver, Colorado • Oxford, England

Library of Congress Cataloging-in-Publication Data

Dority, G. Kim, 1950–
  LIS career sourcebook : managing and maximizing every step of your career / G. Kim Dority.
       pages cm
  Includes bibliographical references and index.
  ISBN 978-1-59884-931-8 (pbk.) — ISBN 978-1-59884-932-5 (ebook) (print) 1. Library science—Vocational guidance—United States. 2. Library science—Vocational guidance—Canada. 3. Information science—Vocational guidance—United States. 4. Information science—Vocational guidance—Canada. 5. Library education—United States. 6. Library education—Canada. I. Title.
  Z682.35.V62D66 2012
  020.23'73—dc23   2012025250

ISBN: 978-1-59884-931-8
EISBN: 978-1-59884-932-5

16 15 14 13 12   1 2 3 4 5

This book is also available on the World Wide Web as an eBook. Visit www.abc-clio.com for details.

Libraries Unlimited
An Imprint of ABC-CLIO, LLC

ABC-CLIO, LLC
130 Cremona Drive, P.O. Box 1911
Santa Barbara, California 93116-1911

This book is printed on acid-free paper ∞

Manufactured in the United States of America

This book is dedicated to the students I have had the privilege to teach over the past ten years in my University of Denver MLIS Alternative LIS Careers course. I have learned so much from you.

Contents

Acknowledgments

One of the unique joys of working as a library and information science (LIS) professional is the extraordinarily collaborative, supportive nature of the profession. Students, colleagues, fellow discussion group members, teachers, professional association members you connect with online, people you meet at a conference—all become part of the rich mix of knowledge and insights we share with each other over the course of a career.

This book is just such a collaborative effort, and for that I would like to thank Libraries Unlimited Acquisitions Editor Barbara Ittner for proposing the idea for this book; the members of the LinkedIn LIS Career Options group who have shared so generously their experiences, insights, and information with all of us; the University of Denver students I have had the privilege to work with over the past 10 years in my Alternative LIS Careers course; and the support and encouragement of three colleagues who daily inspire me with the possibilities of this profession: Mary Ellen Bates, Marcy Phelps, and Scott Brown.

Introduction

The rumors of my death have been
greatly exaggerated.

—Mark Twain

Trying to chart a career path in today's library and information science (LIS) universe is, to say the least, challenging; trying to figure out what things are going to look like 10 or 20 years down the road, pretty near impossible. But to quote Amazon founder Jeff Bezos, "We're stubborn on vision and flexible on the details." When it comes to your LIS career, it's going to pay to be committed to your goals, but flexible on how (and when) you get there.

Here's what we know: the nature, mission, and services of traditional libraries are being fundamentally restructured in response to changing user needs, technology advances, demographic changes, and budget impacts, to name but a few of the trends driving change among traditional libraries. Similarly, the nature of special librarianship is in flux, with some types of special library work contracting while others are increasing in demand. In addition, the range of information necessary to create, manage, and distribute content for companies with an online presence is growing exponentially. Bottom line: LIS jobs will most definitely be available, they just may look a bit different than you were expecting.

Nevertheless, it's likely that your career will probably follow some pretty predictable growth points. You'll need to decide what kind of professional education choices best support your career goals (at least for the time being). You'll face the challenge of job hunting. You'll go through that adventure known as being the new person on the job and trying to figure out how to contribute (and how to get the copier to work).

Once you've figured out the copier and become a valued team member, you'll start thinking about growing your skill set. You'll also be growing your professional community and establishing your professional reputation.

You may then find yourself moving into management and possibly into a leadership position. Or you may decide the independent path of information entrepreneurship is for you.

And as you work through these steps in your career, you're also likely to have any number of side trips, transitions that take you in a different direction for a time—or permanently. These can be taking time out for family commitments, relocating, moving into a new career direction, losing a job (pretty much a rite of passage for all of us), or even retiring. The really terrific news: if you have an attitude that embraces flexibility and resiliency, the LIS career you've chosen can mirror that flexibility and resiliency.

The ideas, recommendations, and resources included here are intended to help you navigate these key career growth points. Some are drawn from the LIS field, but many others are from other disciplines, for example, business or psychology or social media. My goal has been to place LIS work in the broader context within which it often operates, while also drawing on the best resources, regardless of the audience for which they were initially intended.

I have purposely not included (for the most part) general library blogs, Twitter feeds, Facebook groups, and Yahoo and Google groups for two reasons: the first is that there is such an astounding number of really high-quality LIS resources among these that it would be impossible to include them all but also unacceptable to exclude any. The second is that I have tried to keep the focus of the book on LIS career-related resources and topics rather than on the resources that enable you to do your LIS work. However, I would like to emphasize how important these tools are for continuing to grow your knowledge, network, and professional brand. I would encourage you to consider the online social tools relevant to your professional interests to be an important part of your continued career development.

Regardless of which LIS career path(s) you choose, I believe you have chosen a profession of expanding opportunities, even though those opportunities may not be the ones you'd originally envisioned. Perhaps the best way to approach such a dynamic professional universe is to keep in mind author Henry Miller's wise words, "All growth is a leap in the dark, a spontaneous unpremeditated act without the benefit of experience." Happily, you have many friends, colleagues, and resources to help you successfully make those leaps.

1
The LIS
Career Universe

Library and information science (LIS) careers range across a broad and constantly changing landscape of types of work, knowledge and skill sets, employers (or clients), and job structures. In fact, trying to get a handle on the vast range of ways a Master of Library and Information Science (MLIS) degree can be deployed can prove immensely challenging.

How challenging? Consider these examples of LIS work:

- school librarian for traditional, charter, or online high school
- cataloger for public library
- bibliographic instructor for academic library (campus-based or on-line, traditional or private sector, research university or community college)
- embedded librarian for a federal agency
- corporate librarian for a *Fortune 500* company
- information and web manager for community nonprofit

- records manager for media company
- independent researcher for healthcare management industry
- technical documentalist for Cirque du Soleil
- prospect researcher for philanthropic foundation
- metadata specialist for major Internet player (think Google)
- taxonomist for content-focused start-up
- archivist for a state historical society
- digital asset manager for multi-state law firm
- information architect for web development company
- database designer for green technology engineering firm
- knowledge manager for local economic development organization
- independent information professional specializing in patent research
- literacy specialist for ESL populations

These positions and titles represent a very small selection of the stunning diversity of roles to be found among LIS professionals. Needless to say, this can make it a bit challenging when it comes to exploring—let alone choosing—an LIS career path. On the other hand, that very vastness of career options is one of the true benefits of having an MLIS degree and its accompanying skill set.

Framing Your Career Options

Nevertheless, if you're thinking about a career based on library and/or information skills, it helps to have some ways to frame your choices—so you at least have a starting point! The following categories of options may help you identify which one(s) might be of greatest interest to you.

Traditional

Although anyone who works in traditional libraries will tell you there's pretty much nothing traditional about the work they're doing these days, the profession generally uses this term to denote jobs in school, public, and academic libraries. Examples might include

- being a school librarian in a public, private, or charter K–12 school,
- being a public librarian in a large urban library or a small rural library, and
- being an academic librarian in a community college, four-year, public or private, for-profit or not-for-profit, online on campus-based college or university.

Although jobs in traditional libraries haven't been as plentiful as the profession (and recent graduates) would hope, there are still jobs available.

The likelihood, however, is that they may start out at a paraprofessional or part-time level, they may require relocating, and they may start at lower salaries than desirable. At this point it's not clear how these trends may play out in the coming years, but it's probable that the traditional library job market will continue to be pretty competitive.

In addition to the American Library Association (ALA) and the Canadian Library Association (CLA), the associations most closely aligned with traditional library career paths are the American Association of School Librarianship (AASL) and Canadian Association for School Libraries (CASL), the Public Library Association (PLA), the Young Adult Library Services Association (YALSA), the Association for Library Service to Children (ALSC), Canadian Association of Public Libraries (CAPL), the Association of College and Research Libraries (ACRL), and the Canadian Association of College and University Libraries (CACUL). Each of these associations offers valuable career-related information on its website, and the ALA site in particular offers useful data and profiles for US-based library careers under its *Education & Careers > Careers in Librarianship* section.

Library-Related

These types of jobs involve working with the library profession, but not necessarily in a librarian role. For example, these could be positions with regional consortia, the state library, vendors, or perhaps one of the LIS media companies. Examples might include

- doing product development for Cengage, a learning-solutions, training, and educational publishing company,
- recruiting for LAC, a California-based national LIS placement and staffing firm,
- being a sales rep for Baker & Taylor, distributor of physical and digital content to libraries,
- writing for *EContent* magazine, and
- being a client systems trainer for Lyrasis, a regional membership organization for libraries.

There is an exceptionally wide range of salaries for these types of jobs, depending on the size and type of organization as well as the work that you're performing. Generally speaking, however, it's safe to assume that a for-profit venture is going to pay higher salaries for your information skills (and library contacts).

A great way to get a sense of how many (think hundreds) library-focused vendors there are is to check out the online listing in the *Librarian's Yellow Pages.* This will give you a sense of both what the vendor categories are and the companies within the various categories. Another great way to learn more about library-related organizations is by checking out the annual *Library and Book Trade Almanac* (formerly *The Bowker Annual*), which is not only packed with statistical and trend information about libraries, but also provides an approximately 150-page Directory of Library and Related Organizations. Lastly, many of the trade publications identified in the resource section of Chapter 4 have several annual special sections that overview all of the players in a specific industry sector, for example, database providers.

Organization-Based

This is the traditional special library model, where an individual or a team of librarians acquires or licenses, organizes, distributes, and maintains information resources that support the strategic goals of the organization, including for-profits, nonprofits, and government agencies. Examples might include

- being the library director for a professional medical association,
- heading up the library for an alternative magazine,
- being the director of an engineering company's business information center,
- managing library services for the local botanical gardens, and
- being the head librarian for a Native American rights foundation.

Although the term *special libraries* is becoming a catch-all for an increasingly wide range of career paths, the three largest segments are corporate librarianship, law librarianship, and medical librarianship. The organizations that provide advocacy, information, and professional support to these groups are the Special Libraries Association (SLA) and its multiple special interest divisions and sections, the Canadian Association of Special Libraries and Information Services (CASLIS), the American Association of Law Libraries (AALL), the Canadian Association of Law Libraries (CALL), the Medical Library Association (MLA), and the Canadian Health Libraries Association (CHLA). However, there are additional special-interest special library groups, such as the Church and Synagogue Library Association (CSLA), the Art Libraries Society of North America (ARLIS), and the Major Orchestra Librarian's Association (MOLA), to name a few. When in doubt, type "library association" and your key phrase into any search engine to see if there's a group that aligns with your career interests.

Embedded Librarianship

Another area of special librarianship is embedded librarianship. This type of LIS work entails deploying your information skills as part of an operational team or department within an organization, generally as an outpost of the corporate/organization library. Examples might include

- using the company Info Center's databases to do competitive intelligence as part of the business development team,

- working with the compliance department team to organize key legal department documents within the Info Center's intranet,
- joining one of the product development teams do market research for a proposed product, and
- working as the full-time patent research for the engineering department.

Embedded librarianship is a role that is evolving, but promises to provide career opportunities for information professionals with strong business knowledge who might otherwise have been working within the corporate information center. From a job security standpoint, this type of work demonstrates every day the value of the skills contributed, and is much less likely to be seen (and budget cut) as overhead than is a centralized information center staffed with multiple LIS professionals.

The best resource for information about this emerging career path is David Shumaker's *Embedded Librarian* blog and his book, *The Embedded Librarian: Innovative Strategies for Taking Knowledge Where It's Needed.* A faculty member at Catholic University of America's School of Library and Information Science, Shumaker pioneered embedded librarianship while at MITRE Corporation, so brings both an academic and practitioner viewpoint to the topic.

Information Skills Work, Not Connected to an Organization Library

The major skills areas in this category are an ability to research (including analysis and synthesis), an ability to organize information (from metadata to taxonomies to information architecture), an ability to design and execute information systems (websites, intranets, business intelligence dashboards, etc.), and/or an ability to create content. Examples might include

- doing prospect or donor research for a nonprofit,
- creating inventory taxonomies,
- establishing a trade association archive,
- designing and building management information systems (MIS), and
- researching, writing, and then promoting web-posted position papers via social media for a political candidate.

Generally, the information resources and organizations related to these types of career paths are as numerous as the career options themselves (and not necessarily related to the library profession). So, for example, prospect researchers might belong to and follow the best-practice guidelines of APRA (although they don't reveal the meaning of the acronym these days, it's basically the prospect researchers' association).

Taxonomists might belong to the Taxonomies and Controlled Vocabularies special interest group (SIG) of the American Society for Indexing or read Heather Hedden's excellent *Accidental Taxonomist*. All types of archivists would want the knowledge of the Society of American Archivists (SAA) or the Association of Canadian Archivists supporting their work, whereas systems designers working on an MIS design would probably find the most collegial support (and relevant knowledge) among members of the American Society for Information Science & Technology (ASIST) or Canadian Association for Information Science (CAIS). Those dealing with documents and/or records management would gain most from being a member of ARMA or ARMA Canada, which are now broadening from their initial focus on records management to encompass legal and compliance responsibilities. Content developers, on the other hand, would want to be following Kristin Halvorson's *Brain Traffic* blog after having read, re-read, and extensively marked up her *Content Strategy for the Web*.

Bottom line: These types of work engagements typically move you well beyond the universe of library information resources, so it will be necessary for you to research the best information sources and professional groups to help keep your skills sharp (and get your questions answered) in these areas.

Transferable Non-LIS Skills Work

Many people develop basic business skills such as project management, people management, marketing, vendor licensing negotiation, and/or public relations while working in a traditional library setting. Because these skills are highly transferable into any organizational setting, they could provide the bridge for you to re-career into another profession should you so desire. Examples might include the following:

- A library director becoming executive director of a small nonprofit organization
- A district director becoming a city manager
- An instructional services librarian becoming a trainer for a tech start-up
- A school librarian becoming a tutor for a learning-services company

As with the previous type of work, the information for these career paths would very much depend on which direction you were taking your career. However, since this is such a *major* professional shift, you might want to check out one of the better books on re-careering, such as Pamela Mitchell's *The Ten Laws of Career Reinvention* or Barbara Sher and Barbara Smith's classic *I Could Do Anything If I Only Knew What It Was*.

Going Independent

All of the LIS skills that you can provide to an employer can also be provided to a client. Being self-employed involves offering an information-related product or service to customers or clients, whether on a project basis, ongoing contract, hourly engagement, product licensing, or some other financial arrangement (that enables you to pay your bills!). Examples might include the following:

- Providing competitive intelligence for clients
- Creating and selling subscriptions to an industry trends alerting service
- Doing contract book indexing for publishers
- Patent searching for pharmaceutical research and development (R&D) groups
- Creating information/content strategies for start-up web portals

The most important starting point for any type of independent information business, regardless of the type of product or service you might offer, is Mary Ellen Bates's *Building & Running a Successful Research Business: A Guide for the Independent Information Professional,* 2nd ed. Although it says research in the title, it's basically a great how-to guide for any information offering. The key association for independents is the Association of Independent Information Professionals (AIIP), although many AIIP members also belong to SLA or CASLIS for their subject-specific special interest groups. Many independents also belong to the Strategic and Competitive Intelligence Professionals (SCIP) organization. Patent researchers may want to consider membership in The International Society for Patent Information and its Patent Information Users Group, whereas independent indexers and abstractors will probably belong to the American Society for Indexing or the Indexing Society of Canada.

Who Needs What Information?

For each of the non-LIS types of work identified, it's important to understand how, in general, organizations (both for-profit and nonprofit) use information to achieve their goals. This lets you develop a clearer picture of where and how your skills will add value, and will also help you identify what roles may make the most of your information smarts, even if they don't say "librarian" or "information" in the job description.

Although every organization structures its operations a bit differently to fit its unique circumstances, market, and mission, generally speaking, their activities broadly fall into the major categories of creating a product or service, marketing/selling that product or service, and managing the ongoing operations (finance, legal, HR, etc.). Even nonprofits and libraries to some extent follow these same lines of responsibility. So keeping in mind that every organization is different, the following departmental descriptions should provide a very basic overview of the different types of activities that take place in organizations, and where your information skills might fit it.

Engineering, Product Development, and Production Teams

Responsible for developing the products an organization takes to market, these teams rely heavily on not only engineering skills but also project management, team collaboration, and often STEM (science, technology, engineering, and mathematics) research skills. They may work with product managers as well as sales and marketing staffers to gather user feedback, and also work with suppliers. These groups are held accountable for delivering products that meet technical and budget specifications; meeting production deadlines (for which project management tools and skills are invaluable); identifying and implementing best practices and processes to maximize their product's value to consumers while minimizing production costs; and managing supply-chain logistics ("supply chain" refers to the multiple vendors and interactions that go into providing the materials that make up the end product).

The types of information that would help these teams meet their responsibilities might include, for example, findings about best practices and performance benchmarks; vendor/provider/supplier background research, evaluations, comparisons; and alerts about recent advances in engineering and materials sciences.

Sales, Marketing, and Public Relations Teams

These are the folks who move that recently-created product into the hands of purchasers. The public relations (PR) team is responsible for creating a positive image of the company and its products/services in the minds of consumers, the marketing department is responsible for promoting interest in and desire for specific products through various channels (think advertising, social media, cool website content, etc.), and the sales team is charged with ensuring that consumers are actually purchasing those products in ever-increasing quantities. The sales and marketing people may work closely (or not) with their company's product developers, engineering and development, and finance (for product pricing issues) teams. In addition, public relations may either be part of the marketing group or a broader corporate communications team that includes product and service PR as well as community affairs, corporate outreach, crisis communication control, and so on.

Some of the activities these groups engage in include performing market research and market segmentation (of the 10 gazillion people in the world who *might* purchase this product, which two million represent the realistic, potential market segment *likely* to purchase—and why); creating and executing marketing and sales campaigns; documenting return-on-investment (ROI) of marketing campaigns (for every dollar spent on this marketing initiative, how much sales income resulted?); and setting and meeting sales goals. Marketing departments are also increasingly being tasked with taking responsibility for their organizations' customer experience management programs (including call centers, customer service, etc.).

In terms of information needs, these groups are some of the highest users of both external and internal information, including market, customer, and competitor information (includes demographics, purchase drivers, product response, trends and changing patterns); sales data on which to base predictive models (who's likely to purchase what, and why); effective sales channels and approaches; statistical information; market research—characteristics of potential opportunities; and call center and customer service best practices and benchmarking findings. In addition, the PR people are always on the lookout for good quotable statistics, media research (especially social media insights), issues research, and speech/article background information.

Information Systems/Technology Department

The information technology (IT) group often deploys its departmental staff and skills throughout the entire organization, possibly supporting new product development, working on the organization's knowledge management infrastructure, pitching in on website development (depending, often, on the size of the organization), architecting the records-management system, and supporting employees' individual computer needs, among other tasks. Responsibilities often include not only creating and sustaining an enterprise-wide IT infrastructure that aligns with company needs and strategy, but also allocating budget to reflect often-competing strategic priorities, evaluating new technologies in terms of long-term enterprise needs, participating in the design and creation of any IT aspects of new products or managing the relationship with vendor-partners responsible for this activity; and supporting legal requirements and compliance by knowing and following records retention best-practice policies.

Information needs (and needed skills) for the IT department obviously depend on how wide-ranging its mandate is, but at the very least there's a need to have information that will enable the IT staff to stay apprised of emerging information technologies, evaluate potential vendor/contractor partners, and draw on state-of-the-art, current evaluations and comparisons of existing technologies and providers. In addition, the IT department may also need professionals well-versed in information access and retrieval concepts, taxonomy building, user experience, website design, and similar types of information organization skills. (*Note*: These activities may alternatively fall within the marketing, legal, or other departments depending on the organization.)

Human Resources

The human resources (HR) department is generally in charge of hiring staff, training and development of the organization workforce, and ensuring the company's compliance with all labor-related legal requirements. Some of HR's responsibilities include aligning workforce abilities with company needs (essentially, do they have the right people in the key spots in the organization, and if not, how do they fix that); recruiting, on-boarding, and retention of staff; providing appropriate learning opportunities to help staff maintain competitive skills; creating and managing competitive benefits and compensation programs; and managing the HR aspects of contract and outsourced/off-shored employee relationships.

HR departments play a critical role in any organization, especially because they juggle so many responsibilities. So their information needs can encompass legal issues related to personnel matters; staying current with HR trends; evaluating training and development (T&D) options as well as benefits, and compensation best practices; and monitoring new advances in recruiting, hiring, and compensation approaches. That means they may need information about multiple HR-related best practices and benchmarks, background information about potential job candidates and/or recruiting firms, analysis of and comparisons among the many training and development resources available, and possibly monitoring and alerts regarding any emerging legal issues related to staffing activities.

Finance

Responsible for monitoring the overall financial health of the organization, the finance department usually works with other department heads as well as key company strategists and decision-makers to develop annual financial goals (and budgets), monitor progress, and institute cost-cutting measures if deemed necessary. In a publicly held company (i.e., one that has issued stock and has public shareholders), the finance department also works closely with the legal department to ensure compliance with all federal reporting requirements as well as with internal and outside auditors, Securities and Exchange (SEC) representatives, and often key investors and industry analysts.

Depending on the specific responsibilities tasked to the finance department, its members may need information about industry comparisons and ratios; legal issues related to financial requirements; the financial strength of the organization relative to similar companies; competitive intelligence related to potential joint venture partners, acquisitions, or hostile takeovers; market trends (for financial forecasting); and/or regulatory or market developments that may impact revenues.

Legal

The legal department is the group responsible for ensuring that the organization is in compliance with all legal/regulatory restrictions. This includes ensuring the legality of all HR policies, ensuring that contracts are not only legal but represent the best interests of the organization, and, if necessary, working with outside counsel in the event of a lawsuit.

In order to stay on top of these responsibilities, legal departments need ongoing monitoring and updates regarding legal and regulatory changes, legal decisions and proceedings, and, if a public company, any pending SEC issues. So information professionals' ability to use key legal databases and online resources, analyze and synthesize key findings, and communicate critical information concisely can be especially valuable here.

Be sure to keep in mind that every organization has information needs specific to its business (or nonprofit mission) and the products and services it delivers. Just consider this a starter overview to get you thinking about where and how your information skills could add value within your current organization or one you'd like to work for.

Exploring Your Career Options

A great way to get a good sense of what many of these potential career paths may look like is to check out the career profiles in books such as Priscilla K. Shontz and Richard Murray's *A Day in the Life* or Shontz's *The Librarian's Career Guidebook,* Rachel Singer Gordon's *What's the Alternative,* and Laura Townsend Kane's *Working in the Virtual Stacks.*

You may also want to explore some of the other excellent LIS career-focused titles that provide advice and counsel for finding one's way in the expanding universe of information work. Check out, for example, Denise Fourie and David Dowell's *Libraries in the Information Age: An Introduction and Career Exploration,* which provides a comprehensive overview of traditional library career paths. For an overview of technology-focused careers, see the excellent *The New Information Professional: Your Guide to Careers in the Digital Age* by Judy Lawson, Joanna Kroll, and Kelly Kowatch (see especially the career maps for various skill sets). Or for advice focused more on overall LIS career development and strategy, consider Ulla de Stricker and Jill Hurst-Wahl's *The Information and Knowledge Professional's Handbook: Define and Create Your Success* or my book, *Rethinking Information Work: A Career Guide for Librarians and Other Information Professionals.*

In addition, many professional associations such as those listed in the resource section at the end of this chapter provide extensive career (and often salary) information on their websites. Other options include monitoring the key trade publications for your area of interest, joining relevant LinkedIn groups to follow their discussions and possibly reach out to other group members for information interviews, and/or checking in with your MLIS program (whether student or alumni) to see if there are graduates working in fields that interest you and with whom you could connect for further information.

The great thing about a career focused on information work is that there is an almost infinite need for credible, reliable, authoritative information on the part of individuals, communities, businesses, and governments. There is an equally compelling need to have it organized and accessible. Although the way that information is being delivered is in flux, as are the titles we use to describe how we do it, the opportunities to find or create meaningful work based on our skills will continue to grow. They may not be the jobs we expected to be doing when we started our careers (or degrees), but in many ways they can be just as rewarding as the path we initially set out on.

Also, remember that your career will unfold and build over a long period of time, and the path you may choose to pursue today is only the choice you are making for today. Half the fun of creating an LIS career is getting to pursue cool new opportunities as you continually expand your professional expertise.

Resources

Starred titles are mentioned in the chapter.

Major North American LIS Associations

Note: Many of these organizations offer student memberships at a steep discount. (If you've joined as a student, don't forget to renew your membership the day before you graduate!) Also, many ad hoc groups are using social media sites such as LinkedIn groups, Yahoo groups, Facebook, wikis, and other social collaboration tools to form around areas of special interest, so you'll want to check these sites as well to see if there are any relevant (and free) groups you may want to participate in. Also, keep in mind that the websites and blogs of many professional associations also provide valuable information about careers in their fields.

**American Association of Law Librarians (AALL)

www.aallnet.org

AALL represents more than 5,000 professionals working in multiple organization settings, including law firms, corporate legal departments, local, state, and federal courts, government agencies, and law schools, among others. The website includes information about AALL caucuses, chapters, and special interest sections, AALL online professional development offerings; and its Competencies of Law Librarianship statement, which is especially valuable for students considering this career path.

**American Association of School Librarians (AASL)

www.ala.org/ala/mgrps/divs/aasl/index.cfm

AASL works to ensure that all members of the school library media field collaborate to: provide leadership in the total education program; participate as active partners in the teaching/learning process; connect learners with ideas and information; and prepare students for lifelong learning, informed decision-making, a love of reading, and the use of information technologies. The website provides a section on education and careers, including information on Federal Student Loan Forgiveness for librarians.

**American Library Association (ALA)

www.ala.org

ALA's mission is to provide "leadership for the development, promotion, and improvement of library and information services and the profession of librarianship in order to enhance learning and ensure access to information for all." Representing public, academic, and school libraries, ALA is the only library organization that seeks to promote strong libraries of all types throughout society. Membership includes a subscription to the monthly *American Libraries* magazine. See especially the information on Careers in Librarianship in the Education & Careers section.

American Library Association—Allied Professional Association (ALA-APA)

www.ala-apa.org

Focuses on two primary areas: certification of individuals in specializations beyond the initial professional degrees and direct support of comparable worth and pay equity initiatives, and other activities designed to improve the salaries and status of librarians and other library workers.

American Medical Informatics Association (AMIA)

www.amia.org

Medical informatics is an area of potential opportunity for those with technology-focused LIS skills and an interest in medicine/healthcare. AMIA is included here as an example of a non-LIS association that, although not specifically targeted to those with "library" skills, may offer connections into these types of emerging alternative career paths.

**American Society for Indexing (ASI)

www.asindexing.org

Professional association for those involved in indexing, abstracting, and database building. Content-rich website offers a directory listing of indexers, links to resources of interest to indexers, articles and position papers about indexing, and information about ASI's special interest groups, which include a range of specializations (business, psychology/sociology, sports/fitness, culinary, web, and science and medicine, among others). For career info, see So You Want to Be an Indexer in the Become an Indexer section.

**American Society for Information Science & Technology (ASIST)

www.asis.org

With a primary mission of "leading the search for new and better theories, techniques, and technologies to improve access to information," the ASIST organization draws its membership from an extraordinary range of professional disciplines, including chemistry, computer science, education, engineering, law, librarianship, linguistics, management, and medicine, among others. Website includes information about the society, its goals and programs; memberships (discounted for students); and many special interest groups and chapters, including multiple student chapters.

**APRA

www.aprahome.org

Although this international organization overall supports those who specialize in fundraising research, analytics, and relationship management, the research piece is donor prospecting, an area of opportunity for LIS professionals with research skills. APRA offers educational programs, networking opportunities, publications, and career resources (see Career Center in the left-hand menu). Formerly the Association of Prospect Researchers for Advancement.

**ARMA International
www.arma.org
Billing itself as "The Authority on Managing Records & Information", ARMA is the oldest organization focusing on records and information management, a field that has undergone substantial changes since its inception more than 50 years ago. (Due to legal requirements, records management is now central to the compliance operations of almost every major corporation.) ARMA Canada (www.armacanada.org) is a regional arm of ARMA International comprising 14 chapters that represent Canada from coast-to-coast.

**Art Libraries Society of North America (ARLIS/NA)
www.arlisna.org
ARLIS/NA aims to enable "excellence in art librarianship and visual resources curatorship for the advancement of visual arts." Despite its relatively small size (approximately 1,000 members), ARLIS/NA is very active, with an annual conference, online job listing, publications, and multiple divisions, chapters, sections, and special interest groups.

Association for Information and Image Management (AIIM)
www.aiim.org
Also known as the enterprise content management (ECM) association, AIIM's mission is to help its members "understand the challenges associated with managing documents, content, records, and business processes." Check out the content-rich website for overviews of key topics, downloadable Industry Watch reports, and an excellent resource center.

**Association for Library Service to Children (ALSC)
www.ala.org/alsc/
An exceptionally active ALA division with more than 60 committees, ALSC's membership includes more than 4,200 librarians, educators, and others dedicated to connecting children and youth with literature, literacy, reading, and books in all their forms. Provides multiple publications and support resources for those advocating for early literacy, excellence in children's literature, and multilingual/multicultural reading opportunities.

Association for Rural & Small Libraries (ARSL)
www.arsl.info
ARSL's mission is to "provide a network of people and materials to support rural and small library staff, volunteers, and trustees to integrate the library thoroughly with the life and work of the community it serves." In addition to its annual conference, the group shares information through a blog and discussion group.

**Association of Canadian Archivists

http://archivists.ca

The 600 members who comprise the ACA are dedicated to an organizational mission that focuses on "the preservation and accessibility of Canada's information resources and its documentary heritage." In addition, the ACA actively promotes and supports Canadian archivists in their ongoing efforts to preserve and provide access to that heritage. Includes student chapters and several special interest sections. Formerly the Archives Section of the Canadian Historical Association (CHA).

**Association of College & Research Libraries (ACRL)

www.ala.org/ala/acrl

With a membership comprising academic librarians from all types of higher education institutions, ACRL's mission is to enhance "the ability of academic library and information professionals to serve the information needs of the higher education community," while also improving its members' ability to "improve learning, teaching, and research" related to the practice of academic librarianship. ACRL publishes *College & Research Libraries, College & Research Libraries News, Choice,* and a number of highly-regarded monographs. At its website, see especially the Career Opportunities from Across the Country listings for descriptions of academic jobs throughout the country.

**Association of Independent Information Professionals (AIIP)

www.aiip.org

Key resource for anyone considering a career as an independent information professional. Membership in the organization brings access to the AIIP electronic discussion list, perhaps the most valuable learning tool available for independents, and a community of colleagues who will cheer your every success. Check the website for career information, publications, and information about the organization and its events.

Association of Research Libraries (ARL)

www.arl.org

Although ARL is an organization whose 123 members are institutions (i.e., universities) rather than individuals, its website nevertheless offers a rich collection of resources for everyone. See especially the sections on Diversity, Career Resources, and the Leadership and Career Development Program.

**Canadian Association for Information Science (CAIS)

www.cais-acsi.ca

Mission is to "promote the advancement of information science in Canada, and encourage and facilitate the exchange of information relating to the use, access, retrieval, organization, management, and dissemination of information." Membership includes information scientists and archivists, librarians, computer scientists, documentalists, economists, educators, journalists, psychologists, and others who support the CAIS objectives.

Canadian Association for School Libraries (CASL)
www.cla.ca/AM/Template.cfm?Section=CASL2
A division of the Canadian Library Association, CASL is focused on the support and promotion of Canada's school libraries. It advocates for excellence in school libraries while also providing professional development opportunities for its members. In addition, CASL actively promotes reading and information literacy across multiple environments (e.g., library, classroom, home, etc.).

Canadian Association of College and University Libraries (CACUL)
www.cla.ca/AM/Template.cfm?Section=CACUL
CACUL's mission is twofold: to provide its nearly 700 academic-librarian members with professional development opportunities (e.g., workshops, conferences, etc.) and to enable them to communicate with each other and build community through an online discussion list. Check the website for professional development resources and CACUL publications, and the association's online discussion list.

Canadian Association of Law Libraries (CALL)
www.callacbd.ca
Focuses on "developing and supporting legal information specialists." Check the website for publications, professional development initiatives, special interest groups, a listing of legal research links, and other valuable resources.

Canadian Association of Public Libraries (CAPL)
www.cla.ca/AM/Template.cfm?Section=CAPL2
A division of the Canadian Library Association, CAPL is the primary advocacy, support, and information exchange organization for public librarians and libraries in Canada. Check the website for career information, public library resources, and the CAPL newsletter.

Canadian Association of Research Libraries (CARL)
www.carl-abrc.ca
Leadership group for the Canadian research library community, including 29 major Canadian academic research libraries, Library and Archives Canada, the Canada Institute for Scientific and Technical Information (CISTI), and the Library of Parliament.

Canadian Association of Special Libraries and Information Services (CASLIS)
www.cla.ca/caslis/index.htm
The diverse membership of CASLIS includes special libraries personnel, information specialists, documentalists, vendors, and others involved in delivering special library services throughout the country. A division of the Canadian Library Association.

Canadian Health Libraries Association (CHLA)
www.chla-absc.ca/
Focuses on professional development, networking, and advocacy for Canada's health sciences librarians and libraries. Check the website for blog posts and full-text articles from the association's journal.

**Canadian Library Association (CLA)

www.cla.ca

CLA is the umbrella organization for libraries and librarians in Canada, comprising more than 57,000 library staffers, public library board members, and students in library-focused graduate or community college programs throughout the country. The organization includes 22 special interest groups (e.g., action for literacy, entrepreneurship in librarianship, library and information services for older people) and numerous student chapters. Check the website for library career resources.

**Church and Synagogue Library Association (CSLA)

http://cslainfo.org

CSLA has an exceptionally strong mission of information dissemination in service of its members' needs. To this end, it offers CSLA members training sessions, publications, a peer community, an annual conference focused on continuing professional education and networking, a monthly publication, and a series of topical guides in areas such as selecting and cataloging materials, reference services, and handling archival materials, among others.

**Indexing Society of Canada (ISC)

www.indexers.ca/

Although the majority of its members specialize in indexing, ISC members also do "cataloguing, fact checking, glossary writing, HTML encoding, project management, teaching, thesaurus construction—and of course abstracting."

**Major Orchestra Librarians' Association

www.mola-inc.org

Primary focus is improving communication among orchestra librarians, with a secondary focus of "assisting librarians in providing better service to their orchestras, presenting a unified voice in publisher relations, and providing support and information to the administrations of performing arts organizations." If this is a potential career choice for you, be sure to read "The Orchestra Librarian: A Career Introduction," listed under Resources > MOLA Publications.

**Medical Library Association (MLA)

www.mlanet.org

More than 4,700 individual and institutional members based in the health sciences information field. Focus areas include education of health information professionals; health information research; and promoting universal access to health sciences information, both national and international. The MLA website includes information about the organization, a solid collection of career resources, and descriptions of and links to the association's two dozen sections (e.g., cancer librarians, dental section, hospital libraries, medical informatics, etc.).

Music Library Association (MLA)

www.musiclibraryassoc.org

Music librarians can be found in "large research libraries such as the Library of Congress or the New York Public Library; in the music section or branch library in universities, colleges, and conservatories; in public libraries; in radio and television station libraries; with music publishers and dealers; with musical societies and foundations; and with bands and orchestras." The Music Library Association represents librarians from all of these arenas, with a focus on music librarianship, its materials, and its careers. For those interested in music librarianship as a possible career path, check out Music Librarianship—Is It for You? on the website.

New Members Round Table (NMRT)

www.ala.org/ala/nmrt/nmrt.htm

A sort of terrific on-boarding resource for those new to the profession (as well as for those almost in it; i.e., MLIS students), NMRT is intended as a way to help ALA's newest members find ways to participate in ALA's multitude of professional activities. The NMRT electronic discussion list provides a great way to connect with peers across the country.

**Patent Information Users Group (PIUG)

www.piug.org

Provides a forum and resource/information collection for individuals who do professional patent research, with more than 700 active members drawn from 27 countries including the United States. Part of the International Society for Patent Information, PIUG's website notes that it has "nearly 300 patent information professionals who do patent searching for corporations, over 100 patent information consultants, over 80 patent information professionals who do patent searching for law firms, and about 20 searchers based in academic institutions. We are employed in performing patentability, freedom-to-practice, and validity patent searches for Fortune 500 / multinational companies, leading universities and major IP law firms. In recent years, PIUG members have also engaged in patent information analysis as a strategic innovation tool."

**Public Library Association (PLA)

www.ala.org/ala/mgrps/divs/pla/index.cfm

Founded in 1944, PLA supports its more than 9,000 members through a combination of professional development opportunities, advocacy initiatives, programming targeted to key skills and emerging trends, and publishing (membership includes a subscription to the bi-monthly *Public Libraries* magazine). Check out the PLA website for information about PLA committees and advocacy groups, publications, and information resources about public librarianship.

**Society of American Archivists (SAA)

www2.archivists.org

With over 4,000 members, SAA is an extremely active organization in terms of member education, publications, development of policies and standards, and taking a leadership role in the emerging electronic records environment. Check the SAA website for a list of the society's sections and roundtables, career information, and numerous information resources related to archives work.

**Special Libraries Association (SLA)
www.sla.org
Go-to source for professional support and development among U.S.-based information professionals in special library and alternative LIS roles. Most effective when you join and become active in your local chapter and/or one of its multiple special interest divisions and sections. Publishes *Information Outlook;* check out the Career Articles & Resources section on the website for several excellent career resources.

**Strategic and Competitive Intelligence Professionals (SCIP)
www.scip.org
Competitive intelligence (CI) is essentially researching what the competition is up to—a key element in business decision support. SCIP membership represents the very broad skills involved in CI, including LIS professionals, non LIS business researchers, and subject specialists, among others. Members include independents as well as those employed by all types of organizations. Check the website under CI Resources for salary information, white papers, articles, career information, and several overviews of the CI process.

**Young Adult Library Services Association (YALSA)
www.ala.org/yalsa/
The young adult category is basically teenagers, and the more than 5,400 members who make up YALSA—including librarians, library workers, and advocates—are dedicated to ensuring the best possible library services for those 12–18 years old. YALSA publishes the peer-reviewed *Journal of Research on Libraries and Young Adults,* and promotes and provides training and professional development opportunities.

See also the listing of ALA and SLA sections, divisions, and additional LIS special interest groups in the Appendix.

Print Resources

**Bates, Mary Ellen. *Building and Running a Successful Research Business: A Guide for the Independent Information Professional,* 2nd ed. Information Today, 2010. 512p. ISBN 0910965854.
Bates's book is basically required reading for anyone considering going independent as an information professional, regardless of whether that be as a researcher, indexer, taxonomist, content developer, or other type of information specialist.

***A Day in the Life: Career Options in Library and Information Science.* Priscilla K. Shontz and Richard Murray, eds. Libraries Unlimited, 2007. 464p. ISBN 1591583640.
Like having 90 LIS professionals sit down and tell you everything you ever wanted to know about what it's like to do their kind of work.

Includes profiles from those practicing in school, public, and academic libraries as well as numerous nontraditional roles. Multiple voices, multiple career paths—a terrific resource.

**de Stricker, Ulla and Jill Hurst-Wahl. *The Information and Knowledge Professional's Handbook: Define and Create Your Success.* Chandos, 2011. 294p. ISBN 1843346087.
These highly respected, experienced authors provide detailed, practical career advice that comes across as a cross between coaching, mentoring, and, okay, (in the nicest possible way), a bit of nagging. But it's clear their goal is to help readers avoid career potholes if possible. To that end, the tone and format is strongly prescriptive, letting readers know in no uncertain terms how certain situations should be handled in order to help ensure career success.

**Dority, G. Kim. *Rethinking Information Work: A Career Guide for Librarians and Other Information Professionals.* Libraries Unlimited, 2006. 236p. ISBN 159158180X.
Identifies what the options are, which ones might be of greatest interest to you given your personal attributes and values, and strategies and tactics for achieving your career goals. Focusing on actionable information, the book's goal is to help you build a sustainable, resilient career despite the unpredictable state of the profession.

**Fourie, Denise K. and David R. Dowell. *Libraries in the Information Age: An Introduction and Career Exploration,* 2nd ed. Libraries Unlimited, 2009. 308p. ISBN 1591584345.
Intended as an LIS course textbook, *Libraries in the Information Age* presents perhaps the most mainstream take on library work. It presents a thorough overview of types of libraries and librarians, plus their activities (collections, preparing materials for use, circulation, reference service, and evolving library services). Especially useful for those considering more traditional LIS paths.

Gordon, Rachel Singer. *The NextGen Librarian's Survival Guide.* Information Today, 2006. 208p. ISBN 1573872563.
Intended for MLIS students as well as soon-to-graduate or recently graduated librarians in their 20s and early 30s, *Survival Guide* first describes the unique characteristics of this demographic, then recommends approaches to grad school, the job hunt, entry-level positions, and moving forward in your career. Provides solid, practical advice—and lots of it.

**Gordon, Rachel Singer. *What's the Alternative? Career Options for Librarians and Info Pros.* Information Today, 2008. 288p. ISBN 1573873330.
Gordon focuses on a multitude of nontraditional (read: not public, school, or academic) LIS roles, with an emphasis on identifying transferable skills and applying them to a variety of alternative jobs such as knowledge management, competitive intelligence, working for a vendor, or independent work.

**Halvorson, Kristina. *Content Strategy for the Web.* New Riders Press, 2009. 192p. ISBN 0321620062.

LIS professionals may become involved in content strategy not only as the people responsible for developing a strategy that aligns with an organization's goals, but also as the writer, content licenser, taxonomist, cataloger, social media manager, or myriad other ways. This book provides excellent and eminently practical guidance on how to manage the process, the stakeholders, and the ongoing maintenance of compelling website content.

**Hedden, Heather. *The Accidental Taxonomist.* Information Today, 2010. 472p. ISBN 1573873977.

A user-friendly, easy-to-understand and implement guide for those of us who may find ourselves thrown into taxonomy work as part of another project, new job responsibilities, or some other change in job circumstances. Hedden covers all the key bases, ranging from what taxonomies are and taxonomists do, through software explanations, human versus automated indexing requirements, and taxonomy as a career, among other topics.

**Kane, Laura Townsend. *Working in the Virtual Stacks: The New Library & Information Science.* American Library Association, 2011. 167p. ISBN 9780838911.

Updating her previous work, *Straight from the Stacks* (2003), Kane provides another valuable look at career paths for today's information professionals. The book's 34 profiles are grouped into librarians as (1) subject specialists, (2) technology gurus and social networkers, (3) teachers and community liaisons, (4) entrepreneurs, and (5) administrators. Each chapter leads off with an overview of the type of work, environments, responsibilities, skills, and relevant professional associations.

**Lawson, Judy, Joanna Kroll, and Kelly Kowatch. *The New Information Professional: Your Guide to Careers in the Digital Age.* Neal-Schuman, 2010. 200p. ISBN 555706983.

An exceptionally detailed (and useful) look at career options in the emerging digital information world, with extremely helpful career maps of related career paths for specific fields, such as archives and preservation, records management, human-computer interaction, social computing, and information systems management, among others.

***The Librarian's Career Guidebook.* Shontz, Priscilla K., ed. Scarecrow Press, 2005. 592p. ISBN 0810850346.

Imagine hanging out with 63 of your best friends . . . who also happen to be really smart, career-savvy information professionals "from diverse positions, workplaces, and locations." Shontz's contributors offer practical, immediately actionable advice on all sorts of career issues of interest to both LIS students and seasoned practitioners.

***Library and Book Trade Almanac, 2011.* Information Today, 2011. Dave Bogart, ed. 836p. ISBN 1573874124.

Formerly *The Bowker Annual,* this yearly recap covers national library trends, legislation, funding, and grants; LIS education, placement and salaries; research and statistics; reference information such as The Librarian's Bookshelf and Distinguished Books; and a 150-page directory of organizations.

**Mitchell, Pamela. *The Ten Laws of Career Reinvention: Essential Survival Skills for Any Economy.* Dutton, 2009. 272p. ISBN 0525951466.
Based on Seneca's premise that "every new beginning comes from some other beginning's end," *Career Reinvention* guides you through the process of letting go of your previous professional persona and methodically moving toward a new, more rewarding (or less damaging) one. One of the more actionable career-change books.

Nesbeitt, Sarah L. and Rachel Singer Gordon. *The Information Professional's Guide to Career Development Online.* Information Today, 2002. 416p. ISBN 1573871249.
This excellent book may now be over 10 years old, but the process Nesbeitt and Singer Gordon identify for using the Internet to find and apply for jobs in the LIS field still holds up. The four broad topics—learning and growing online, professional involvement, education, and employment—provide the primary organization for the book's chapters, each of which provides practical, sage advice.

**Sher, Barbara and Barbara Smith. *I Could Do Anything If I Only Knew What It Was.* Dell, 1995. 322p. ISBN 0440505003.
The classic book on soulful career introspection and exploration. Sher, a therapist, provides motivation and inspiration, plus lots of checklists, self-analytical exercises, and still-useful insights, despite the book's age.

Shontz, Priscilla K. *Jump Start Your Career in Library and Information Science.* Scarecrow Press, 2002. 208p. ISBN 0810840847.
A practical overview of the steps involved in getting your LIS career started. Shontz has included tips, checklists, resources, and personal stories that all add up to excellent advice for recent (or soon-to-be) MLIS graduates and those wanting to energize their existing careers.

**Shumaker, David. *The Embedded Librarian: Innovative Strategies for Taking Knowledge Where It's Needed.* Information Today, 2012. 240p. ISBN 9781573874526.
The most current and comprehensive examination of the increasing trend for special librarians to become embedded in their organizations' operational units. A must-read for those considering special librarianship as a career path.

Online Resources

**Brain Traffic
http://blog.braintraffic.com/
From Kristina Halvorson, author of *Content Strategy for the Web* (see the previous section), this blog provides a wealth of practical information on online content strategy and development, editorial strategy,

project management, and similar topics of value to online content developers, organizers, and managers.

Career Articles and Resources

www.sla.org/content/jobs/careerportal/index.cfm
A "members-only resource to assist information professionals in becoming indispensable to their clients and organizations." Includes articles, web content, and tools to enhance your career development goals. If you're thinking of a nontraditional career path, this resource provides another terrific reason to join SLA—think of this content-rich repository as your own personal career coach.

Career Development

www.sla.org/chapter/ctor/resources/careerdevindex.asp
A highly valuable collection of annotated bibliographies, articles, white papers, education resources, annotated links, salary surveys, and information on alternative career choices. An excellent starting point for beginning your career exploration, from the Toronto chapter of SLA.

Career Q&A with the Library Career People

www.lisjobs.com/careerqa_blog/
Questions asked and answered about a wide array of LIS career issues. The Library Career People are two smart, experienced professionals (Susanne Markgren and Tiffany Allen) who do a great job of providing useful, practical advice. In addition to their full-time academic library jobs and writing the Career Q&A blog, the two are also coauthoring a forthcoming book, *Career Q&A: A Librarian's Real-Life Practical Guide to Managing a Successful Career* (Information Today).

**Careers in Librarianship

www.ala.org/ala/educationcareers/careers/index.cfm
Check here for coverage of traditional LIS career paths, core competencies, and trends and statistics.

Career Strategies for Librarians

www.liscareer.com/articles.htm
Topics include career exploration, education, job searching, experience, networking, mentoring, interpersonal skills, leadership, publishing and presentations, and work–life balance. On hiatus until early 2012, but still a terrific archive of articles.

**Embedded Librarian

http://embeddedlibrarian.wordpress.com
From embedded librarianship thought leader David Shumaker, this blog presents his thinking and research results related to embedded librarianship and also aggregates key information from others.

Explore a Career in Libraries

www.ala.org/ala/educationcareers/careers/index.cfm
Check here for coverage of career paths, core competencies, and trends and statistics.

Finding a Job—Updated

www.libraryjournal.com/article/CA6250888.html
Companion piece to How to Become a Librarian (see the following entry), both from Rachel Singer Gordon.

How to Become a Librarian—Updated

www.libraryjournal.com/article/CA605244.html
A great primer for those new to the profession, including prospective students considering whether this is the right career choice for them.

Info Career Trends Newsletter

www.lisjobs.com/career_trends/
Put on hiatus in June 2009, *Info Career Trends* was Lisjob.com's bi-monthly electronic newsletter devoted to professional development. A terrific resource for an archives cruise.

Infonista

www.infonista.com
Addresses alternative LIS career paths, career strategies and tactics, profiles of alternative LIS professionals' jobs and career paths, and cool career resources.

Librarian by Day

http://librarianbyday.net/
See especially: So You Want to be a Librarian in the archives.

Librarian of Fortune

www.librarianoffortune.com/
From well-known independent information professional Mary Ellen Bates, with a focus on succeeding in the business of being an independent plus resources, tools, and tactics for doing so.

Librarian Resources, LLRX

www.llrx.com/librarian-resources.htm
Content-rich site focused on law and technology resources for legal and LIS professionals. The topics are highly eclectic, but generally are focused on career skills and information resources of value to LIS practitioners, especially those in law.

**Librarian's Yellow Pages

http://librariansyellowpages.com/
Searchable database of thousands of library-focused products and services vendors. A great place to check for potential employers as an alternative way to use your LIS skills and experience.

Library and Information Careers: Emerging Trends and Titles

http://slisweb.sjsu.edu/resources/career_development/emerging_trends_2011.pdf
An annual survey from San Jose State University's SLIS program that identifies emerging employment trends and the titles associated with them.

Occupational Outlook Handbook: Librarians

www.bls.gov/oco/ocos068.htm

Provides a solid overview of the various aspects of the profession, including the nature of the work, working conditions, employment statistics, education requirements, job outlook, and salary information.

Rethinking Information Careers

www.lisjobs.com/rethinking/

Archived monthly columns written by Kim Dority between December 2007 and July 2010.

2
LIS Education Options

Do You Need an MLIS?

It's an important question to ask, given the changes that are now moving through the profession of traditional librarianship. As noted in the previous chapter, the anticipated wave of new professional-level (i.e., MLS required) jobs opening up with the so-called graying of the profession has simply not materialized.

Two unanticipated trends drove—and are still driving—this employment landscape. First, older librarians decided not to retire, due to financial considerations or simply for a love of the job, at anywhere near the level that was projected and, consequently, their jobs haven't opened up. Second, due to budget constraints, more and more positions that had previously been full-time, professional-level jobs are now being reclassified as either part-time or at a paraprofessional level, or often both. So if your purpose in investing the time and money in an MLIS is to work in a traditional library, you'll want to have a very realistic understanding of what that job market looks like currently and for the foreseeable future.

Does that mean you shouldn't consider an MLIS? Absolutely not! First, there *will* continue to be job openings in traditional libraries—perhaps not as many as we would wish, but jobs will be there nevertheless. If this is the career direction that interests you, that is, working as a librarian in a school, public, or academic setting, the American Library Association (ALA) provides a good starting point with its *Types of Library Jobs* overview. (Another great resource for thinking through these issues is ALA's *What You Need to Know* resource page, which addresses the education issue within the framework of what type of work or position you might aspire to, the probable education requirements, and related information resources.)

Second, you may want to consider broadening the scope of your career aspirations either in case you can't find a traditional library job or simply because you're interested in additional career options. I believe, as do many of my colleagues, that an MLIS skill set can offer an amazing range of career opportunities.

One way to explore some of those additional career options and educational requirements is the Special Library Association's *Career Development* page, which provides an overview of career articles plus alternative career choices and personal development—all of which can help you decide whether a graduate degree is necessary for career options of potential interest to you. And for a useful reading list of articles about LIS careers, a great starting point is Librarian by Day blogger Bobbi L. Newman's post, "So You Want to Be a Librarian? A Guide for Those Considering an MLS, Current Students & Job Seekers."

However, if, in fact, your goal *is* specifically traditional (school or public) libraries and you're not interested in moving into a management role, then you might want to consider less costly alternatives, in terms of both time and money. Paraprofessionals (also called library assistants, library technicians, and parapros) are now doing much of the same work previously reserved only for those with MLIS degrees, and there are several avenues for professional development should you want to learn more but don't feel the need for a graduate degree. (To determine what certification is required by each state for specific types of library work, check out ALA-APA's list of certification requirements by job type.)

Your first option for non-MLIS education may be the library or library district for which you work, which may have good training and continuing professional education (CPE) programs you can take advantage of for free. Second, there are a number of programs for library assistants and technicians at two-year and some four-year colleges. Since there is no current, aggregated list of library technician programs, the easiest way to find one in your region is to search in your favorite search engine for terms such as "library technician programs," "library assistant degrees," and so on.

Third, ALA has created the ALA Allied Professional Association (ALA-APA) to promote the professional interests of librarians and other library workers, for example, paraprofessionals, who seek professional development opportunities not necessarily tied to an MLIS program. Part of this initiative is ALA-APA's Library Support Staff Certification program, designed for library support staff who meet specific criteria (high-school degree or equivalent; have worked—paid or unpaid—in libraries for at least one year). The goal of the Support Staff Certification program is to provide an official credentialing process to recognize professional achievement, to improve service delivery, and to increase the skills and knowledge of library support staff.

If, on the other hand, you think you may want to move into a management or leadership position (or would at least like to keep that option open), or you would like the broad information-focused skill set that an MLIS can provide, then you may want to consider getting that graduate degree.

Finding an MLIS Program

Where to start? There are currently 63 ALA-accredited master's degree programs in the United States, Canada, and Puerto Rico. According to ALA's statement on its website,

> ALA accreditation indicates that the program has undergone an external review and meets the ALA Committee on Accreditation's *Standards for Accreditation of Master's Programs in Library and Information Studies*. These standards evaluate a program's mission, goals, and objectives; their curriculum, faculty, and students; their administration and financial support; and their physical resources and facilities.

How important is ALA accreditation? Very. Assume that almost *no* professional-level traditional library positions will accept an MLIS from a program that is not ALA-accredited, and many other special-library positions will stipulate an ALA-accredited degree as well. (However, if you are planning a nontraditional information career path for which a library credential is irrelevant, you may want to seriously consider whether the degree is critical to your job plans.)

Fortunately, ALA has provided an easy way to see what programs are available via its Searchable Database of ALA-Accredited Programs, which you can search by state/Canadian province or name of institution, while also filtering by distance education options (from some distance education elements to 100 percent online), areas of concentration/career pathways (e.g., archival studies, health sciences librarianship/health informatics, public librarianship, etc.), and other degree opportunities (bachelor's, nondegree continuing education, dual/joint degree, PhD, and post-master's certifications).

In addition, the American Association of School Librarians (AASL) has compiled a directory of nationally reviewed and recognized NCATE/AASL school
librarianship education programs by state. (*Note*: NCATE has now become
part of a broader accrediting body, The Council for the Accreditation of Educator Preparation [CAEP].)

Evaluating MLIS Programs

Now that you have a starting point from which to explore possible
programs that match your interests and career goals, what criteria should
you use to do so? ALA's *Guidelines for Choosing a Master's Program in
Library and Information Studies* provides a good overview of key considerations.

Another option for evaluating potential programs, however, is within
the framework of how well they'll do at helping you create job prospects. In
that case, you may want to explore the programs from a slightly different
angle, considering the following program characteristics.

Faculty Makeup

There are a number of elements to consider here. In the academic universe, scholarly/research credentials signify accomplishment and value. However, if a program has mostly full-time tenured faculty who focus primarily
on scholarly work (which undoubtedly has value), they'll be unlikely to have
many professional connections or experience outside academia, which means
they'll not be able to assist much when it comes to helping you find great
internships and/or jobs. Another consideration is who teaches in the subject
areas that interest you. Are they publishing interesting papers, exploring
new applications, leading interesting projects (that you could participate in)?

A third consideration is how many adjunct faculty teach in the program,
and the quality of their teaching. Adjunct faculty are usually practitioners
who have had successful experience in the topic they're teaching and can
bring real-life insights (and a practitioner's network of connections) to the
subject at hand. On the other hand, some adjuncts can have poor teaching
skills, poor communication skills, and little understanding of how to help
students master the material. So if you're getting serious about a program,
you'll want to learn more about the faculty, and perhaps research them online to see if their strengths align with what you'll be looking for.

Career Services

The level (and effectiveness) of career support for students differs radi-
cally from school to school. Some MLIS programs have dedicated career-
services counselors, while others share one of the main campus's career-center
staffers. Some schools provide a tremendous amount of career information

and support resources online (see, for example, San Jose State University's Career Development section on its website), but others almost none. So when talking with school representatives about their program's strengths, be sure to ask about what resources and support they provide for career counseling and job placement.

Internships

Internships are a great way to (1) gain job experience, (2) test out potential career paths, and (3) build professional connections. Does the program have internships set up with organizations that reflect your career-path interests? Are the internships paid or unpaid, virtual or onsite, or a blend of both? If possible, ask to speak to someone who's done an internship in your area of interest. If the school doesn't help with internships or practicum placements, it's sending a pretty clear signal that you're also going to be on your own when it comes to finding a job when you graduate.

Corporate Relations

Related to the internship question, does the program have any relationships established with key employers? If so, how will those relationships benefit you as a student? That might be via internships, opportunities to participate in real-life business projects, working with professional mentors, willingness to do information interviews with you, or even job placement for top students. Your job is to see if these relationships are in place and how they benefit program students and graduates.

Professional Associations

Does the program have active student chapters of the professional associations relevant to your interests? If not, this can either signify a great opportunity for you to step into a leadership role and create the chapter *or* it can indicate that no one else in the program shares your professional interests, which might mean it's not the right school for you.

Alumni Network

A great alumni network can be a major career asset for students. Alumni can mentor students, be available for informational interviews, make wonderful guest speakers, and connect you to their professional network for job contacts. They can also show you career directions and paths you might not have considered. So you'll want to ask about the program's alumni network— What is it? How does it work? and Would it be possible to speak with some alumni in your potential field?

Employment Statistics

Where do students go to work once they've graduated (what organizations or types of organizations, what roles or job titles)? How long on average did it take them to get a job? Some schools don't have this information, but if they can discuss even anecdotal data with you, it means that they realize how important it is for students (and prospective students) to find decent jobs as quickly as possible when they graduate.

Advisory Board Makeup

Who's on the advisory board for the program? Is it mostly people from industry, mostly from traditional libraries, a mix? Any non-LIS folks? The makeup of the advisory board can often signal what types of LIS paths are most highly emphasized in the program.

Technology Focus

Two questions dominate this category. First, how much is technology used in the program? Organizations today are looking for employees who are adept at using a wide range of collaborative and communications technologies, and it's a lot easier to master these tools in grad school where there is (potentially) faculty and IT department support. Second, how many courses in the program focus on technology-based LIS skills? If few, you have to assume that you'll be graduating without the most in-demand professional knowledge and skill set, and will be competing for jobs against other new grads who *do* have those skills.

What about Online Programs and iSchools?

Two other considerations to weigh when choosing a master's degree program are (1) online versus on-campus and (2) MLIS or iSchool.

More and more schools are beginning to put at least part of their programs online as the knowledge surrounding effective online teaching has grown and delivery methods have improved. As noted, ALA's Directory of ALA-Accredited Programs allows you to search on "online availability" as a filtering criterion, so it's easy to quickly see a list of schools offering online options.

As of this writing, 20 schools provide degree programs entirely online. However, more and more MLIS programs are beginning to experiment with incorporating a select number of online courses into their more traditional on-campus offerings, or are exploring the uses of blended courses, which are courses that have both on-campus and online elements. If this is an important consideration for you, you'll want to be sure to inquire about online options.

Another alternative to consider is the iSchools. According to their mission statement as stated on the group's website, the iSchools are

interested in the relationship between information, people and technology. This is characterized by a commitment to learning and understanding the role of information in human endeavors. The iSchools take it as given that expertise in all forms of information is required for progress in science, business, education, and culture. This expertise must include understanding of the uses and users of information, as well as information technologies and their applications.

Essentially, their focus is specifically not on libraries and librarianship, but rather on information, information technology, and the "relationships between information, people, and technology." Some traditional MLIS programs have expanded their mandate to embrace the iSchool approach and curriculum, some schools are running dual programs, and some schools offer only the iSchool curriculum. More information about iSchools can be found on the iSchools' website, which identifies iSchool programs and explains their conceptual basis. This may be an option of interest to you if you want to ensure that your education includes a strong grounding in information technologies.

In addition, another new entrant into the field of graduate-level information studies is Columbia University's M.S. in Information and Knowledge Strategy. Part of the university's School of Continuing Education, the degree is geared toward individuals aspiring to knowledge strategist or knowledge strategy executive positions within organizations.

What Courses to Take

One of the questions most likely to get impassioned responses from those who've been in the profession for a while is what courses students should or shouldn't take in grad school. Naturally, a lot depends on what type of work you'd like to do when you graduate, but generally speaking your career path, at least initially, may follow one of these directions:

- archives and/or preservation
- content development
- digital asset management
- information organization (access and retrieval, cataloging and metadata, taxonomies, etc.)
- information systems and technology, information architecture
- public services, reference, readers advisory, community outreach
- research (business, nonprofit, medical, law, community, etc.)
- technical services
- web design, development, and user experience

Undoubtedly many more areas of specialization will emerge (or will have emerged by the time this book is published), but despite the wide range of potential LIS career paths, most grads and practitioners agree on some basics. Specifically, that you should take as many technology courses as you can, you should take classes outside the LIS program if possible on topics like management, psychology, marketing, budgeting, and organizational development (if available), and you should take a course on either cataloging or information organization/access and retrieval so you are at least familiar with the concepts underlying so many aspects of information work.

Additionally, when this question was posed to members of the LinkedIn LIS Career Options group with a focus on core skills and concepts that would transfer from one library setting to another, some of the answers included knowledge management, online searching, marketing, customer relationship management, information architecture, resource sharing and library networks, information-seeking behavior, science/technology information resources, social media strategies and tactics, information analysis, business writing, indexing and abstracting, instructional design/teaching, archiving and indexing, human resources management and management of information systems (both from the MBA program), web authoring/design and user experience (UX), and records management.

And almost universally, respondents indicated that internships were invariably one of the most useful aspects of their degree experiences, and recommended them for students whenever possible.

Financial Aid Sources

If you decide that a master's degree in library and information science will help advance your career goals, and you've tentatively decided on a school or two, your next question may be what financial aid resources are available to help you pay for your program. Fortunately, there are a number of avenues for securing financial aid, possibly through grants, scholarships, or loans.

Some places to check include the following:

- your state library association
- your employer (ask what the tuition reimbursement options are)
- the school(s) to which you will be applying
- local community organizations
- professional organizations such as SLA that may have student scholarships available
- special-interest groups, for example, groups supporting education for minorities, women, and other special populations (in your favorite search engine, search on "financial aid," "scholarships," "grants," and similar terms plus the appropriate special-interest phrase)

In addition to these sources, ALA has a wide range of financial aid programs as well as information resources. Per the association's ALA Scholarship page,

> The American Library Association (ALA) is committed to promoting and advancing the librarian profession. To demonstrate this commitment, the ALA and its units provide more than $300,000 annually for study in a master's degree in library and information studies from an ALA accredited program, or for a master's degree in school library media program that meets the ALA curriculum guidelines for a National Council for Accreditation of Teacher Education (NCATE) accredited unit [note: NCATE has now become part of a broader accrediting body, The Council for the Accreditation of Educator Preparation (CAEP)].

This includes general scholarships, scholarships by specialty or practice area (for example, service to children, young adults, and teens), scholarships for support staff working on their MLS/MLIS, and financial aid for underrepresented groups (such as minorities or those with disabilities). Another program identified separately is the ALA Spectrum Scholarship Program. Established in 1997, the goal of the Spectrum Scholarship program is to increase the success of national diversity and recruitment efforts for the library profession.

Yet another option, provided by ALA's Office for Human Resource Development (HRDR), is its annual aggregation of state-by-state financial aid sources. The *ALA Financial Assistance for Library and Information Studies, Academic Year* (2010–2011) report identifies financial assistance for students offered by state library agencies, state library associations, education institutions, and local libraries for the United States, Canada, and Puerto Rico, as well as U.S. and Canadian national and regional awards.

Lastly, consider the loan forgiveness programs offered by the federal government (see an overview of this option at ALA's Federal Student Loan Forgiveness page). Designed to encourage public and school librarians to join the profession and begin working in high-need areas, the loan forgiveness program is definitely something to check out.

Does Getting an MLIS Make Sense?

As the profession continues to undergo disruptive changes and an unpredictable future, it makes sense to really think through the decision to get an MLIS (and take on the accompanying student debt). Although I believe the degree can still be a pathway to substantial career opportunities, I also believe potential students deserve to be given the straight skinny when it comes to connecting a graduate degree to a job.

Reality check: Although the long-anticipated graying of the profession is in fact underway (i.e., more and more of us are sporting gray hair), the projected result—all sorts of professional-level jobs opening up for new grads—is simply not materializing. Nor are those entry-level professional jobs likely to ever open up again in large numbers. The result? An extremely competitive job market for those hoping to go into school, public, and/or academic librarianship.

Because of this competitive job market, MLIS students and graduates need to assume that although they may, indeed, find jobs in the school, public, or academic libraries they've prepared for, those jobs are likely to

- take several months (at a minimum) to find,
- require previous experience (paid is preferable, but volunteer experience is a good alternative),
- offer less-than-stellar salaries (as is the case in any profession with an excess of job candidates),
- require relocating (especially if your grad-school program is located in a highly popular region), and
- possibly require starting at a paraprofessional level (discouraging, but assume you'll be in line for professional jobs that may open up).

It's especially important not to assume that this is a temporary situation that will improve if/when the economy improves. We can hope, but the smarter betting is on the continued downsizing of traditional library jobs—welcome to Library Profession 2.0.

Despite this, why do I still believe that getting an MLIS may still be a worthwhile investment? Because what you learn from that degree can provide you with incredibly valuable skill set: you know not only important stuff about information, you also know many cool and smart things to do with it.

You need to clearly understand when you start your MLIS program that your grad school can't guarantee you a job, and has no responsibility for doing so. But what they *should* be able to guarantee you is an invaluable skill set that can be deployed in many different ways. You just need to make sure that you approach your degree program with an open mind and realistic set of assumptions as to how you will use your degree.

Think of your MLIS as guaranteeing you the ticket you need to start pursuing a job; it will be up to you to turn that ticket into a job opportunity. When you graduate (and throughout your career) the more realistic you are about the types of jobs you intend to go after, the dues you will need to pay to successfully land them, and the likelihood that you may need to rethink your career course should the nature of those jobs change, the more successful you will be.

Note: do yourself a favor and, if you can, work while you're in grad school, even if part time. The best-case scenario is that you work in a library doing any sort of work, or if you can't work in a library, try to work in some environment or role that enables you to use the information skills you are learning. The worst option is to go straight from undergrad school to full-time graduate study. If you have no relevant work experience when you graduate, or at the very least relevant volunteer experience, you will have a much more difficult time getting a job after graduation.

Resources

Starred titles are mentioned in the chapter.

Associations

**ALA-Allied Professional Association (APA)

http://ala-apa.org

ALA-APA provides services to librarians and other library workers in two primary areas: certification programs for paraprofessionals and library technicians/assistants and library supervisory staff (post-MLS), and direct support of comparable worth and pay equity initiatives, plus other activities designed to improve the salaries and status of librarians and other library workers. Publishes the monthly *Library Worklife: HR E-News for Today's Leaders.*

**Career Development Page / SLA

http://units.sla.org/chapter/ctor/resources/careerdevindex.asp

When considering whether to pursue an MLIS, and in what direction to focus your studies if so, you may want to explore the career paths and resources provided by SLA's Career Development page (information provided by SLA's Toronto chapter). Although all of the materials are in dire need of updating, there are nevertheless some good basics here, including a career reading list, jobsites, resume and interview tips, and compensation information.

A Career in Libraries / CLA

http://www.cla.ca/AM/Template.cfm?Section=A_Career_in_Libraries_& Template=/CM/HTMLDisplay.cfm&ContentID=11905

Central spot on the Canadian Library Association's website for exploring library career information. Links to LIS and library technician programs in Canada, as well as those offering ALA-accredited master's programs.

**Certification Requirements by State / ALA-APA

http://ala-apa.org/certification-news/stateregional-certifications/

According to ALA-APA, "Although more than half of the 50 states offer or require certificates or certification for public library workers, the standards for certification are not universal and the requirements vary from state to state. The greatest difference among states was required education." This resource lists both MLS and non-MLS state certifications while also identifying the rationale behind those certifications.

**Directory of ALA-Accredited Programs / ALA

> www.ala.org/ala/educationcareers/education/accreditedprograms/directory/search/index.cfm
> Listing of more than 50 ALA-accredited MLIS programs in North America. Each entry includes contact information, program name, date through which it is accredited, and whether the program offers distance education opportunities. Searchable by state/province, distance education options, degree type, and institution name.

**Federal Student Loan Forgiveness / ALA

> www.ala.org/ala/educationcareers/education/financialassistance/loanforgiveness/index.cfm
> Explains the loan forgiveness provisions enacted by the 2008 Congressional legislation and where further details about loan forgiveness programs for librarians can be found, including Federal Perkins Loan Teacher Cancellation and Public Service Loan Forgiveness.

**Financial Assistance for Library & Information Studies Directory / ALA

> www.ala.org/ala/educationcareers/education/financialassistance/2010
> 2011_FALIS_Booklet.pdf
> Fifty-four pages of scholarship sources offered by state library agencies, state library associations, educational institutions, and local libraries. Organization is by country (United States, Canada, Puerto Rico) and state within the United States, including for each entry: granting body and/or name of award; program level (e.g., master's); type and amount of assistance; academic and other requirements; and application information and deadline. Updated annually.

**Guidelines for Choosing a Master's Program in Library and Information Studies / ALA

> www.ala.org/ala/educationcareers/education/accreditedprograms/guidelinesforchoosing/index.cfm
> These guidelines are designed to help prospective students select the program that best meets their individual needs. In choosing a program, several factors should be considered, including future career plans, specialization options, geographic mobility, distance-learning opportunities, and financial aid resources.

Info*Nation / CLA

> www.cla.ca/infonation/welcome.htm
> A site for exploring (and promoting) librarianship as a career choice. Includes both solid information and great profiles of Canadian information professionals.

LibraryCareers.org / ALA

> www.ala.org/ala/educationcareers/careers/librarycareerssite/home.cfm
> Resources for those considering a career as a librarian; includes a wide range of information resources, plus a great picture of nationally recognized librarian and author Nancy Pearl, the only librarian known to have been the inspiration for her own action figure (which this author has sitting on her office bookshelf as an ongoing source of inspiration).

**Library Support Staff Certification / ALA-APA

http://ala-apa.org/lssc/

ALA-APA offers two certification programs: the Library Support Staff Certification Program and the Certified Public Library Administrator Program. If you're a paraprofessional and/or library technician (and you're not interested in a management position), you may want to consider the Library Support Staff Certification Program as an alternative credential to the MLS. You'll want to first consult with your library's management to determine the value (and benefits) of the credential to your organization.

**Nationally Reviewed and Recognized NCATE/AASL School Librarianship Education Programs / AASL

www.ala.org/ala/mgrps/divs/aasl/aasleducation/schoollibrary/ncateaasl reviewed.cfm

State-organized list of approved degree programs for school librarians, with links to those programs. (*Note*: NCATE has now become part of a broader accrediting body, The Council for the Accreditation of Educator Preparation [CAEP].)

New Members Round Table (NMRT) / ALA

www.ala.org/nmrt/

A sort of terrific on-boarding resource for those new to the profession (as well as for those almost in it, i.e., MLIS students), NMRT is intended as a way to help ALA's newest members find ways to participate in ALA's multitude of professional activities. The NMRT electronic discussion list provides a great way to connect with peers across the country.

**Scholarship Program / ALA

www.ala.org/ala/educationcareers/scholarships/index.cfm

An overview of (with links to) ALA's four MLIS scholarship categories: general, by specialty or practice area, for library support staff, and for people from underrepresented groups. Scholarship applications are accepted between October and March, and can be submitted online.

**Spectrum Scholarship Program / ALA

www.ala.org/ala/aboutala/offices/diversity/spectrum/index.cfm

Per its mission statement, "the Spectrum Scholarship Program is ALA's national diversity and recruitment effort designed to address the specific issue of under-representation of critically needed ethnic librarians within the profession while serving as a model for ways to bring attention to larger diversity issues in the future." Check here for information about requirements and the application process and online forms.

**Standards for Accreditation of Master's Programs in Library and Information Studies

www.ala.org/ala/accreditedprograms/standards/index.cfm

Identifies the criteria that ALA's Committee on Accreditation (COA) uses to accredit (or not) graduate library and information science programs, including a glossary of accreditation terminology.

Student Chapters / ALA
www.ala.org/ala/mgrps/affiliates/chapters/student/studentchapters1.cfm
Central resource page for information related to starting or joining an
ALA student chapter at your graduate school. For a list of all ALA student chapters, see www.ala.org/ala/mgrps/affiliates/chapters/student/
directory/studentchapterdir.cfm.

Student Chapters / ASIS&T
www.asis.org/Chapters/chapters-student.html
Billing itself "the information society for the information age," ASIS&T
has perhaps the strongest focus on the technology aspects of LIS work.
Consequently, its student chapters are a great way to connect technology track students with trends, issues, and people likely to be of interest
to them when they graduate.

Student Groups / SLA
www.sla.org/content/community/sgroups/index.cfm
SLA works with its MLIS student groups through its seven-member
Student and Academic Affairs Advisory Council, which acts as a liaison
between the student groups and the SLA executive team. For a list of
student chapters, see www.sla.org/content/community/sgroups/sgf.cfm.

**Types of Library Jobs
www.ala.org/ala/educationcareers/careers/librarycareerssite/typesof
jobs.cfm
A quick overview of the types of jobs and roles people may have in public libraries, from pages to directors, with salary or hourly pay ranges
for each. Also includes a list of resources for additional information, although these are pretty out of date.

**What You Need To Know / ALA
www.ala.org/ala/educationcareers/careers/librarycareerssite/whatyo
uneed.cfm
An overview of education requirements by type of library position, as
well as an exploration of whether you need a library science associate's
or master's degree, and how to choose a library school if you do.

Print Resources

Johnson, Marilyn. *This Book is Overdue! How Librarians and Cybrarians
Can Save Us All.* Harper Perennial, 2011. 304p. ISBN 0061431613.
In the midst of the profession's hand-wringing and anxiety attacks,
Johnson has written a delightful, witty, and spot-on paean to the amazing
work librarians do as educators, archivists, and community knowledge
curators. For those considering the profession, this is an upbeat and
positive take on the profession's future as well as its future opportunities.

The Portable MLIS: Insights from the Experts. Ken Haycock and Brooke E.
Sheldon, eds. Libraries Unlimited, 2008. 316p. ISBN 1591585473.
If you're wondering whether a career as a librarian is for you, *The Por-
table MLIS* is a great place to start. With enthusiastic entries by some

of the profession's best-known practitioners and leaders, this book will give you an insider's sense of what a career as a librarian might offer—both challenges and rewards.

Rubin, Richard. *Foundations of Library and Information Science,* 3rd ed. Neal-Schuman, 2010. 471p. ISBN 1555706908.
   The introductory textbook for many if not most MLIS programs, this work provides an excellent overview of what is involved in library and information work, and will help those unsure of this career path to have a more realistic sense of what librarianship involves (and whether it's a good fit for them).

Shontz, Priscilla K. and Richard Murray. *What Do Employers Want? A Guide for Library Science Students.* Libraries Unlimited, 2012. 140p. ISBN 1598848283.
   This practical guide focuses on two aspects of becoming an LIS professional: first, how to make the most of your student experience while in school, and second, how to find a job with your new graduate degree. The authors are well-known and respected contributors to the profession (Shontz is editor of the career site LIScareer.com, Murray is the co-author of several LIS books as well as the metadata librarian, digital collections program, at the Duke University Libraries). A valuable resource for students and graduates—plan to mark your copy up.

The Whole Library Handbook 4. Compiled by George M. Eberhart. American Library Association, 2006. 596p. ISBN 0838909159.
   A fun, fascinating, total-immersion dive into the library profession for students and those new to the profession. Chapters include "Libraries," "People," "The Profession," "Materials," "Operations," "The Underserved," "Promotion," "Technology," "Issues," and "Librariana" (great for Trivial Pursuit moments!). The *Handbook* is also a pretty solid resource for researching a lot of those assignment papers.

Online Resources

Note: In addition to the online resources listed here, be sure to consider joining your school's student and alumni group on LinkedIn (if there is one), and keep an eye out for student blogs, of which new ones leap into existence with delightful regularity. Or, consider starting one yourself to connect with other students!

By (and for) Students & New Librarians
   http://libland.wikispaces.com/by_student_new
   Part of the LibLand wiki hosted by ALA, this page aggregates "a sampling of cyberspace connections (outside of ALA) for students and new librarians (outside of ALA)." Includes blogs, wikis, podcasts, examples of librarians/libraries using social networking, and listservs. A good overview of key current resources for those new to the profession or soon to be.

**Career Development Center > Career Direction / San Jose State University

http://sliswcb.sjsu.edu/resources/career_development/index.htm

A broad and deep aggregation of LIS career information. See especially the information under Career Direction and the research study Library and Information Careers: Emerging Trends and Titles, updated annually.

Career Strategies for Librarians > Career Exploration

www.liscareer.com/careerplanning.htm

For individuals considering whether to pursue an MLIS and/or the direction to take their studies once enrolled (if so), this extensive compilation of (and links to) articles provides a wealth of advice, information, and stories on which to base those decisions.

Hack Library School

http://hacklibschool.wordpress.com/

By, for, and about library school students, Hack Library School is a terrific window into the world of MLIS students and their challenges, issues, trends, and observations.

**iSchools

www.ischools.org/site/

Whereas many of the traditional MLIS programs focus on the more traditional aspects of librarianship, the iSchools place a stronger emphasis on the relationship between information, people, and technology. Check out the website for a listing of iSchools and additional information about their specific offerings.

"Learn by Doing: Hands-On Education through Internships"

http://lisjobs.com/career_trends/?p=515

From Eamon Tewell, a former MLIS student who used multiple internships to broaden his classroom learning, open up additional career opportunities, and demonstrate his initiative and work ethic. His advice on how to approach and perform an internship is excellent, including his four points to help you decide when an internship is the right option for you.

Library Workers: Facts & Figures

http://dpeaflcio.org/wp-content/uploads/Library-Workers-2011.pdf

An overview of "library staff in the workforce, where library staff work, their diversity, the role of women in the profession, issues of pay and pay equity, the union difference for library staff, and the impact the recession has had on libraries and library staff." This aggregates a broad range of statistics for traditional (public, school, academic) library employees, and paints a realistic picture of the job situation. Keep in mind, however, that this overview does not include any of the hundreds of nontraditional LIS career opportunities.

**LinkedIn LIS Career Options

www.linkedin.com/groups?gid=3126663&trk=hb_side_g

A LinkedIn group focused on every possible aspect of LIS career options, including students, practitioners, those considering librarianship, LIS recruiters, and vendors. The group's 4,000-plus members are from more than 30 countries, and are engaged in more than 450 discussion threads as of this writing. A subgroup of ALA's LinkedIn group (you don't have to be a member of ALA, only its LinkedIn group, to join).

**M.S. in Information and Knowledge Strategy / Columbia University
http://ce.columbia.edu/Information-and-Knowledge-Strategy
A new approach to information work that focuses on strategy more than implementation, with a strong focus on knowledge/information planning, design, and evaluation initiatives in such diverse environments as corporations, government agencies, and educational and nonprofit institutions.

New Librarians' List (NEWLIB-L)
http://walternelson.com/dr/newlib-l
A listserv for MLIS students and recent graduates that provides a forum for exchanging ideas, advice, concerns, and job information. Check the website for sign-up information.

"Skill Check: Utilizing Your Nontraditional Library Education"
http://lisjobs.com/career_trends/?p=523
Author Andrea D. Reed suggests that "Unlike some careers such as law or medicine, which require a relatively standard education track for those wishing to join the profession, librarianship's strength lies in its members' diverse work and educational backgrounds." She outlines an excellent and very practical approach to using your nonlibrary experiences to both enrich your degree-program experience and broaden your career opportunities.

"Slow Down: Making the Most of Library School"
http://liscareer.com/katopol_school.htm
A great argument from adjunct faculty member Patricia Katopol on the importance of taking a slower route through your LIS program. Rather than racing through with a focus on grades, this approach will enable you to build connections, work experience, problem-solving expertise, and other professional-level experience through attendance at course lectures and events, discussions with faculty and guest speakers, and similar connections.

**"So You Want to Be a Librarian? A Guide for Those Considering an MLS, Current Students & Job Seekers"
http://librarianbyday.net/2010/09/01/so-you-want-to-be-a-librarian-a-guide-for-those-considering-an-mls-current-students-and-job-seekers/
From *Librarian by Day* blogger Bobbi L. Newman, this aggregation of articles related to LIS careers provides a great starting point for deciding if a job as an LIS professional is for you. Articles are grouped within the categories of The Degree, The Job Search, General Professional Advice, and Skills. Very helpful decision-support information if you're debating whether to pursue an MLIS.

Ten Tips for Building Your Career While You're in Grad School
http://infonista.com/2010/ten-tips-for-building-your-career-while-you're-in-grad-school/

Grad school's not only an opportunity for you to develop your LIS skills and expertise, it's also an opportunity for you to build a professional platform that will help launch your career. These 10 tips will help you do just that.

"What Do You Wish You'd Learned—or What Classes Do You Wish You'd Taken, But Didn't—in Grad School?"
http://linkd.in/sfCl92
From the LinkedIn LIS Career Options group, 49 members weighed in with their recommendations for what classes they'd make sure to take if they had a chance for a grad school do-over.

3
LIS Job Hunting

Chapter Highlights

Chapter Highlights

- Decide on Potential Job Opportunities/Career Paths
- Research the Relevant Job Market(s)
- Understand Your Value Proposition
- Polish Your Job-Hunting Tools (E-Portfolios, Resumes, and Cover Letters)
- Build Your Professional Brand Online *before* Applying for Jobs
- Launch Your Job Search
- Interviewing and Negotiating
- Should New Grads Take Non-LIS Jobs?
- Temping as an Interim Job Solution

Whether you're a student soon to graduate and getting ready to hit the job market, an employed professional seeking to make a job change, or a now-unemployed practitioner trying to identify or create new opportunities, job hunting can be a challenging undertaking. In a depressed economy, things can quickly move from challenging to daunting.

According to David E. Perry, coauthor of *Guerrilla Marketing for Job Hunters 3.0: How to Stand Out from the Crowd and Tap into the Hidden Job*

Market Using Social Media and 999 Other Tactics Today, "Every job search is a sales and marketing campaign." Although, generally speaking, sales and marketing don't come naturally to LIS students and professionals, if you approach looking for the right job as a process to move you from point A to point B (okay, and include some sales and marketing), both the job search— and your spirits—can be more easily managed to a positive end.

Decide on Potential Job Opportunities/ Career Paths

As noted in Chapter 1, the universe of potential jobs that align with your skills and strengths is large and diverse, so the challenge becomes how to narrow things down a bit. To frame your possibilities, starting thinking through the following.

What Industry Might You Want to Work In (Including Traditional Libraries as Either the Education Industry or Government)?

When you consider this question, two of the issues you want to think through are (1) does this industry have very many employers in areas where I'd like to live (or currently do live), and (2) is this a growing or contracting industry? To research industries, their prospects, and some of the major employers, consider exploring the relevant entries for the *Plunkett's* publications, *Hoover's* database, annual trend and forecast issues for the major trade publications, and the Bureau of Labor Statistics' *Industries at a Glance* overviews. Also be sure to check out the leading professional associations through either an online search on your key terms or, if you have access to them, Gale/Cengage's comprehensive tools, *Encyclopedia of Associations* (print version), or the associations component of the online resource, Gale Directory Library.

What Type of Organization (Library, Company, Nonprofit, Association, Government Agency, etc.) Might You Want to Work For?

Each of these types of organizations offers very different working environments, opportunities for growth, job flexibility, and compensation. Also, think about whether you'd prefer a small, medium-sized, or large organization, a start-up or a long-established company, and/or a local organization or one that has a national or international reach (and job opportunities). To find out more about potential employers in the business world, check resources such as *Hoover's Online, Vault Reports,* or *Wetfeet* for starters, then go further and explore their company websites, LinkedIn pages, Facebook pages, and articles about them online and in commercial databases available through the library. Another great company resource that continues to expand its insider insights is *Glassdoor,* which provides information and interviews about companies, salaries, and organizational culture.

To learn more about libraries as potential employers, consider informational interviews. One way to approach this is to search LinkedIn for individuals who either currently work with or were previously employed by your potential employer, and contact them to see how they would describe the organizational culture. (This works well for non-LIS organizations as well.)

Which Department Might You Work For?

Within any type of organization, each department has different responsibilities, and therefore different types of information needs. For example, one department may need a skilled business researcher, another an experienced records manager, yet another someone with strong website building and managing expertise. (If you're unfamiliar with how most businesses and nonprofits are structured and the information needs of their departments, check out "Who Needs What Information?" in Chapter 1.)

What Work Might You Do?

As you progress through your career, you'll probably find that the work you do changes in ways completely unanticipated when you began your career. Usually those changes are an outgrowth of your original core work. For the LIS skill set, this generally falls into the categories of (1) research skills and information roles; (2) information organization roles (ranging from taxonomy-building to information architecture and beyond); (3) content roles (writing, developing online content, editing, acquiring content); (4) customer service/teaching or training/sales roles; and (5) information resources, people, or project management roles. Needless to say, there are many exceptions to this framework, but it can provide you with a starting point for thinking about broad types of work that might appeal.

Once you've narrowed the field by thinking through these options, then you'll have a better sense of both what types of jobs to look for and where to look for them.

Research the Relevant Job Market(s)

Depending on the type of jobs you're interested in, you'll want to monitor several job sources to figure out what specific jobs are called, what skills they require, and how many job opportunities there are in your area of interest. Key job research sources include the following:

- general LIS job posting sites such as *ALA Joblist, LISJobs.com, Library Job Postings on the Internet,* and Naomi House's LIS jobs aggregator, *INeedaLibraryJob*
- more general job posting sites (especially for nontraditional LIS jobs) such as *Monster.com, Indeed.com,* or *Idealist* (for nonprofit jobs)

- industry- or job-specific job boards (the easiest way to find these is to search on "[industry name or job type]" and "job boards" in your favorite search engine; for example, "green industry" and "job boards"
- job postings from your grad school, professional associations you belong to, and/or your state library association
- company websites
- social media resources such as LinkedIn, which aggregates job postings from (and for) members and allows you to set up alerts by keywords

Naturally, these will also be useful resources when you're ready to start applying for jobs. Keep in mind, however, that according to the U.S. Bureau of Labor Statistics, employers fill the majority of job openings through the unadvertised, hidden job market, that is, the job market accessibly only through networking—which should clarify where your strongest efforts should be directed when you're ready to go after job opportunities.

Understand Your Value Proposition

Once you have a good sense of what types of jobs you find interesting and the skills required for those jobs, your next step is to clearly understand how to position your strengths for a potential employer in a way that aligns with the organization's needs as identified in the job postings you've read.

Overall, you want to target all of your messages, that is, your resume, cover letter, and interview responses, toward one key value statement: *I am the solution to your problem*. When you're ready to apply for a job, your goal is to learn, from the job posting and doing as much research on the organization as possible, what problem, challenge, or opportunity it's trying to address through the posted position, and then focus entirely on the value you bring that will help it successfully do so.

Basically, your communications should showcase four things.

You Have the Skills, Expertise, and Track Record Necessary to Fix the Problem

This may include education, credentials, work experience, and/or volunteer engagements that relate to the challenge the company needs to address. Whether in your resume, cover letter, or interview, your communications need to be about the professional value you bring that lets you help the organization resolve its pain points. You may also have professional connections that will be of value to your potential employer—if so, be sure to point that out.

You Deliver Results

Prospective employers pay attention when you can point to quantifiable results from work you did (solutions you provided). Being able to say that you increased customer retention by 15 percent or led a project that came in 20 percent under budget or achieved some other measurable positive result means that you have a track record of delivering actual results. How to frame this? Companies generally focus on two bottom-line benefits: an increase in revenue or decrease in costs (for nonprofits, this may translate to increased membership or donations or similar metrics). If you're able to point to achievable results in any of these areas, make sure potential employers know it.

You Learn Fast

Almost any new job is going to involve a learning curve where you're trained on existing systems, processes, and practices. The faster you can master these and actually start producing value (i.e., being the solution), the happier your employer. So be sure to highlight any experiences that demonstrate how you quickly mastered new information and were able to apply that knowledge in previous situations.

You're Easy to Work with and Will Fit in with—Rather than Disrupt—Their Team

In terms of being that great solution, think seamless transition. Make it clear that your great people and team skills have helped drive successful solutions in the past, and will do so now as well.

Part of the process of understanding your value is to do a bit of self-assessment. Not only is it helpful to know your *Myers-Briggs* profile, but it's also valuable to be able to identify and highlight your strengths. A great resource for this is Marcus Buckingham and Donald O. Clifton's *Now, Discover Your Strengths,* and the assessment follow-up by Tom Rath, *Strengthsfinder 2.0,* both of which will help you be able to confidently describe and provide examples of your value in an interview situation.

Polish Your Job-Hunting Tools (E-Portfolios, Resumes, and Cover Letters)

Whether you're a student, a job-seeking new graduate, or a seasoned practitioner looking for a new job, having some sort of body of work you can point to will help potential employers be able to quickly identify evidence of the value you could contribute. Today's online information sharing tools (e.g., e-portfolio tools or something as simple as a robust LinkedIn profile) make this much easier to do.

Resumes will be your primary job-application tool. Given how many different ways you may want to deploy your skills, assume you'll need to tailor your resume for both print and online delivery, as well as to reflect specific skills and accomplishments relevant to the jobs you're applying for. A good guide to help you get started is Robert R. Newlen's *Resume Writing and*

Interviewing Techniques That Work!: A How-to-do-it Manual for Librarians. However, for more up-to-date tips and techniques, consider making an appointment with your school's career services resume review people (usually you can do this as a student or alumni), checking with your state library association to see if they have a resume review service, or, if you're a member of a professional association, taking advantage of any resume review options they offer. Additionally, check out the resumes, interviews, and cover letter advice provided by Rachel Singer Gordon in her helpful *Finding a Library Job-Updated* on the *Library Journal* website.

Since not all potential LIS jobs will be library jobs, however, it also makes sense to consider some of the more popular non-LIS resume and cover letter resources, such as Martin Yates's series (*Knock 'em Dead Resumes, Knock 'em Dead Cover Letters*), or the Magic series, for example, Wendy S. Enelow's *Cover Letter Magic,* 4th ed. and Susan Britton Whitcomb's *Resume Magic,* 4th ed., and *Interview Magic.*

Ready to assemble your online/e-portfolio? For a great overview of online portfolios, see Susanne Markgren's articles "Ten Simple Steps to Create and Manage Your Professional Online Identity" and "Using Portfolios and Profiles to Professionalize Your Online Identity (for Free)." Markgren, one of the two Career Q&A with the Library Career People experts, has also created an excellent example of an effective e-portfolio, based on a WordPress platform.

Also, if you're new to the profession, one of the reasons you may want to join ALA's New Members Round Table is to be able to take advantage of its Resume Review Service. Lastly, consider searching the Resume entries in Career Q&A with the Library Career People as well as the Job Searching Articles section found in the LIScareer.com archives.

Build Your Professional Brand Online *before* Applying for Jobs

Social media can be a great tool for job-hunting, but it's also a must-do for creating an easily accessible way for potential employers to check you out and get a good sense of your value and strengths. These days, almost no hiring manager considers moving the applicant (that would be you) to interview stage without first running an online search on your name to see what pops up.

What you want to have pop up is indicators and evidence of your substantial professional worth. And in order for that to happen, you've got to build an online presence that speaks to your strengths. Roughly translated: put up a killer profile on LinkedIn, think about creating a blog and/or career-focused Facebook page, and consider tweeting on topics that engage you professionally.

LinkedIn is perhaps the easiest social media tool to get started with, because it's pretty simple to get up and running with a minimal learning curve. Having a LinkedIn profile is quickly becoming as expected as having an up-to-date resume. In fact, HR types and hiring managers almost *all* check out applicants' LinkedIn profiles before considering them for job openings, and would be surprised not to find one for you.

The following LinkedIn basics will get you started.

Complete Your Profile

If you haven't created a profile yet, it's easier if you check out a couple of other profiles of people whose careers you admire, then gather/write the information you want to put in your own profile before you actually start inputting the data. And be sure to include a photo. It doesn't need to be a high-priced professional job; a decent photo taken with a digital camera (avoid bad hair days) should work just fine. You want to look professional, and you want to be sure you're smiling.

Use Business Language to Showcase Your Strengths in Your Summary

Your summary is a short paragraph that describes your expertise and capabilities. Use the keywords employers are likely to search to find someone with your skills. For example, if database management is the term people use in your field, make sure you've included it in your summary; that way potential employers can find you when they're looking for your skill set.

Reach Out and Start Building Links

You don't need hundreds of connections, but having *zero* LinkedIn connections makes people wonder why no one likes you. LinkedIn offers an easy way to request a link, so find at least 10 willing connections (colleagues, former classmates, friends, clients) to add to your network.

Ask for Recommendations

These can be from colleagues, bosses, classmates, teachers, people who have volunteered with you, just about anyone who can comment on how smart you are and what a delight you are to work with. Naturally, you'll offer to reciprocate. But the point is to have these recommendations visible to potential employers. The recommendations that carry the most weight are from people who have supervised your work.

Not sure how to ask? Try "Hi, [name], hope all is going well with you! I'm in the midst of building my LinkedIn profile, and was wondering if you would be willing to write a brief recommendation for me about the work we did together at [company / school / volunteer project / etc.]. I would, of course, be happy to do the same for you."

Join a Group or Two

Go to the Groups tab at the top of the LinkedIn page, and check out the Groups You May Like option for groups matching keywords in your profile, or search on Groups Directory using some topics that interest you.

Being part of a group lets you connect with people with whom you share an interest, and provides a natural way to reach out to them if you'd like. You may also want to start building your professional visibility by asking or answering questions in the group's discussions, after lurking for a bit to get a feel for how the discussions work.

These steps will help you start building your visibility for potential employers on LinkedIn. For more coaching, check out the New User Starter Guide on the LinkedIn homepage, then click on the More tab at the top of the page, and then Learning Center.

In addition to LinkedIn's career-building focus, Facebook, Twitter, and several other social media tools are also emerging as valuable ways to both position for and find jobs. The best, most current books on this topic (as of this writing) include Joshua Waldman's *Job Searching with Social Media for Dummies,* Susan Britton Whitcomb's *The Twitter Job Search Guide,* and Kristen Jacoway and Jason Alba's *I'm in a Job Search—Now What???: Using LinkedIn, Facebook, and Twitter as Part of Your Job Search Strategy.*

Launch Your Job Search

Once you've laid the groundwork for your job search, you're ready to launch that search. The best way to do this (if possible) is to stay employed in a current job while you are searching for a future job—all things being equal, potential employers tend to prefer to hire people who are currently employed. The key take-away is: don't leave the job you have now until you've lined up your next job.

However, you may be launching your job search after being recently laid off. In that case, you want to approach searching for a job as if it *is* your job. That means you need to be organized, commit a substantial amount of time (as in eight hours a day if you're unemployed), and be diligent with follow-through. However, be sure you also schedule in enough goofing-off time to keep your spirits up—looking for a job can be exhausting and discouraging in a poor economy, and distracting yourself with something (or someone) fun regularly can help you maintain a positive and engaged attitude.

What might your job search process look like? Searching for a job involves numerous steps, including

- identifying what types of jobs require the skills you offer (which, presumably, you've been discovering as you research the job market);
- finding relevant job openings (visible or unadvertised);
- applying for those jobs; and
- following up as appropriate.

Each of these steps can be organized into a daily schedule that keeps you on track, but still sane. So, for example, you might search for job openings from 9:00 A.M. to 11:30 A.M., take an exercise break or meet a friend for lunch, then further research any jobs you've found (who do you know who works for the target company or knows someone who does, what can you discover about the nature of the job and/or the company, etc.) from 1:30 P.M. to 3:30 P.M. From 3:30 P.M. to 5:00 P.M., you might create tailored cover letters and resumes and submit them, or, if there are no jobs to apply for on a given day, spend that time reaching out to individuals in your network to continue your job hunt via your connections. Naturally, if you're currently working full- or part-time for another employer, these steps may either be condensed to fit within the amount of time you can spend on them, or move into the evening hours.

The goal is to have a regular process in place to help you organize and follow through on your job search efforts. You may want to use a spreadsheet to track your efforts, noting where and when applications have been submitted, with whom you've spoken or e-mailed (if applicable), and any follow-up actions you've undertaken or added to your to-do list. Note which people in your network you've reached out to, their recommendations and introductions, and any other relevant information (including when you sent them a thank you e-mail and updated them on the outcome of their information). And make sure you've updated you running to-do list before you wrap up for the day so you'll know where to quickly get started the next day.

Three things to keep in mind as you work on your job search. First, you'll be ahead of the game if you focus as much on *who* you know as on *what* you know. The standard numbers are that 15 percent of new hires come from public sources such as job postings online, and about 70 percent via referrals. Although these numbers seem to go up or down depending on which source you check, the reality is that employers vastly prefer to hire someone who's been recommended by someone else they trust. So your job is to make sure that you let everyone in your network help if they can. They need to know you're job-hunting, and what sorts of jobs you're looking for. You need to remain upbeat and positive about your prospects in any conversations or communications with your contacts, but keep them apprised of your status every so often so they don't forget to connect you with a job opportunity should one arise.

Second, given today's hiring environment, it's possible that your job search may take you far from your current location. Consequently, it's important to consider before applying for distant jobs just how you feel about moving to a different city or state. If you live close to your family, will you be comfortable moving away from them? Are you okay with leaving friends and colleagues to start building connections with a new community? Under what circumstances might you be willing (or not) to move for a job opportunity? As you think through these questions, keep in mind that such a change of location isn't necessarily forever, and sometimes it may be the fastest way to jumpstart your LIS career.

Third, assume no employer or hiring manager is going to follow up with you after you've submitted an application (or sometimes, even after you've had an interview), and don't take it personally. It's rude, it's crazy-making for the job applicant, and it's the reality in today's job market. Occasionally, some kind soul in an HR department will feel compelled to do the right thing and let an applicant know they've been rejected, but this is such an exception to the rule these days that these individuals almost qualify for sainthood. This is yet another reason to go the get introduced by a friend/colleague/former boss route: people seem to feel more responsible for letting you know you've not gotten the job when there's a personal connection involved.

Interviewing and Negotiating

The good news is: they liked your resume and cover letter, liked what they found out about you online, and they're considering you for the position. The bad news is: now you've got to ace the interview! Happily, there are a lot of great resources available to help you prepare for this often anxiety-producing experience. Some of these are geared toward any job interview situation—for example, Quintessential Careers' *Job Interview Collections for Job-Seekers* provides a wealth of interview prep questions, while Tony Beshara's *Acing the Interview: How to Ask and Answer the Questions That Will Give You the Job,* and Vicky Oliver's *301 Smart Answers to Tough Interview Questions* both provide more general interview advice.

Others specifically address interviewing for LIS-related jobs. For example, the University of South Carolina's School of Library and Information Science has a great list of 54 frequently asked interview questions, while Libgig's "Top Ten Questions to Ask in a Job Interview" turns the tables and puts you in question mode. The Annoyed Librarian blog has an excellent post from 2008, "Job Interviewee Questions," on how to watch for red flags (indicators that this is not an organization you want to work with) in an interview situation, and Mr. Library Dude's "Library Interview Questions" blog post provides links to 15 mostly LIS-focused articles on interview questions. In addition, academic librarian John Glover's "Telling Stories to Get the Job" article on the LIScareer.com site presents a great overview on how to use telling stories about your accomplishments to demonstrate not just what you know, but what you can *do* with what you know.

What about the dreaded salary issue? As with interviewing, successful salary negotiation is all about being prepared—to ask for what you're worth, and to back it up with knowledge.

Know the Going Rate

What do other people doing this type of work get paid? These are your salary comps, or comparables. Check out Salary.com, Payscale.com, GlassDoor.com (employees at specific companies sharing their salaries), and relevant professional association salary surveys to determine the going rate. Depending on what type of position you're applying for, you may also want to check out the annual *Library Journal Placements and Salaries* report.

Keep in mind that geographic and industry circumstances will influence these numbers. For example, jobs in large cities and on the coasts tend to pay higher (often because of higher costs of living). Also, positions in emerging rather than shrinking industries tend to pay more, for example biotech versus manufacturing.

Know Your Added Value

Most companies have a salary range for a given position; sometimes it's posted, other times not. If it's posted, you'll have a pretty good idea of the negotiating range going in. More likely (especially when applying online), the prospective employer will insist that you name a number or a salary range as part of your application. Rely on the salary comps you've identified, and hit mid- to mid-high range. (Too low and interviewers will question your skills, too high and you'll price yourself out of the running.)

Once you're in an interview situation, you'll want to focus on selling your extraordinary value to the organization, so that by the time you get to the salary negotiation point your interviewer is highly motivated to bring you on board. Although the ideal strategy is to get the interviewer to identify a proposed salary first, most often you'll be pressured to name a number to initiate the discussion.

At that point, you'll be able to say "I know that the pay range for this position is generally $45,000 to $60,000, and I believe my skills put me at the high end of that range." Be ready to identify your unique, value-adding skills and how they'll benefit the company if you're in an interview situation. But also be sure to add "depending on the full benefit package" when you specify a salary number. This will give you the flexibility to ask for additional consideration (for example, more vacation days, stock options, working from home one day a week, etc.) *or* a higher salary if the benefits are skimpy.

Understand Your Own Priorities

As part of preparing your salary negotiation strategy, you'll want to think through what would really be valuable for you. Help with childcare expenses? Tuition reimbursement? Health insurance with no 90-day wait? Know what you're willing to compromise on versus what's truly a deal-breaker.

Be Prepared to Ask for It

Rehearse your lines as often as needed until you're comfortable saying "I'd really love to work with you, but it's important to me to be fairly compensated for the value I'll be contributing. Is there a way we can work together to get to this number?" If you don't ask, you won't get the salary you deserve. For the best coaching on how exactly to jump into this conversation with confidence, you'll want to read, re-read, and probably read again Linda Babcock and Sara Laschever's landmark *Ask For It: How Women Can Use the Power of Negotiation to Get What They Really Want* (equally useful for men and women).

Should New Grads Take Non-LIS Jobs?

One of the questions new LIS grads (or even those who have been employed until recently) ask is whether taking a job that's not in the traditional area of librarianship (school, public, or academic) they're seeking will hurt their chances of eventually landing a job in their chosen field.

Given the somewhat challenging nature of today's current job market for new LIS grads, this question is assuming greater relevance for the profession. Several of my students have mentioned hearing about an unspoken bias among librarians that if you've started your post-grad career in a nonlibrary role, it's much more difficult to be seen as someone dedicated to the profession, and thus you're less likely to be hired for traditional library positions when they do open up.

I asked numerous colleagues who are public and/or academic librarians what advice they would give on this issue, and the consensus seemed to be that while being able to pay your bills pretty much takes precedence over anything else, there are some strategies that will help you position yourself for an eventual transition to the type of work you seek should you need to make this choice. Those strategies were the following.

Stay Connected

Maintain your library association memberships, stay current with library issues, continue to hang out with your friends in the library community. Assume your current job is a temporary one, and that you need to remain engaged with issues of concern to your chosen professional community even if you're not presently working within it.

Stay Visible

If possible, maintain a blog on LIS topics that interest you, comment on others' blogs, use social media to maintain an LIS presence. Find ways to work with your state library association on committees and roundtables, and participate in professional events.

Volunteer

A great way to demonstrate your continued interest in an LIS opportunity is to volunteer in the type of library you'd like to work in, even if only for a couple of hours a week. This will keep your skills up-to-date, provide you with an opportunity to build your LIS professional network, and also give you a group of practitioners who (assuming you are a terrific volunteer!) will be happy to (1) keep an eye out for possible openings in the district for you, (2) provide you with glowing references, and (3) grab you in a heartbeat for any openings their own library may have.

Focus on Transferable Skills

I thought this strategy was particularly smart (and can take no credit for it—it came from friend, colleague, and independent information professional Scott Brown). Basically, it involves looking at your non-LIS/pay-the-bills job as an opportunity to develop some transferable skills that will then enable you to stand out to potential employers because of your combination of LIS-applicable skills and a fresh viewpoint. For example, say your job involves customer service, training, presenting, web development, or perhaps project management. Even though your current use of these skills may not be focused on library patrons, they will certainly be valuable to library employers, especially when you can offer additional insights into how to most effectively use them, based on your previous experience. Your job will be to sell the transferability of those skills to potential LIS employers, but this should be fairly easy to do.

Given the outlook for library jobs for the foreseeable future, it's likely that, at least in the interim, many new grads are going to end up in jobs not in traditional library fields. If work in a public or academic library is your career goal, the tactics outlined above should help keep you headed in that direction.

However, you might also keep in mind that some jobs, those non-LIS positions you hesitated to take, can open up unforeseen opportunities for you to grow and contribute professionally, and reward you handsomely for doing so. You may want to be open to that possibility as well.

Temping as an Interim Job Solution

Working a temporary job, or temping, can be a job-hunter's best friend.

In addition to providing some much-needed professional experience for recent LIS grads, it can also be a great solution for those in the midst of career transitions or life changes, those who've just moved to a new community and need to build professional contacts, or even those who prefer the variety of temporary or project work to the predictability of a permanent position.

In terms of career benefits, temporary work can be equally helpful. It can provide you with opportunities to

- try out different types of work to get a first-hand sense of pros and cons,
- get to know potential employers, and have an opportunity to dazzle them as a temp before you approach them for a permanent position—essentially positioning yourself as a known, and valuable, commodity,

- start building a professional network of references, contacts, and sources of potential job openings if you're either just starting out in your career or have recently moved to a new community,

- start building your professional reputation and brand among multiple groups of colleagues,

- start building a portfolio of projects and accomplishments, and

- potentially position yourself for permanent employment if that's what you seek.

There are three ways to approach finding temporary jobs: (1) sign up with temporary staffing/project agencies that focus on information work, such as LAC or C. Berger Group, (2) sign up with general staffing/project agencies in your region, and highlight your information skills as a stand-out professional value, and/or (3) for companies of interest, scan their website job sections for announcements of project or temporary work. Additionally, don't forget that some of the general job sites, such as Indeed.com and Career Builder.com, also include search options for temporary or contract positions.

Resources

Starred titles are mentioned in the chapter.

Associations

Note: Many associations have their own job boards; sometimes these are available to members only, other times to the public. Below are several examples of LIS-related job boards provided by large associations, but there are many others. A wise strategy would be to check out any and all associations that correspond to your career interests, and then check to see (1) if they post job openings, (2) if you have to be a member to access them, and (3) roughly how many new job openings they post per month (to see if this is a resource worth monitoring). Consider also the major special interest sections and divisions within the associations, which may also have their own job listings.

Careers > Find a Job / Canadian Library Association (CLA)

www.cla.ca/AM/Template.cfm?Section=Library_Careers
Searchable by province or as an aggregated list, the jobs posted here run the gamut from traditional library jobs to more technology-oriented specialties, for example Senior Information Architect for the Ontario House of Commons. An encouraging number (though not a majority) of the jobs post salary ranges.

Job Announcements / American Association of Research Libraries (ARL)

www.arl.org
Membership organization of 126 research libraries (rather than individuals) in North America. Although most of ARL's activities and initiatives take place at the institutional level, the website does offer job

announcements, a list of internships, and a database of LIS graduate student resumes for those six to eight months from graduating.

Jobline / American Society for Information Science and Technology (ASIST)

www.asis.org/jobline.html

View jobs (138 when last checked), create a personal job alert, and/or a jobseeker account. Mostly technical/digital resources management jobs for academic institutions or corporations.

**Joblist / ALA

http://joblist.ala.org/

In addition to aggregating library job openings (primarily for the traditional library paths of school, public, and academic), ALA Joblist also provides several articles per month by practitioners about job search strategies, career-development topics, and related information, all of which are uniformly well-written, knowledgeable, and practical.

Jobs in Library and Information Technology / Library Information Technology Association (LITA)

www.ala.org/lita/professional/jobs

An example of an ALA division with a robust job listing program, where employers can post jobs and job-seekers can research potential job opportunities.

**Resume Review Service / New Members Round Table

www.ala.org/ala/mgrps/rts/nmrt/oversightgroups/comm/resreview/resumereview.cfm

For members of the NMRT, this service is based on volunteers from all types of libraries reviewing and critiquing submitted resumes. In addition, the (conference) onsite Resume Review Service is open to any job-seeker attending either the ALA annual or midwinter conferences (for more information, see the website).

Print Resources

**Babcock, Linda and Sara Laschever. *Ask for It: How Women Can Use the Power of Negotiation to Get What They Really Want.* Bantam, 2009. 336p. ISBN 0553384554.

A follow-up to their earlier landmark work, *Women Don't Ask: The High Cost of Avoiding Negotiation—and Positive Strategies for Change* (2007), *Ask for It* moves readers from an assessment of the problem to practical tactics for negotiating effectively. Read, re-read, and rehearse your lines before you go to the interview.

**Beshara, Tony. *Acing the Interview: How to Ask and Answer the Questions That Will Give You the Job.* McGraw-Hill, 2010. 224p. ISBN 0071738886. Think job interviewing as a verbal martial arts workout: how to prepare for not only the usual questions but also those designed to put you on the defensive, to see how you handle them. Beshara also arms you with the questions you'll want to be sure to ask to ferret out any tell-tale signs of the workplace from hell.

**Buckingham, Marcus and Donald O. Clifton. *Now, Discover Your Strengths.* Free Press, 2001. 272p. ISBN 0743201140.

Basic premise: most of us put our energies into trying to improve our weaknesses rather than building our strengths to a point of excellence. This book will help you identify your strengths, and learn how to invest in them in order to become your professional best self. Highly recommended as a starting point for understanding, then being able to build upon, your innate strengths.

**Enelow, Wendy S. and Louise M. Kursmark. *Cover Letter Magic: Trade Secrets of Professional Resume Writers*, 4th ed. JIST Works, 2010. 448p. ISBN 1593577354.

A comprehensive, step-by-step guide to creating successful cover letters—basically, everything you could ever want to know about cover letters (and more), but all useful information. Related titles are Susan Britton Whitcomb's *Resume Magic*, 4th ed. and *Interview Magic,* 2nd ed., from the same publisher.

Gordon, Rachel Singer and Sarah L. Nesbeitt. *The Information Professional's Guide to Career Development Online.* Information Today, 2002. 401p. ISBN 1573871249.

Gordon not only managed to anticipate many of the trends that are today expected practice, she also provided a timeless, solid approach to methodically building one's career using online platforms as a means, rather than the end. Whenever I am asked to identify the top 10 books on career-building and job-hunting for library and information science students and professionals, Gordon's book is among them. Provides a firm foundation on which to build other, more tool-specific (e.g., Twitter, LinkedIn, Facebook, etc.) strategies.

How to Stay Afloat in the Academic Library Job Pool. Teresa Y. Neely, ed. ALA Publishing, 2011. 152p. ISBN 9780838910801.

Those who have negotiated (or attempted to negotiate) the academic library job process know that it can often be complex, confusing, and opaque—why *is* that search committee waiting for six months before making a hiring decision? Neeley and her contributors, academic librarians at the University of New Mexico and experienced search-committee members, explain how the academic library search process works, what to expect, and how to best position yourself to succeed in your quest for a library job in academe.

**Jacoway, Kristen and Jason Alba. *I'm in a Job Search—Now What??? Using LinkedIn, Facebook, and Twitter as Part of Your Job Search Strategy.* Happy About, 2010. 136p. ISBN 1600051707.

A quick read that presents more than 100 resources and tips for using social media tools to advance both your job search and your career. If you're not already using social media sites for career promotion (networking, visibility, etc.), assume you'll come away with at least several dozen solid action items to improve your job-search odds.

**Levinson, Jay Conrad and David E. Perry. *Guerrilla Marketing for Job Hunters 3.0: How to Stand Out from the Crowd and Tap into the Hidden Job Market Using Social Media and 999 Other Tactics Today.* Wiley, 2011. 315p. ISBN 9781118019092.
Covers creative ways to approach personal branding, key elements of a successful attitude, and tools and tactics for cracking the hidden job market; coaches you through your research plan, provides a resume writing and cover letter boot camp, and lays out the why-to's and how-to's of networking; walks you through LinkedIn and other social media tools and tactics, then describes how to get in front of the people you want to meet with; and explains how to use the force multiplier effect (the military discipline of using multiple tactics at the same time to create synergy—and overwhelm the target) to land the job you seek. Perry's in-your-face style may be bit much for some readers, but there's so much practical info here, you're sure to pick up many, many useful ideas and action items.

**Newlen, Robert R. *Resume Writing and Interviewing Techniques That Work! A How-to-do-it Manual for Librarians.* Neal-Schuman Publishers, 2006. 206p. ISBN 1555705383.
One of the publisher's familiar How-To-Do-It-Manuals for Librarians titles, this work is useful for both jobs in traditional library fields and those outside them. Updating Newlen's earlier *Writing Resumes That Work* (1998), this guide provides an excellent framework for shaping and then presenting your achievements.

**Oliver, Vicky. *301 Smart Answers to Tough Interview Questions.* Sourcebooks, 2005. 384p. ISBN 1402203853.
One of the best of many books designed to help you field challenging interview questions, Oliver's book preps you for questions that are designed to throw you off your game, and helps you take control with answers that showcase your strengths as well as your calm under duress.

**Rath, Tom. *StrengthsFinder 2.0.* Gallup Press, 2007. 183p. ISBN 159562015X.
First read *Now, Discover Your Strengths* (Buckingham, above), then turn to this book to get the clearest assessment of your particular strengths. Comes with an access code for taking the online strengthsfinder assessment. Knowing your unique strengths, and being able to discuss them effectively in an interview, will help you make the case to a hiring manager that you can be a high-value contributor.

Tieger, Paul D. and Barbara Barron-Tieger. *Do What You Are: Discover the Perfect Career for You Through the Secrets of Personality Type,* 4th revised updated ed. Little, Brown and Company, 2007. 416p. ISBN 0316167266.
Think of this as the "what to do with your Myers-Briggs results" guide. The authors have been so successful with this excellent resource that it

has continued as a best-seller through multiple editions. A must-read for those in the midst of career exploration.

**Waldman, Joshua. *Job Searching with Social Media for Dummies.* For Dummies, 2011. 360p. ISBN 0470930721.
Social media (SM) tools (read: LinkedIn, Facebook, Twitter, and a multitude of niche sites) are increasingly important to the job search process for all professions. Waldman provides a step-by-step process for using SM resources to research companies and jobs, make connections that will help you land targeted job openings, and position yourself online— where hiring managers are likely to be researching *you,* as well.

**Whitcomb, Susan Britton, Chandlee Bryan, and Deb Dib. *The Twitter Job Search Guide: Find a Job AND Advance Your Career in Just 15 Minutes a Day.* JIST Works, 2010. 192p. ISBN 1593577915.
Although Twitter might be considered much more high maintenance than, say, LinkedIn, for those who are comfortable with its format Twitter can be a dynamite tool for career-building's big three: networking, professional brand-building, and job searching. This title can be a good starting point if you're not familiar with Twitter, or can furnish additional job-searching insights if you're already an experienced user.

Woodward, Jeannette. *A Librarian's Guide to an Uncertain Job Market.* ALA Editions, 2011. 112p. ISBN 0838911056.
Written for at-risk librarians (i.e., those at risk of losing their jobs) in a supportive yet still authoritative style, *Uncertain Job Market* walks you through the steps necessary to be prepared for the worst, even as you hope for the best. Woodward's focus is on understanding how to recognize impending changes in the profession or your workplace that signal potential jobs in jeopardy, preparing for the economic and emotional fall-out of unemployment, and laying the groundwork to transition into alternative job opportunities and paths.

**Yates, Martin. *Knock 'em Dead Resumes: Standout Advice from America's Leading Job Search Authority,* 9th ed. Adams Media, 2010. 320p. ISBN 144050587X.
Yates, who has several equally successful job-related knock 'em dead titles, here focuses on resumes, and how to create ones that will help you differentiate yourself from the 800 other resumes that have landed in the hiring manager's in-box. See especially the information about online resumes.

Online

Note: Many of the following resources provide good overviews of multiple industries and companies. Keep in mind, however, that whenever the library profession is described in terms of trends and employment, the most reliable numbers will be for traditional librarianship (i.e., school, public, and academic), because that data is consistently tracked. The broader scope of information work, including all of the nontraditional or alternative career tracks, are rarely reflected in these employment numbers.

Also, many of the associations related to your career path or interest undertake their own regular (often annual) overview of their discipline, and make these findings available to their members and sometimes the general public—you'll want to check the organizations' websites for availability. In addition to the resources listed below, check also for job openings posted by your state library, for possible career centers at LIS conferences you may be attending, and any job opportunities posted by your MLIS program for students and/or alumni.

"Building Your Virtual Brand"

http://americanlibrariesmagazine.org/columns/your-virtual-brand
From Meredith Farkas, this *American Libraries* article lays out the benefits of creating an online or e-portfolio, especially for those just beginning their professional careers.

**CareerBuilder

www.careerbuilder.com
In addition to this site's job postings, see its information-rich Career Advice section, especially the articles under Cover Letters & Resumes and Getting Hired.

CareerOneStop

http://careerinfonet.com/
Extraordinarily rich source of information about government jobs and careers in general. Research industries, careers, salary information, and more here. Data is generally pulled from the Bureau of Labor Statistics, which means that most of the information you find based on a search for librarian or library will reflect traditional library positions.

Careers in Federal Libraries

https://groups.google.com/forum/#!forum/careers-in-federal-libraries
Federal librarian Nancy Faget has organized this popular and highly engaged group (nearly 2400 discussion threads/job posts), which provides a terrific entry into seeing what federal library jobs may be open, as well as information about applying for those jobs. According to Nancy, not only are there a good number of federal library job openings, they pay well—so if you're willing to consider relocation, this is a resource you'll want to check out.

Chronicle of Higher Education

http://chronicle.com/section/Jobs/61/
The go-to resource for academic library jobs. Searchable by keyword and location, the jobs listing also allows you to restrict your search to community colleges only.

**Encyclopedia of Associations

[online access varies]
Available as the associations component of the Gale Directory Library online resource, a database licensed by many public and academic

libraries, or through the DIALOG and LexisNexis database services, or as a multivolume print directory. Entries include name, contact information, history and mission, membership numbers, estimated budget, presence of a library, publications, events, and type of organization for each association covered. An invaluable resource for researching potential association/nonprofit employers.

**e-Portfolio (Susanne Markgren)

http://smarkgren.wordpress.com/

Markgren is one of the two Library Career People of Career Q&A with the Career Library People (see Resources, Chapter 1), and her e-portfolio provides an excellent example of how to create a simple but very effective e-portfolio. The goal is to bring together in one online location the various types of information that document not only what you know, but what you have done with that knowledge.

**54 Frequently Asked Interview Questions

www.libsci.sc.edu/career/invufaqs.htm

From the University of South Carolina, this list provides a great starter point for identifying (and preparing for) some of the most commonly asked LIS interview questions that you're likely to encounter in traditional library settings.

**"Finding a Library Job—Updated"

www.libraryjournal.com/article/CA6250888.html

From one of the experts in library job-searching, this online article by Rachel Singer Gordon provides a great overview of the steps needed to break into the library profession for those new to the LIS job market. Practical, realistic, but also encouraging in that Gordon clearly believes that landing a library job is doable.

"From Temporary to Permanent—Making the Best of Your Time as a Temp"

http://liscareer.com/bridgewater_temp.htm

Although author Rachel Bridgewater's experience was with academic libraries, her wise advice about using a temp job to position yourself for permanent opportunities is applicable across all temporary employment situations.

Furthering Your Library Career

www.ala.org/ala/educationcareers/employment/index.cfm

Main page for links to ALA's job-seeking resources: the Get a Job! interactive website, JobLIST, the LITA job site, the Placement Center (active during conventions), and ALA's Human Resource Development and Recruitment (HRDR) Library Employment Resources (in need of updating and building out).

**Glassdoor

www.glassdoor.com

Glassdoor's mission is to help job-seekers "find jobs and see company salaries, reviews, and interviews—all posted anonymously by employees."

Information provided includes North American companies as well as those outside North America, and is drawn from both current and former employees. Searchable by company, industry, and highest-rated company. Also includes best places to work rankings.

**Hoover's Online

www.hoovers.com/

Hoover's company and industry information is primarily available as an online database through academic and/or large public libraries, since its primary market is large companies doing market or competitive research. But if available to you, Hoover's can be a good source for descriptions of key companies in a given industry, as well as for overviews, analysis, and forecasts for those industries themselves.

"How to Find That First Job: Tips and Techniques for LIS Students"

www.lisjobs.com/career_trends/?p=80

Although written in 2001, this article by Lisa Taylor continues to provide relevant and useful advice to those soon to graduate and looking for their entry into the profession.

**Idealist

www.idealist.org

Central clearinghouse for social-good organizations and the jobs and internships they have available.

**Indeed

www.indeed.com

Aggregates postings from job sites, newspapers, associations, and company career sites; searchable by job title, keyword, or company name plus location.

**Industries at a Glance

www.bls.gov/iag

This Bureau of Labor Statistics (BLS) resource provides "a 'snapshot' of national data obtained from different BLS surveys and programs" as well as additional industry detail, including state and regional data, when available. Searchable by alphabetical industry index or by industry numerical order (North American Industry Classification System/ NAICS), this is a good place to start gathering information about industries of potential interest for employment purposes.

**I Need a Library Job

http://inalj.com/

Librarian Naomi House, working with a dedicated team of volunteers, intends to aggregate every single LIS job posting not only in North America but globally as well. Updated daily; sign up for the e-mail alerts to be apprised of an ongoing flow of new job opportunities.

Info Career Trends

www.lisjobs.com/newsletter

Check the archives for an astounding number of still-valuable issues, articles, and practical insights on job interviewing, resumes, and the process of applying for jobs. See especially "Library Interviews: Improving Your Odds" by Karen Evans in the September 2004 issue, and the articles in the January 2001 issue, whose theme is The Library Job Hunt. Although these articles were written years ago, the general advice still resonates.

The Info Pro's Survival Guide to Job Hunting

http://www.infotoday.com/searcher/jul02/mort.htm

Written in summer 2002, this *Searcher* article by Mary-Ellen Mort still provides an excellent overview of how to approach job hunting for LIS professionals, whether just starting out or as someone well into his or her career. Although some of the resources are dated, the advice is not; this is a timeless and useful resource for all LIS job hunters.

"Informational Interviewing: The Neglected Job Search Tool"

http://interview.monster.com/articles/informational/#

Informational interviewing is a key strategy for those exploring career options, and Monster contributing writer Carol Martin describes ten steps necessary to make the most of your interview. This offers useful information for any job exploration or search strategy, both within and outside of the LIS field.

Is an Employment Agency for You?

www.lisjobs.com/rethinking/?p=73

Overview of the different types of employment agencies and what they do, questions to ask about their services (and whether your skills are a match for their jobs/projects) and a list of the major temporary/project/recruiting firms.

Job Hunters Bible > Counseling, Testing & Advice

www.jobhuntersbible.com/counseling/sec_page.php?sub_item=047

The online component of John Bolles' classic job-exploration manual, *What Color is Your Parachute*. Within the Counseling, Testing & Advice section see especially the Online Personality & Traits Tests and the Online Careers Tests entries.

**"Job Interview Collections for Job Seekers"

www.quintcareers.com/interview_question_collections.html

Tons of interview preparation questions, from Quintessential Careers, a content-rich site geared toward helping job-seekers navigate their careers and career change.

**Job Interviewee Questions

http://annoyedlibrarian.blogspot.com/2008/02/job-interviewee-questions.html

A terrific and highly entertaining discussion about what questions or other problematic signals library job applicant should be on the look-out for that may indicate a dysfunctional work environment (translation: excuse yourself from further consideration as a potential job candidate as quickly and gracefully as possible!).

**Job Searching Articles / LIScareer.com

www.liscareer.com/jobhunting.htm
More than 50 job-search advice and coaching articles from the LIScareer. com archives. Covers a wide range of topics, including crafting effective resumes, punching up your portfolio, considering international librari- anship options, and multiple articles on resumes and interviewing.

Job Seekers Salary Calculator

www.jobsearchintelligence.com/NACE/jobseekers/salary-calculator.php
From the National Association of Colleges and Employers (NACE), this salary calculator is one of several reliable sources to check when gathering salary comparables in preparation for negotiating your com- pensation.

Jobshark

www.jobshark.ca
Job aggregator for open positions in Canada, supplemented by addi- tional services like a salary calculator, connections with volunteer op portunities, and resume writing services.

LibGig

www.libgig.com
Sponsored by LAC, the recruiting, placement, and temporary agency, LibGig is a content-rich source of information about the profession, in- cluding a career Q&A section, several excellent blogs, news, career pro- files, events, newsletters, and links to LIS schools. Of specialist interest for job-seekers is its job board and job alerts.

LibInfoSciJobs

http://twitter.com/#!/LibInfoSciJobs
Yet another way to track LIS job openings, this Twitter feed describes itself as "a researched compilation of digital library & information man- agement internships & jobs."

Librarians' Yellow Pages

www.librariansyellowpages.com
This site doesn't list job openings, but instead provides a centralized lo- cation for you to see the wide range of LIS-related vendors (with links to their websites), so you can identify possible employers in the LIS vendor space. Potential jobs may include product development and/or management, sales, customer relations, account management, product training, creating taxonomies, creating online content, competitive in- telligence, market research, and other opportunities.

**Library Interview Questions

http://mrlibrarydude.wordpress.com/nailing-the-library-interview/library- interview-questions/
This post has two parts: the first is a list of 23 sites dedicated to help you identify, prepare for, and navigate tricky interview questions, and the second is a list of some 50 job questions Mr. Library Dude has himself fielded during his career.

**Library Job Postings on the Internet

www.libraryjobpostings.org/

Compiled by Sarah Johnson since 1995, this is a great starting point for identifying job sources in specific states. A monumental effort by a single librarian; thank you, Sarah!

Linkedin > Companies

www.linkedin.com/companies?trk=hb_tab_compy

An alternative route for signing up to follow companies that have a LinkedIn presence. Monitor information updates, press releases, new job postings, etc. (Requires that you have a LinkedIn account as well.)

LinkedIn > Jobs

www.linkedin.com/jobs?displayHome=&trk=hb_tab_findjobs

Job listings posted by the thousands of companies with a LinkedIn presence. Search by company name, keywords, or industry, and/or sign up to start following specific companies to receive alerts about recent developments, employees who have recently joined, left, or been promoted by companies of interest, and receive information about job openings. (Requires you to have a LinkedIn account, which is free.)

**LISJobs.com

www.LISjobs.com

Run single-handedly by Rachel Singer Gordon for years, this resource is now paring down to its core functions, i.e., find a job, post a job, browse and/or post resumes, and Career Q&A with the Library Career People. Search by job title and/or state, or browse the reverse chronological listing of postings. If you're in job-search mode, you'll want to subscribe to the RSS feed for regular job-opening updates.

**Monster

www.monster.com; www.monster.ca

Similar to CareerBuilder, Monster provides not only job listings and the opportunity to post resumes but also a robust collection of job-hunting articles in their Career Advice section under the headings of Interview Center, Resume Center, and Job Search Basics.

**Myers & Briggs Foundation

www.myersbriggs.org/

The go-to resource for identifying your MBTI (Myers-Briggs Type Indicator®) profile and understanding the basic concepts related to personality type. Assume at least one interviewer will be interested in knowing your Myers-Briggs type; this will provide the information you need to respond knowledgeably.

Navigating the Salary Question

http://slisapps.sjsu.edu/blogs/career/?p=103

Q&A follow-up to one of San Jose State University's SLIS program career development workshops. Excellent source of specific language to use when attempting to avoid the salary question during the initial interview.

**Payscale

www.payscale.com/

One of the best-known salary calculators, based on "salary and career data from more than 30 million people, covering 12,000 job titles and 1,100 distinct industries in 150 countries."

"A Permanent Alternative: Temporary, Part-Time Library Work"

http://liscareer.com/johnston_temporary.htm

Written in 2004 by academic librarian Jennifer Johnston, this helpful article explores the pros and cons of temporary positions, how to find them, and how to make the most of them. Probably has even more relevance for today's job seekers than when first written.

**Placements and Salaries [year]

http://features.libraryjournal.com/placements-and-salaries/

Undertaken annually by *Library Journal,* this survey reports on who's getting jobs, where, and at what salary. This will help you identify what salary range to target for specific jobs.

**Plunkett Research

www.plunkettresearch.com

Like the Hoover's information, Plunkett's data is now primarily available as an online database via academic or large public libraries. Although Plunkett's does publish print industry guides, their cost is generally prohibitive for the average job-seeker, so best bet is to check your local libraries to see if any of them include Plunkett among their online resources. If so, check out their industry overviews, company write-ups, and trends and forecast information.

**Resumes / Career Q&A with the Library Career People

www.lisjobs.com/CareerQA_blog/?cat=10

From the Career Q&A with the Library Career People archives, this collection of advice is exceptionally practical, useful, and realistic (as are all their responses). Check out for various aspects of resume best practices.

**Salary.com

www.salary.com

Search by title and location to see a list of relevant options (for example, a search on librarian in a specific zip code brought up information for "Librarian," "Librarian—Higher Ed," "Librarian Assistant," "Chief Medical Librarian," and "Database Librarian," among others). The site provides both free information as well as more detailed, fee-based information.

Simply Hired

www.simplyhired.com

Aggregates more than five million job postings from across the web. Search by keyword and location, or browse by categories such as biotech/science, legal/paralegal, computer/technology, healthcare/nursing, part-time/temporary, and entry level/internships, among others. An especially interesting section is the trends overview section, where you can check out hiring trends, industry trends, benefits trends, and all sorts of other cool trends topics.

"Tactics for Job-Hunting in Hard Times"
www.libraryjournal.com/article/CA6670932.html
Based on a 2009 ALA conference panel sponsored by the ALA New Members Round Table (NMRT), this write-up by Katharine Johnson provides a good overview of the panel's key recommendations, including their three major points: finding a job is a job in itself, there are identifiable best practices to follow when seeking a job (which they enumerate), and it's important to be realistic about prospects and the time involved.

****"Telling Stories to Get the Job"**
www.liscareer.com/glover_stories.htm
Being able to recount stories that demonstrate and showcase your outstanding professional strengths is quickly becoming a key interview strategy. In this article, John Glover discusses why this can be a valuable tool for you, and how to prepare your best stories using the STAR method: Situation, Task, Action, Result.

****"Ten Simple Steps to Create and Manage Your Professional Online Identity: How to Use Portfolios and Profiles"**
http://crln.acrl.org/content/72/1/31.full
Also from Susanne Markgren, this article provides a walk-through of the steps necessary to create an effective online portfolio, as well as the reasons why this is so important to your job-hunting and long-term career goals.

They Hired the Other Candidate—Now What?
http://infonista.com/2011/they-hired-the-other-candidate—now-what/
How to turn a disappointment—losing a job to the competition—into an opportunity to potentially create additional job possibilities.

****"Top Ten Questions to Ask in a Job Interview"**
www.libgig.com/toptenquestionstoask
Most interview job prep focuses on preparing to answer questions that interviewers will shoot at you, but it's just as important to ask thoughtful questions of your interviewer. This article identifies ten questions to ask, and why.

Transferable Job Skills
www.quintcareers.com/transferable_skills.html
Brings together five practical articles on identifying and showcasing in-demand transferable skills. Three of the articles deal with shaping cover letters so that they most effectively highlight your transferable skills, while the two others speak to their strategic value to your career and provide a detailed list organized by type of transferable skill (communication, research and planning, human relations, organization/management/leadership, and work survival). Not specific to LIS careers, but nevertheless applicable.

USAJobs

www.USAJobs.gov

The job aggregation site for all federal jobs. Search by keyword and location, with special filters for individuals with disabilities, veterans, students and recent graduates, and senior executives.

**"Using Portfolios and Profiles to Professionalize Your Online Identity (for Free)"

www.liscareer.com/markgren_portfolio.htm

Another helpful article from digital librarian and LIS career expert Susanne Markgren, this is an excellent overview of the what, why, and how-to of e-portfolios.

**Vault Career Intelligence [Vault Reports]

www.vault.com

Most of the Vault content is fee-based, so your best option if you are a student or recent grad is to check to see if your college career center offers access. You can read the site blogs and a substantial number of well-done career articles for free, but generally Vault is in the business of selling special reports on key industries and job-search topics (or signing up college career centers for their full online offerings).

**WetFeet

www.wetfeet.com

With a mission of equipping "job seekers . . . with the advice, research, and inspiration you need to plan and achieve a successful career," WetFeet provides a wealth of articles, blog posts, insider tips, employee profiles, and industry overviews to help you accomplish that goal. Like Vault, WetFeet is in the business of selling career overviews (e.g., "Careers in Marketing"), but they are generally current and very reasonably priced. While they don't offer a guide on the library profession, they do offer insights into non-LIS career paths that may have relevance to alternative LIS options.

Workopolis

www.workopolis.ca

Search job by keyword/title and city or province, plus browse jobs by broad category (administrative, finance, healthcare, retail, technology, etc.). In addition, post resumes and check out multiple additional career resources such as articles, salary calculators, resume advice, and further education resources. A key resource for Canadian jobs.

Recruiting, Placement, and Temporary Job Firms

Note: The firms listed below have a national presence; for recruiting, placement, and temporary job firms that focus on a specific geographic area (for example, a state or city), try searching online using variations of the terms "recruiter," "placement," and "temporary job," your target location, and the type of LIS work you're interested in, for example cataloging or records management.

Advanced Library & Information Management

www.aimusa.com

Specializes in placing librarians and support staff in special, public, academic, school, and government libraries and information centers throughout the United States.

Bradbury Associates/Gossage Sager Associates

www.gossagesager.com

Specializes in executive searches for all types and locations of libraries.

The Cadence Group

www.cadence-group.com

Woman-owned information and records management consulting firm whose services include temp, temp-to-hire, and direct hire recruiting for clients.

**C. Berger Group, Inc.

www.cberger.com

Helps academic institutions, corporations, trade associations, law firms, public libraries, hospitals and medical libraries, and other U.S.-based organizations recruit librarians and information specialists for staff vacancies. Specializes in executive searches, customized sourcing programs, direct hires, temp-to-hire, and temporary positions for libraries and information centers.

Corbus Library Consultants

www.libraryjobs.com

Works with client libraries and library boards to recruit library directors.

InfoCurrent

www.corestaff.com/Solutions/Pages/Specialized%20Services/Infocurrent.aspx

Focuses on staffing client projects in records management and library science. See their website for an interesting list of the areas they cover, which mirror many of the emerging career paths for LIS professionals.

Information International Associates, Inc.

www.iiaweb.com

Contract information services firm that provides library management and other professional services to numerous clients, but especially government agencies.

John Keister & Associates

www.johnkeister.com/library/

Executive search firm specializing in executive-level candidates for corporations and directors for libraries.

Labat-Anderson Inc.

www.usis.com/Information-Management-Support-Services.aspx

Provides many types of specialized contract expertise to clients, including information management and support services (records management, litigation support, and library services such as cataloging, serials management, and loose-leaf filing).

**LAC

www.lac-group.com

Encompasses a wide range of information-based client services, staffing for consulting and project management, information and asset management, library and research services, and legal services, among others. LAC also does recruiting for client firms. Formerly called Library Associates.

PRO LIBRA Associates, Inc.

www.prolibra.com

Focuses on providing experienced library personnel who specialize in all aspects of library service and maintenance to corporations, public organizations, and individuals. Pro Libra provides consulting services, personnel staffing (direct hire/temp/temp-to-hire), and project management.

PTFS

www.ptfs.com

Contract information services firm providing expertise and project staffing in the areas of enterprise contract management, Freedom of Information Act (FOIA) and declassification solutions, open source ILS and DLS systems, professional support services, systems integration and content management solutions, and digitization and content conversion.

4
Start Your
Career off Right

Chapter Highlights

- Communicating Effectively
- Becoming an Effective Team Player
- Responding Positively to Change
- Getting Things Done
- Staying Professionally Current
- Importance of Self-Leadership to Your Career

When starting your career as an LIS professional, you'll want to make sure that you take every opportunity to establish yourself as an outstanding contributor. On the other hand, you'll also want to demonstrate to your colleagues that you understand the importance of paying dues and that you respect their knowledge and experience. It can be a tricky path to navigate, but literally everyone who starts a new job (or career) has had to deal with this challenge, so no doubt you'll succeed with flying colors!

What does being an outstanding contributor entail? It means contributing your best to your team's priorities, your organization's goals, and the profession of which you've chosen to be a part.

However, transitioning into that outstanding contributor role can be relatively uncharted territory for new MLS grads, as Elisabeth Doucett points out in her *What They Don't Teach You in Library School,* an overview of the professional, people, and job-performance skills that you need to succeed in your LIS career. In what area do you want to develop specialized skills? How will you continue to develop professionally? What about networking and building your professional brand? All part of taking charge of your fledgling career and starting off right.

To boil it down to its most basic elements, in order to become a strong contributor, you'll need to master four key skills. These are

- the ability to communicate effectively up, down, and across—in other words, with your managers, your peers, and your subordinates;
- the ability to work effectively in a team environment, either as a team member or leader;
- the ability to respond positively to change and help others do so as well; and
- the ability to get things done.

Communicating Effectively

According to Joan C. Curtis, author of *Managing Sticky Situations at Work,* there are six messages in any conversation:

- what you *mean* to say
- what you *actually* say
- what the other person *hears*
- what the other person *thinks* he/she hears
- what the other person *says*
- what you *think* the other person says

No wonder communication can get so complicated so fast. Yet only by knowing what to say, how to say it, and when to say it—whether written or verbally, one-on-one or with a group, with customers, clients, patrons, board members, and across multiple generational and cultural lines—can you contribute positively to your organization.

Each one of these exchanges can provide its own set of challenges, but fortunately there are some great resources to call on to ace most communications challenges. One of the most basic (and also one of the oldest) but still valuable resources: *How to Win Friends and Influence People* by Dale Carnegie. Writing in 1937, Carnegie asserted that "the ability to express ideas, assume leadership, and to arouse enthusiasm among people" was key to succeeding in life and in business. Carnegie emphasized communicating with others in ways that let them know you appreciate and value their ideas and contributions.

Another excellent resource for developing your people skills in general, including communication, is *PeopleSmart: Developing Your Interpersonal Intelligence* by Melvin L. Silberman. He identifies eight key "smart skills" that provide the basis for positive interpersonal communication, including the ability to (1) understand people, (2) express yourself clearly, (3) assert your needs, (4) exchange feedback, (5) influence others, (6) resolve conflict, (7) be a team player, and (8) shift gears, that is, taking steps to reframe a difficult pattern of interpersonal exchange. *PeopleSmart* will be especially effective for you when you find yourself dealing with people whose own communications styles are, shall we say, less enlightened.

You may also want to explore resources for more specific communication issues. For example, when dealing with gender communications issues, the classic work is Deborah Tannen's *You Just Don't Understand: Women and Men in Conversation*—an overview of the different ways that men and women interpret statements, tone, and meaning in conversations. She addresses workplace specific communications in her related book, *Talking from 9 to 5: Women and Men at Work*.

For understanding how to communicate (and work) most effectively in a culturally diverse world at both the local and global level, David Livermore's *The Cultural Intelligence Difference: Master the One Skill You Can't Do Without in Today's Global Economy* provides valuable insights into how to embrace, respect, and work collaboratively with people of diverse backgrounds and life experiences.

And for understanding communication issues among the four to five generations that we now have in many workplaces, Linda Gravett and Robin Throckmorton's *Bridging the Generation Gap: How to Get Radio Babies, Boomers, Gen Xers, and Gen Yers to Work Together and Achieve More* offers interesting insights into the challenges of cross-generational communication that we will continue to face in libraries as well as nonlibrary workplaces for years to come.

Crossing all of these groups, however, is Tom Rath and Donald O. Clifton's *How Full is Your Bucket? Positive Strategies for Work and Life,* which explores and champions the role of positive psychology in creating healthy, supportive human interactions in the workplace as well as outside it. The powerful effect of positive reinforcement and a trust-based environment makes *all* communication effective communication.

Bottom line: It's tough to beat Steven Covey's fifth habit as described in his popular *The Seven Habits of Highly Effective People:* seek first to understand, then be understood.

Becoming an Effective Team Player

Smart organizations (and smart bosses) create work environments that encourage and support the concept of high-performing teams—that is, groups of people who are committed to achieving stated goals together by helping each other contribute at their highest levels. If you're just starting out in your career you're more likely to be a team member (rather than leader), which provides you with the perfect opportunity to practice being a high-value contributor by learning from the best (and sometimes worst) practices of your fellow team members. And you'll find that there are plenty of both.

Patrick Lencioni, author of the best-selling *The Five Dysfunctions of a Team,* summed up the challenge of creating effective teams this way:

> Not finance. Not strategy. Not technology. It is teamwork that remains the ultimate competitive advantage, both because it is so powerful and so rare. (vii)

It's not surprising, then, that being able to work effectively in a team setting is becoming one of the most sought-after attributes when hiring managers are asked what characteristics their company is most in need of among new hires.

How do you become an effective team member and contributor? Concentrate on the following actions.

Be Reliable

If you agree to accomplish something by a specific time, do it. Consistently. The ability of other team members to complete their tasks may be dependent on your deliverable, so let them know they can count on you.

Actively Listen

Team meetings can often disintegrate into power plays, expressed as who interrupts whom the most often, also known as *I'm the important person here so I'm not going to listen to a thing anyone else says.* File this under Worst Team Practices, and be smart enough to realize that high-performing teams only result from mutual respect and actively listening to each other.

Communicate Your Views Honestly, Then Support the Final Decision

Your job is to contribute your best professional judgment, which at times will put you in conflict with others' ideas. State your opinion and the rationale underlying that opinion, but understand that if you're not in charge, your job is to implement the decision your boss has made to the best of your abilities.

Share Information

One of the most exciting changes that the younger staffers are expected to bring into the workplace with them is an eagerness to share, rather than hide, information. The mantra *information is power* has been used often as a way to compete with or undermine others; it is equally damaging to team effectiveness. So be generous and open with the information your fellow team members need to succeed and they'll be likely to reciprocate.

Engage and Assist

Being an effective team member requires you to engage in the team's goals, to assume mutual responsibility for their achievement, and to help other team members when necessary to accomplish those goals, if and when *occasionally* necessary. (If it's necessary to bail out another team member on a regular basis, then it's time for the team leader to take another look at individual responsibilities.) But generally speaking, the goodwill and positive energy that comes from generously helping each other out when the need arises is a powerful contributor to team effectiveness and success

Responding Positively to Change

In "Managing Personal Change," digital libraries guru Roy Tennant points out that, at his age, he has "probably *forgotten* more technologies than many of our young librarians have ever known," and that "they will know more than I have ever known in my lifetime." The result of our increasing pace of change is, suggests Tennant, simply something we must get used to.

Tennant is right, of course, but nevertheless the ability to respond positively to change, and to help others do so as well, can be challenging for all of us. It's disruptive, disorienting, and almost always is accompanied by a sense of loss, even if the ultimate outcome of a given change turns out to be positive. However, just as surely as being change-resistant is often hardwired into our psyches, so, too, is the inevitability of change hardwired into our lives and workplaces.

Spencer Johnson's classic (and endlessly parodied) parable on change, *Who Moved My Cheese,* makes the point that the wisest (and least damaging) approach to change is to anticipate it, be ready to let go of the way things were, and be courageous about embracing new directions. But another way to look at change is to develop the habit of finding the opportunity embedded in it. As Mary Catherine Bateson noted in *Composing a Life,* "At the center of any tradition, it is easy to become blind to alternatives. At the edges, where lines are blurred, it is easier to imagine that the world might be different. Vision sometimes arises from confusion." The reality is, more and more of us in the LIS profession are operating at the edges on a regular basis, and it's highly likely that the growth in the profession—and your career opportunities—is going to be there as well.

Whether you're new to the profession or you're a seasoned practitioner, you'll likely find yourself in the midst of ongoing changes, hanging around those edges, in the coming years. Traditional libraries are restructuring, special libraries are being decentralized, but information skills are also in increasing demand in an expanding range of organizations. So this is the perfect time to start developing your resiliency skills, chief among them being your ability to respond positively to change. Those changes may be in your job responsibilities, your organization's management (i.e., your boss), or even throughout your profession, but regardless of where they occur, your attitude will determine whether you move forward with change or are de-railed by it.

In *The Resiliency Advantage: Master Change, Thrive Under Pressure, and Bounce Back from Setbacks,* author and resiliency expert Al Siebert states that "highly resilient people are flexible, adapt to new circumstances quickly, and thrive in constant change. Most importantly, they *expect* to bounce back and feel confident they will." As a new professional, one of the best career skills you can develop will be just this resiliency in the face of change: rather than staying stuck in defensiveness or denial, you'll be the one able to help your coworkers move forward positively toward new solutions.

Getting Things Done

Self-management skills involve setting and meeting goals, both per-sonal and professional. In the workplace, your ability to get things done (or lack thereof) will influence people's confidence in your professional judg-ment and their willingness to rely on you—both important contributors to your ability to assume higher levels of responsibility. But for many people, especially those just starting their careers, skills like self-leadership, time management, and goal-setting may be unfamiliar at best, frustratingly dif-ficult at worst. The good news: these are skills that can be learned.

One of the best-known experts on personal productivity and goal-setting is Brian Tracy, who has a multimedia empire based on coaching those strug-gling with both the idea and execution of achieving goals. A good starting point for learning more about both is his book *Goals! How to Get Everything You Want—Faster Than You Ever Thought Possible.* Despite the title's high hype factor, the book actually does a solid job of explaining both the process of goal-setting and then the actions necessary to achieve the goals you've set. Although Tracy focuses on both personal and professional goals, you'll find his ideas especially helpful if you're struggling to complete tasks or projects at work.

Author Henriette-Anne Klauser takes a different, more right-brain ap-proach to goal-setting in her *Write it Down, Make It Happen: Knowing What You Want and Getting It.* Strong on writing down goals as a means of visual-ization and generating the power of intention and commitment around those goals, Klauser supports her metaphysical underpinnings with additional ex-ecution steps, a combination that has led to success for both the book and its readers.

At a perhaps more micro level is David Allen's *Getting Things Done: The Art of Stress-Free Productivity,* which, to put it mildly, has generated hundreds of thousands of impassioned advocates. (Yes, I've actually seen "What would David Allen do?" stickers in friends' offices.) No touchy-feely guy here, Allen instead methodically lays out an approach to personal and office organization that is tightly focused and based on daily organizational habits strictly adhered to. The good news is that although the upfront, "take control of the chaos" effort can be substantial (depending on the actual level of chaos into which you've descended), once you're up and running on the Getting Things Done (GTD) program, it becomes quite doable and it actually does work for most people.

At the other end of the spectrum is Regina Leeds's *One Year to an Organized Life: From Your Desk to Your Deadlines, the Week-by-Week Guide to Eliminating Office Stress for Good,* which takes a more Zen-like approach to getting organized. Leeds is low-tech and upbeat, and perhaps the best choice (at least initially) for those traumatized by the mere thought of dealing with physical and mental clutter.

Staying Professionally Current

In addition to mastering the four basic skills of becoming a strong contributor, you'll also want to develop a process for staying on top of issues, emerging trends, and important developments in both the profession at large and in your own areas of interest or specialization. The good news? There are many, many information sources to keep you current. The bad news? There are actually more like gazillions of information sources to help you out here—so which ones do you focus on?

The easiest way to deal with your own personal case of information overload is to put together a systematic process for staying on top of the information you need—and avoiding the rest of the bombardment. So as a first step, determine the types of information you want to monitor. For example, print periodicals such as *Library Journal, Searcher, School Library Monthly, Journal of Academic Librarianship,* and *EContent* and online publications such as *D-Lib Magazine* will provide authoritative, in-depth analyses of key topics. Information aggregators like *LLRX, Docuticker,* the *Internet Public Library/ipl2 newsletter,* and other topic-specific information aggregators will do the work of scanning multiple information sources for you. The professional associations you belong to may have their own electronic discussion lists, which you'll want to stay abreast of. And social media tools such as hundreds of LIS blogs, Facebook pages, Twitter feeds, YouTube videos, podcasts, and similar resources will enable you to gain from others' ideas and insights about the LIS profession. (Your job is to decide which ones to monitor—a good starting point is to ask professionals you admire what they track.)

A good environmental scanning or current awareness program needs to be easy to keep up with, consistent, and as automatic as possible—you want information to come to you rather than having to go find it. So now is the time to be really, really grateful for the tech geniuses who came up with

RSS feeds. Not only can you subscribe to most blogs, discussion lists, and e-newsletters via RSS feed, but as LIS tech guru Meredith Farkas points out in her article "Current Awareness through RSS," many database vendors and journal publishers provide RSS feeds for journal tables of contents—so you can identify what publications you want to monitor and have their tables of contents e-mailed to you automatically if you have access to their databases.

Another important source for staying professionally current is attending professional conferences at the local, state, regional, and national levels. These may be LIS conferences, conferences related to your area of specialization, or even conferences for your employer's industry—but your goal is to learn as much as you can about emerging trends, technologies, and issues in your field. Not able to attend conferences? Look at the online conference programs to find presentations of interest, and then check after the conference to see if any of these have been posted online by their presenters. If not, research the presentation topic on your own to learn more, and/or contact the speaker for additional information.

The goal here is get into the career-long habit of staying up to date on not only where the profession is, but where it's headed. This provides you with two important career benefits. First, it enables you to increase your value—through increased knowledge—in your current position. But also it ensures that over the duration of a decades-long career, your skills and expertise remain up-to-date and valuable.

Importance of Self-Leadership to Your Career

Lastly, in order to become a high-value contributor on your team, in your workplace, and long-term throughout your career, it's critical to understand and embrace the concept of self-leadership. That means that you *take* responsibility for determining all of your goals and *accept* responsibility for all of your outcomes.

Why? Two reasons. First, most managers are way too busy to provide the ongoing level of feedback and coaching that many younger staffers may have previously received from the adults in their lives, so moving to self-leadership puts *you* in the significant adult role—where you'll want to be, as someone aspiring to professional respect.

Second, one of the first things a career-savvy professional learns is that regardless of who you're working for, we're all self-employed. That means that it's up to you to take charge of your career path, including determining what else you intend to gain from your current position besides a paycheck. Because, given this economy and the unemployment realities of today's job environment, part of what you should be doing from an employment perspective is identifying what additional things you can do in your current job to position yourself for your next one, whether that's a year or ten years down the road.

For example, consider the following questions.

What Do You Need to Learn, and How Will You Learn It?

Given how quickly existing skills become outdated, it's important to keep learning just to stay current in your field. Figure out what you need to learn to keep your skills competitive, and how, where, and when you'll do that. Does your employer offer in-house training, support for conference attendance, tuition reimbursement? Take advantage of all of it.

How Will You Build, Nurture, and Expand Your Network?

Professional relationships are critical to opening up career opportunities. Part of your career development plan will be to find ways to connect: participate in professional associations, contribute to online communities, reach out to help others in your network. Make as many connections as you can both on and off the job (vendors, by the way, can be exceptionally valuable network connections). Join relevant professional associations and get active at the local level. Then make sure that you have a personal record all of your network contact information, rather than just storing this data on your office computer.

What Actions Will You Take to Grow Your Professional Brand?

Today's online tools make it easy to showcase your strengths to the world. Establishing your professional brand *outside of your employer* provides an opportunity for others to learn more about the value you could bring to their organization and the contributions you've made to others'. Determine what actions you will take on a regular basis to position yourself not just as the person who has XYZ job, but as an expert on the relevant topic. At an absolute minimum, make sure you have a robust LinkedIn profile, and are an active participant in at least one or two professional groups.

Can You Work with a Mentor?

A mentor relationship can be formal or casual, but either way your objective is to find someone you respect who can help coach you through your job challenges and perhaps even counsel you through your more challenging career decisions. Many organizations have mentor programs in place; if your employer is one of them, take advantage.

What Portfolio-Building Activities Can You Engage In?

Volunteer to lead a new initiative, participate in a key team effort, learn a new system, and teach other staffers. Part of your agenda will be to keep an eye out for these types of opportunities, and then step up.

The key take-away here is that in order to become a high-value contributor throughout your career, it will be up to you to create and deliver that value well beyond the information skills you learned in grad school. There are many resources—both information and people—that can help you learn to do so, but it will be up to you to seek them out and implement their lessons.

Resources

Starred titles are mentioned in the chapter.

Associations

ALA Connect
http://connect.ala.org
Another useful resource from ALA, this common virtual space is intended to provide a forum for exchanging information, connecting with other group members, posting events (in person and virtual), and sharing documents. It provides yet another way to continue to build your professional knowledge.

ALA Emerging Leaders Program
www.ala.org/ala/educationcareers/leadership/emergingleaders/index.cfm
Leadership development program intended to have newer library workers in the United States "participate in problem-solving work groups, network with peers, gain an inside look into ALA structure, and have an opportunity to serve the profession in a leadership capacity." Applicants must be under 35 years old or be a new library professional of any age with fewer than five years' experience (professional or parapro) in the field; able to attend both annual and midwinter conferences (and willing to work virtually in between); willing to volunteer with ALA or an ALA group (e.g., Division) upon completion of the program; and be an ALA member and/or member of the sponsoring organization. Submission deadline is generally August 1 and 75 participants are chosen each year.

New Members Round Table (NMRT)
www.ala.org/ala/mgrps/rts/nmrt/index.cfm
An ALA group comprising more than 2,000 members, NMRT is designed to "help those who have been association members less than ten years become actively involved in the association and the profession." To that end, NMRT focuses on providing opportunities for involvement and/or training for committee engagement, programs to inform those new to the profession, leadership training and opportunities, and programs for MLIS students to encourage professional involvement and networking. The NMRT electronic list, NMRT-L, is an especially valuable resource for information sharing; the group also publishes a newsletter (*NMRT Footnotes*) and an online peer-reviewed publication (*Endnotes*).

Print Resources

Periodicals

Following is a representative sample of LIS publications, some general in scope, others more specialized. But it's fair to assume that no matter what area of information work you're involved in, there will be a trade or association publication that covers it.

American Libraries. American Library Association, 1970– . monthly. ISSN 0002-9769.
http://americanlibrariesmagazine.org
Provides an update and analysis of the current state of affairs for the country's traditional libraries. ALA's official publication, *American Libraries* reflects a combination of organization news and information plus other contributed articles on key library topics.

Association of College and Research Libraries, 1956– . monthly. ISSN 0010-0870.
http://crl.acrl.org
A referred/peer-reviewed publication, *College & Research Libraries* provides articles of interest to those working in college and research libraries. Topics covered include research studies, case studies, new projects and initiatives, and discussions of relevance to academic librarians. The website includes archived articles abstracts, but full-text versions are available to ACRL members only.

Computers in Libraries. Information Today, 1980– . 10 issues/yr. ISSN 1041-7915.
www.infotoday.com/cilmag/
Monthly magazine providing complete coverage of the news and issues in library information technology. Check the website for sample full-text articles.

***EContent: Digital Content, Media and Publishing Strategies.* Information Today, 1976– . 10 issues/yr. ISSN 1525-2531.
www.econtentmag.com/
A must-read for professionals (including executives and decision-makers) in the digital publishing, media, and marketing content markets. Covers the emerging issues, tools, trends, and thought leaders in the digital content universe. Check the website for sample full-text articles.

***Journal of Academic Librarianship (JAL).* Mountainside Publishing, 1975– . bimonthly. ISSN 0898-1752.
www.elsevier.com/wps/find/journaldescription.cws_home/620207/description
A refereed/peer-reviewed publication, *JAL* provides academic librarians a forum through which to share ideas, discuss issues, and explore future scenarios. Much of the content is research-based, which ensures rigorous authority.

Knowledge Quest. American Association of School Librarians, 1997- . 5 issues/yr. ISSN 1094-9046.
www.ala.org/ala/mgrps/divs/aasl/aaslpubsandjournals/knowledgequest/kqweb.cfm
Knowledge Quest focuses on topics relevant to building-level media specialists, supervisors, and library educators involved in managing or

teaching about school library media centers. Check the website for excellent archived articles; students considering this career path should be sure to check out Carol A. Brown's article, "Trends and Issues: What's Important for the 21st Century School Librarian?" The official journal of AASL.

****Library Journal.** Reed Business Information, 1876– . 20 issues/yr. ISSN 0363-0277.
   www.libraryjournal.com
   Key resource for broad-based coverage of libraries, the library profession, and the industries that support it. *Library Journal* issues include news items, an events calendar, industry analyses, vendor overviews, features, profiles, and several special issues per year. Its book reviews are relied on by librarians for their objectivity and usefulness. The website is an extraordinarily content-rich resource with archived articles, salary surveys, a career resource center, and job postings; all are publicly accessible for free.

Online: Exploring Technology & Resources for Information Professionals. Information Today, 1975– . bimonthly. ISSN 0146-5422.
   www.infotoday.com/online/default.shtml
   Online is a key resource for librarians and other information professionals who need the most current information about online resources, research techniques, and research tools. Content includes how-to articles, product reviews, case studies, and coverage focused on the selection, use, and management of digital information products. The website provides sample full-text articles.

Public Libraries. Public Library Association, 1961– . bimonthly. ISSN 0163-5506.
   www.publiclibrariesonline.org/
   This official publication of PLA covers industry news, association updates, and articles, columns, and feature stories of value to those managing the country's more than 9,000 public libraries.

School Libraries in Canada Online. Canadian School Library Association, 1980– . 4 issues/yr. ISSN 0227-3780.
   www.clatoolbox.ca/casl/slic/
   Official publication of CASL, covering trends, insights, and issues among Canada's school libraries.

School Library Journal. Reed Business Information, 1961– . monthly. ISSN 0362-8930.
   www.schoollibraryjournal.com
   Information, resources, and insights for school and children's librarians, with an emphasis on integrating libraries into the school curriculum. In addition, *School Library Journal* content is geared toward helping readers become technology, reading, and information literacy leaders. Check the website for an archive of articles and a subscribers-only career center.

**School Library Monthly*. Libraries Unlimited, 1983– . monthly. ISSN 0889-9371.
www.schoollibrarymonthly.com/
Coverage includes practical classroom-tested instructional strategies, effective advocacy and leadership initiatives, inquiry learning strategies, and program, professional development, and management ideas and strategies. Check the website for additional content related to topics covered in the print edition.

**Searcher*. Information Today, 1993– . monthly. ISSN 1070-4795.
www.infotoday.com/searcher/default.asp
A must-read for professional database searchers, such as those who do competitive intelligence, market research, and other types of business research. Check the website for sample full-text articles.

Teacher Librarian: The Journal for School Library Professionals. Rockland Press, 1998– . bimonthly. ISSN 1481-1782.
www.teacherlibrarian.com
Previously known as *Emergency Librarian,* this publication explores topics of interest to school librarians with a focus on their teaching mission. Articles address such areas as collaboration, leadership, technology, and management. Check the website for a useful (and free) collection of annotated links, articles, guides, and white papers.

Books

**Allen, David. *Getting Things Done: The Art of Stress-Free Productivity.* Penguin, 2002. 267p. ISBN 0142000280.
The book that launched a thousand—okay, a hundred thousand—GTD disciples. David Allen lays out a very specific process for gaining control over all aspects of your life, and a systematic structure for avoiding falling back into those oh-so-familiar bad habits that led to chaos in the first place.

**Bateson, Mary Catherine. *Composing a Life.* Grove Press, 2001. 256p. ISBN 0802138047.
Daughter of anthropologists Margaret Mead and Gregory Bateson, the author explores the lives of five high-achieving women (including herself) with the goal of establishing a common thread among women's lives, that is, that they compose their own life narratives. Although her premise is appealing, it's probably much more realistic to say that all of us, men and women, *improvise* our lives on a daily basis. And it's that ability to improvise—to adapt—that is the heart of resiliency.

Buckingham, Marcus. *Go Put Your Strengths to Work: 6 Powerful Steps to Achieve Outstanding Performance.* Free Press, 2010 320p. ISBN 07432[.
Buckingham gained fame for his previous book, *Now, Discover Your Strengths* (Free Press, 2001), which asserted that people tend to ignore

their strengths and focus instead on fixing their weaknesses, with the result that weaknesses are only minimally improved and strengths are never honed to excellence. This work applies his strengths theme to helping individuals excel in the workplace. Although written for managers, the book is equally useful to individuals who would like to help introduce the key concepts to their team members and bosses.

**Carnegie, Dale. *How to Win Friends and Influence People.* Pocket Books, 1998. 288p. ISBN 0671027034.
It seems unbelievable that a simple book first published in 1937 could continue to wield such influence over how thousands of today's most influential, successful leaders approach their work relationships, but yes, it does. (It's said that the only diploma that hangs in Warren Buffett's office is his certificate from Dale Carnegie Training.) Packed with basic advice about how to build positive relationships and influence positive outcomes, Carnegie's classic work is a great resource for those looking for coaching about how to work effectively with others.

**Covey, Stephen R. *The Seven Habits of Highly Effective People.* Free Press, 2004. 384p. ISBN 0743269519.
The classic work on personal productivity and effectiveness, Covey's *Seven Habits* can be a valuable primer on the key elements of creating individual value for your family, community, and employer. The applicability of his ideas is evident in the sustained popularity of the book and its offshoots (e.g., CDs, DVDs, speaking engagements, calendars, etc.). Two favorite Coveyisms: you cannot talk your way out of something you have acted your way into, and seek first to understand, then be understood.

**Curtis, Joan C. *Managing Sticky Situations at Work: Communication Secrets for Success in the Workplace.* Praeger, 2009. 213p. ISBN 0313362785.
Curtis is a communications coach, and her guidance here on how to navigate workplace interactions is thoughtful and, with some practice, easy to apply. Organized around the Say It Just Right model, chapters cover sticky situations with your boss, coworkers, clients, subordinates, and others.

**Doucett, Elisabeth. *What They Don't Teach You in Library School.* ALA Editions, 2010. 160p. ISBN 0838935923.
You may have graduated with killer LIS skills, but how much do you know about the basic professional and business skills that will enable you to excel in your first job? If you're feeling like you could use a bit of help here, Doucett's guide is just the ticket. She focuses on three broad categories: when you're looking for that first job, when you've landed it and you're new on the job, and when you've had a bit of experience on the job and are ready to learn more to expand your skill set—and value to your employer.

Goleman, Daniel. *Emotional Intelligence: Why It Can Matter More Than IQ.* Bloomsbury Paperbacks, 2010. 368p. ISBN 1408806169.

Originally published in 1995, this landmark work set forth the idea that emotional intelligence, including the ability to control your impulses, self-motivation, an ability to feel empathy for others, and social competence in relations with others, among other skills, is a stronger predictor of success in all areas of life than is simply having a high IQ. Emotional intelligence (EQ) is now widely accepted as an important element of creating successful management and leadership relations, and a key strength in potential employees.

The first of several EQ-focused titles Goleman has published, this book focuses on EQ's 12 self-mastery competencies and 13 key relationship skills to help you understand how you can contribute to—or create—a more positive and high-performing workplace (and career).

**Gravett, Linda and Robin Throckmorton. *Bridging the Generation Gap: How to Get Radio Babies, Boomers, Gen Xers, and Gen Yers to Work Together and Achieve More.* Career Press, 2007. 222p. ISBN 156414898X.

Yep, working with someone who could be your grandparent –or your grandchild—is creating some pretty interesting interpersonal dynamics in the workplace these days. Gravett and Throckmorton focus on recruiting and retaining the best employees from all generations based on their unique motivations; case studies demonstrate how to implement the authors' advice. Expect more research studies, books, *Harvard Business Review* articles, workshops, and conference presentations on this topic in the coming years.

Heath, Chip and Dan Heath. *Switch: How to Change Things When Change is Hard.* Crown Business, 2010. 320p. ISBN 0385528752.

An engaging, amazing book on how individuals process and react to change in their lives, *Switch* will help you understand your own reactions to change and manage them in a more effective, positive manner. Since change is a constant factor for anyone growing their career in new directions, this book will be a welcome companion as you push beyond your comfort zone to increase your level of contribution on an ongoing basis.

**Johnson, Spencer and Kenneth Blanchard. *Who Moved My Cheese? An Amazing Way to Deal with Change in Your World and in Your Life.* Putnam's Sons, 1998. 96p. ISBN 0399144463.

This is one of those books you love or hate, with very few readers landing in between. Johnson's parable, about how people do or don't deal effectively with change, uses as its central narrative mice in a maze who suddenly have their cheese moved to a new spot. The different responses of two pairs of mice are used to illustrate the importance of always being ready to respond to change in a proactive, curious, and positive manner. A quick read, it's worth perusing *Who Moved My Cheese?* if for no other reason than to understand the multiple references to it when people are discussing change-resistance issues.

**Klauser, Henriette Anne. *Write It Down, Make It Happen: Knowing What You Want and Getting It.* Fireside Books, 2001. 250p. ISBN 0684850028.
A more right-brain approach to goal-setting and achieving than most books on this topic, *Write It Down* focuses more on the psychological, spiritual, and self-exploratory aspects of setting goals. Inspirational and motivational, while ultimately also being practical and actionable.

Kotter, John and Holger Rathgeber. *Our Iceberg Is Melting: Changing and Succeeding Under Any Conditions.* St. Martin's Press, 2006. 160p. ISBN 031236198X.
Kotter, the leading authority on corporate change and author of *Leading Change* (see Chapter 8), here does change management lite, with a fable approach similar to that used in *Who Moved My Cheese?* but with more of an emphasis on large (corporate) team dynamics.

**Leeds, Regina. *One Year to an Organized Work Life: From Your Desk to Your Deadlines, the Week-by-Week Guide to Eliminating Office Stress for Good.* Da Capo Lifelong Books, 2008. 304p. ISBN 0738212792.
Known as the Zen organizer, Leeds lays out an organizing schedule of weekly/monthly action items that advance her three core components of taking control: eliminate, categorize, and organize. Leeds' approach is less structured than David Allen's, but has proven effective for many individuals.

**Lencioni, Patrick. *The Five Dysfunctions of a Team: A Leadership Fable.* Jossey-Bass, 2002. 229p. ISBN 0787960756.
Lencioni uses a fictional story as the basis for his lesson about how teams consistently derail themselves (and often, their organizations): through absence of trust, fear of conflict, lack of commitment, avoidance of accountability, and failure to pay attention to and learn from results. Although this book and its follow-up title, *Overcoming the Five Dysfunctions of a Team* (2005) are intended primarily for managers, this is nevertheless good information for team members as well, since it will enable you to identify and address problematic team dynamics as/if they emerge.

Levit, Alexandra. *They Don't Teach Corporate in College: A Twenty-Something's Guide to the Business World,* rev. ed. Career Press, Inc., 2009. 288p. ISBN 0738212792.
Although the business world is referenced in the title, this practical, conversational guide for those new to the workplace is equally valuable to those beginning their careers in library settings. Levit does a great job of arming young workers with the information they need to (1) behave in a professional manner from day one, (2) avoid on-the-job faux pas, and (3) figure out how to not only fit it, but impress the team.

**Livermore, David. *The Cultural Intelligence Difference: Master the One Skill You Can't Do Without in Today's Global Economy.* AMACOM, 2011. 224p. ISBN 081441706X.
Livermore has become the leading writer on cultural intelligence, whether in the organization working with multicultural teammates or

in the multinational, global arena. For libraries and librarians, cultural intelligence is relevant both in their working environment and with the patrons/students/clients they serve. Going well beyond tired politically correct mantras, Livermore makes the case that knowing how to interact respectfully and effectively in a multicultural world will be mandatory for the long-term survival of most organizations. In addition, it will provide important insights and potential opportunities for long-term information careers.

The New Graduate Experience: Post-MLS Residency Programs and Early Career Librarianship. Megan Zoe Perez and Cindy Ann Gruwell, eds. Libraries Unlimited, 2010. 219 p. ISBN 1591588863.
Residency programs are considered one of the most effective ways to mainstream new professionals into key organizational roles while also helping them learn the ropes in an efficient and supportive manner. This compilation of contributions lays out how and why to implement effective residency programs, and the benefits of doing so.

Pink, Daniel H. *Drive: The Surprising Truth about What Motivates Us.* Riverhead Trade, 2011. 272p. ISBN 1594484805.
One of your responsibilities in the workplace will be to determine what motivates you, so you will then understand both how to motivate yourself and what you need from your job to perform at your highest level. *Drive* helps you identify what those motivations might be: specifically, his research indicates that the three primary motivators for most people are autonomy, mastery, and purpose. A fascinating book with many useful insights for working effectively with others as well.

**Rath, Tom. *Strengthsfinder 2.0.* Gallup Press, 2007. 183p. ISBN 159562015X.
An offshoot of the two bestsellers *First Break All the Rules: What the World's Greatest Managers Do Differently* (Buckingham and Coffman, 1999) and *Now, Discover Your Strengths* (2001), *Strengthsfinder 2.0* is the assessment piece of this series. Understanding your own professional strengths is an important aspect of taking charge of your career outcomes because it enables you to identify or create your areas of greatest—and most rewarding—contribution. The book comes with a key for taking an online strengths assessment.

**Rath, Tom and Donald O. Clifton. *How Full is Your Bucket? Positive Strategies for Work and Life.* Gallup Press, 2004. 128p. ISBN 1595620036.
Clifton first contributed to workplace productivity as coauthor of *Now, Discover Your Strengths* (2001) and Rath as author of *Strengthsfinder 2.0* (see above), both based on the strengths research undertaken by the Gallup Poll organization. The focus of *How Full is Your Bucket* is on positive psychology, and the importance of positive reinforcement as a means to boost productivity, individual and team performance, and personal satisfaction. An important resource for understanding how to help others contribute their best efforts, while also doing so yourself.

**Siebert, Al. *The Resiliency Advantage: Master Change, Thrive Under Pressure, and Bounce Back from Setbacks.* Berrett-Koehler, 2005. 225p. ISBN 1576753298.

For LIS professionals, resilience may be the most importance career skill. Fortunately, it's a skill that can be learned, and given the dynamic nature of the profession, one that you may have a chance to practice regularly. Siebert, director of The Resiliency Center and with a Ph.D. in psychology, makes a great coach; his book lays out five developmental steps (with requisite actions for mastering them) to help you learn to get back up after a career (or life) smackdown.

**Silberman, Melvin L. *PeopleSmart: Developing Your Interpersonal Intelligence.* Berrett-Koelher, 2000. 251p. ISBN 1576750914.

"Strong people skills" is one of the top attributes sought by companies in their new hires, yet this skill is never taught in any grad-school course. In *PeopleSmart,* author Silberman builds on the emotional intelligence concept pioneered by Daniel Goleman to provide a four-step plan for improving your people skills. If you have any doubts about your ability to work effectively and positively with others, this should be considered a must-read.

**Tannen, Deborah. *Talking from 9 to 5: Women and Men at Work.* William Morrow Paperback, 1995. 368p. ISBN 0380717832.

The Georgetown University linguistics professor here takes her basic concept—the misunderstandings that happen as a result of men and women's different communication styles—and applies it specifically to the workplace. The important lesson here is that women's particular tendencies toward supportive, connecting, and/or hesitant language often undermines the perceived value of their ideas and contributions. A must-read for women wondering why they often feel (or are) marginalized in work situations.

**Tannen, Deborah. *You Just Don't Understand: Women and Men in Conversation.* William Morrow Paperback, 2001. 352p. ISBN 0060959622.

Whether you're male or female, by the time you've landed your first job it's probably become clear that, in general, men and women communicate differently. Not a bad thing, but absolutely something to understand and take into consideration when both genders are, for example, in a meeting discussing a key decision. Or working through team assignments. Or discussing a raise. Or evaluating individual and group performance. Or . . . doing just about anything that involves language as a means of communicating ideas and understanding. Although Tannen has a bit of a bias toward the female communication style, the book is nevertheless exceptionally valuable for both genders.

**Tracy, Brian. *Goals! How to Get Everything You Want—Faster Than You Ever Thought Possible.* Berrett-Koehler Publishers, 2010. 288p. ISBN 1605094110.

One of the best-known personal productivity writers, Tracy here explains the seven components of goal setting (example: imagine that you have the inborn ability to achieve any goal you could ever set for your-self; what do you really want to be, have, and do?) and the action items that will enable you to set and achieve your goals. The ability to meet the goals you set for yourself is a key element of becoming a high-value contributor.

Tucker, Cory and Reeta Sinha. *New Librarian, New Job: Practical Advice for Managing the Transition.* Scarecrow Press, 2006. 244p. ISBN 0810858517.
A practical guide for transitioning from grad student to new-on-the-job professional. The tone is upbeat and encouraging, making for a positive introduction to the profession for its intended audience of new public, academic, school, or special librarians.

Online Resources

**"Current Awareness through RSS"
http://americanlibrariesmagazine.org/columns/practice/keeping-20-style
From library tech guru Meredith Farkas, this *American Libraries* article from January 13, 2011 gives clear instructions for setting up RSS feeds to have your current awareness sources sent directly to you via your preferred method (e.g., e-mail client, RSS reader, personalized start page, etc.).

**D-Lib Magazine*
www.dlib.org/
Subtitled "The Magazine of Digital Library Research," *D-Lib* focuses on digital library research and development, including new technologies, applications, and contextual social and economic issues. International and interdisciplinary in scope.

**Docuticker
www.docuticker.com
Aggregates abstracts from gray literature; that is, PDF reports published by government agencies, research institutes and think tanks, nongovernmental agencies, and similar public interest organizations. The website itself is a fascinating browse; sign up for the weekly Docuticker newsletter updates for current awareness.

GTD Times
www.gtdtimes.com/
Although most of the content on the Getting Things Done official website is clearly geared toward selling more materials from David Allen, he does offer a substantial amount of (free) additional information and tips via the Categories section in the left-hand menu. The site's monthly blog post is usually an amplification or clarification of one of the key points in his organization system.

**Internet Public Library/ipl2 Newsletter

http://theipl.wordpress.com/

Topical resources culled from the ongoing IPL survey of best-in-class topical resources. One of the most respected aggregators of credible and authoritative information on the web.

LibGig

www.libgig.com

Sponsored by LAC, the recruiting, placement, and temporary agency, LibGig is a content-rich source of information about the profession, include a career Q&A section, several excellent blogs, news, career profiles, events, newsletters, links to LIS schools, and a job board. A terrific resource for staying current on career topics and job opportunities.

A Librarian's Guide to Etiquette

http://libetiquette.blogspot.com/

How can you not love a blogger who starts one post with the statement "All back-to-school library orientation sessions should include video footage of librarians murdering patrons who don't follow the rules." A delightful but also practical guide to functioning successfully as a library professional.

Librarianship Job Search and Careers

www.linkedin.com/

Created by David M. Connolly as an ALA subgroup with this mission: "Discuss current events, best practices, and industry trends related to library jobs, and network with your professional peers. Brought to you by ALA JobLIST, your #1 source for jobs in Library & Information Science & Technology." To access, you must first join the ALA LinkedIn group (but not necessarily ALA), then go to the More tab at the top of the page, select Subgroups, and then this group.

LIScareer.com

www.liscareer.com

"The library & information science professional's career development center," LIScareer.com aggregates articles, resources, and information on career planning, education, job hunting, professional networking, mentoring, interpersonal skills, leadership, publishing, and work/life balance. Companion to Priscilla Schontz's *Jumpstart Your Career in Library and Information Science*. A key resource.

LIS Career Options

www.linkedin.com

Created by Kim Dority as an ALA subgroup with this mission: "A forum for exchanging information about library and information science careers, both traditional and alternative, for LIS professionals, students, and those aspiring to a career working with information." To access, you must first join the ALA LinkedIn group (but not necessarily ALA), then go to the More tab at the top of the page, select Subgroups, and then this group.

**LLRX

www.LLRX.com

Founded and published by the prolific Sabrina Pacifici (who also authors the daily BeSpacific law and technology news blog), LLRX aggregates a wide range of news items related to legal, social, and technology issues. In addition to signing up for the LLRX RSS feed, you may also want to check the website for the subject-specific resource collections on competitive intelligence, information management, government resources, and other key topics.

**"Managing Personal Change"

http://blog.libraryjournal.com/tennantdigitallibraries/2010/09/29/managing-personal-change/

An insightful *Library Journal* blog post from Roy Tennant on strategies for dealing with change proactively rather than letting it derail you.

Managing Up, Down, and Across

http://www.lisjobs.com/rethinking/?p=18

Advice on how to work effectively with those you supervise (if you do), your colleagues, and your management, from the *Rethinking Information Careers* blog.

Movers & Shakers [Year]

www.libraryjournal.com/csp/cms/sites/LJ/LJInPrint/MoversAndShakers/moversandshakers2011.csp

Every year *Library Journal* surveys the profession to identify and then profile 50 (usually young-ish) movers and shakers who are doing a wide range of innovative things in the profession. The profiles are fascinating to read, and provide a good sense of the diversity of career paths that professionals can take on the road to becoming an outstanding contributor. See also the archive on the *Library Journal* site of all past Movers and Shakers profiles.

New Academic Librarians: Networking to Success

www.linkedin.com/

LinkedIn group created by Sarah Forbes with this mission: "Entering into a new job can be a very daunting period in a librarian's life. This interactive forum will discuss avenues and techniques that new librarians can use when they are looking for or starting a new position in an academic library." To access, from the LinkedIn home page search box at the top right of the page, search on Groups and the title of this group.

The New Librarian's Listserv (NEWLIB-L)

http://walternelson.com/dr/newlib-l

A discussion list intended for "librarians new to the profession who wish to share experiences and discuss ideas, issues, trends, and problems faced by librarians in the early stages of their careers." The list is open to all, and currently includes more than 1,300 subscribers (from North America as well as globally) representing all aspects and types of librarianship. Those contemplating but not yet pursuing an LIS career are encouraged to participate as well.

"An Open Letter to New Librarians"
http://blog.libraryjournal.com/tennantdigitallibraries/2011/02/18/an-open-letter-to-new-librarians/
An outstanding and honest response from technologist and LIS thought-leader Roy Tennant on dealing with the frustrations facing many recent graduates and others new to the library profession. From his *Library Journal* blog.

"Personal SWOT Analysis: Making the Most of Your Talents and Opportunities"
www.mindtools.com/pages/article/newTMC_05.htm
From the career site MindTools, this article and accompanying worksheet help you identify the key questions to ask yourself in order to unearth the information most useful for making career decisions. A great tool for making strategic decisions as you grow your career.

"The Second Time's the Charm: Moving On from Your First Professional Position"
http://lisjobs.com/career_trends/?p=336
An insightful article by Christine Borne about what to look for in your second job, based on what you've learned about yourself in your first job. Favorite quote: "Stay in a job until there is nothing more you can learn from it."

"Smart and Innovative Are Not Enough"
www.lisjobs.com/rethinking/?p=10
A Rethinking Information Work column that brings the considerable wisdom of organizational coach Pat Wagner to bear on setting realistic expectations—both of yourself and others—during your early days as an LIS professional.

SmartBrief on Your Career
www.smartbrief.com/yourcareer/
Daily newsletter that aggregates career articles, columns, and blog posts from multiple online sources such as the *Wall Street Journal, Harvard Business Review,* Forbes.com, CareerRocketeer, etc.

"The Starter Job, Or, Why You Should Consider That Job in Smalltown, USA"
http://infonista.com/2011/the-starter-job-or-why-you-should-consider-that-job-in-smalltown-usa/
Many new MLIS graduates assume that an entry-level job at a small library in an out-of-the-way locale would have little to offer from a career-building perspective, but in fact, just the opposite may be true.

"This Entry-Level Position is NOT What I Expected!"
http://lisjobs.com/career_trends/?p=424
What to do when an entry-level job turns out to be, ah, less than hoped for. A combination of reality check, encouragement, and wise advice in this article from Rachel Augello.

"When You've *Really* Messed Up . . ."

http://infonista.com/2011/when-youve-really-messed-up/

Nobody likes to mess up on the job, but way more important than the actual event is how you handle the aftermath with your boss—which can either cement your professional relationship or irretrievably destroy his or her trust in you.

5
Learning

One of the most powerful ways to open up new career opportunities is to continually expand what you know, and what you can *do* with what you know. It's often critical to being promoted by your current employer, it provides a competitive advantage when you are applying for a new job, and it's frequently the key to bridging existing skills into a new professional arena.

So basically, although it's smart to apply yourself in grad school, consider it just the start of your career learning curve.

The reality is that pretty much no college or institutional, formal learning program can keep up with the pace of change in most organizations and workplaces. They simply can't be sufficiently flexible to reflect recent advances in knowledge. Organizations (including libraries) need to change in response to shifting market environments, or a new opportunity, or the most recent budget cut—so it's wise to assume your career will involve a lot of learning on the fly in response to changing organizational need or your own career aspirations. Happily, you're building your career at a time when

99

the confluence of personal and information technology, communications advances, and new media delivery channels have created an unprecedented environment for supporting self-directed learning. This means that there's a way to learn almost anything you want or need to learn in the way that best suits you.

When thinking about your own career, the questions to ask involve what sorts of skills and knowledge add value to your professional asset base, what options exist for expanding your professional expertise, how you personally learn most easily and effectively, and what steps you can take to ensure your knowledge stays up to date—if not ahead of the curve.

What Will You Need to Learn?

Every year, the National Association of Colleges and Employers (NACE) asks employers what skills are most important when making hiring decisions. In 2011's *Job Outlook: The Candidate Skills/Qualities Employers Want,* the five rated most highly (ranked in order of priority) were the following:

- ability to work as a part of a team
- communication skills (verbal)
- ability to make decisions and solve problems
- ability to obtain and process information
- ability to plan, organize, and prioritize work

So there's your baseline—nice to know you probably already have number four nailed! And you may have picked up some of the other skills in grad school, or along the way throughout your career. But what if not? What types of skills or expertise will add value to your professional portfolio? Although the specific answers will differ for everyone depending on their career aspirations, it may help to think about gaining new knowledge in the following four areas.

Discipline-Specific Professional Skills and Areas of Expertise

This area focuses on the core skills associated with LIS professionals, such as reference and/or research, organizing information, putting together technology-based information systems, developing knowledge collections, creating web content, or providing bibliographic instruction.

In addition, it may also include advanced subject expertise in a specific discipline, say multicultural user experience, medical research, or law. Skills in web portal or intranet design and implementation, competitive intelligence, taxonomy-building, and information architecture would also be considered discipline-specific areas of expertise.

Many of these skills are ones you'll have learned in your MLIS program. However, the farther you get from grad school, or the more far afield your career ranges from your original areas of expertise, the likelier it is that you'll need to either learn skills not mastered in grad school or refresh those you did cover.

General Professional Skills

This type of skill supports your ability to perform your job responsibilities effectively, regardless of what they are. Happily, these skills can be honed in graduate school as well as on the job (just in case you were wondering whether those group projects had any relevance to your professional future!). Some of the most important (and useful) professional skills include

- the ability to use multiple online collaboration tools,
- the ability to do teaching, training, or coaching as needed, and familiarity with the tools to do so online,
- knowledge of budgeting tools and processes,
- knowledge of basic project management tools and processes,
- familiarity with the concepts of database design and construction, and
- familiarity with basic web mark-up languages.

However, these are the skills in demand *today*. We all have to assume that 10 or even 5 years from now, this list might look very different. So the key take-away is that it will be your responsibility to stay current with the technologies that underlie or drive your profession's or employer's opportunities in the coming years.

Business Skills

Based on an understanding of how organizations (not just businesses) operate, these skills are often critical to professional advancement. However, they're rarely covered in any depth in most MLIS programs, which leaves most of us scrambling to pick up this knowledge on the fly. These skills may include

- an ability to analyze and synthesize information, *and* the ability to draw from it and effectively present your conclusions to senior executives;
- an understanding of the product (or program) development lifecycle, with an emphasis on key information components of the process and how your skills support them—whether those are profit-focused products or community outreach programs;
- a familiarity with basic strategic planning approaches (understanding that each organization usually has its own unique variation of these processes), and an ability to plan for your department as well as an ability to contribute to enterprise-wide planning activities; and

- an ability to manage vendor relations, including developing RFPs (requests for proposals), evaluating proposal responses, and negotiating contracts.

Soft Skills

Soft skills are generally those skills that relate to working effectively with others. (To that point, four of the top 10 skills desired by employers relate to employees' abilities to work well with others.) These may include, among others,

- an ability to communicate effectively (verbal, written, or in a presentation) in both group and one-on-one settings,
- an ability to work effectively as a team member or leader,
- an ability to work effectively as part of a multigenerational, multicultural workforce, and help others do so as well, and
- an ability to manage up, down, and across—in other words, to have positive relations with your bosses, peers, and subordinates.

Needless to say, which of these four types of skills are critical to your career path depends on the opportunities you seek out (or the unanticipated responsibilities that land in your lap). But the more of them you can become adept at, the greater the range of opportunities you're likely to have.

How and Where Will You Learn?

Although the likelihood is that you already have some of these skills in your professional tool kit and/or you only need to pick up a few of them at this particular point in your career, it's still helpful to be in an "always learning something new" mindset to be on the upside of changes heading your way.

Following are some ways to get the knowledge you need.

Learn on the Job

A learning organization is an effective and competitive organization, according to Peter Senge's landmark 1990 work, *The Fifth Discipline: The Art & Practice of the Learning Organization.* Senge identified the habits that keep companies from learning from their experiences, and then sharing that knowledge in a collaborative environment. Senge's core insights are just as applicable to individuals. One of his key points, that today's problems come from yesterday's solutions, resonates equally strongly with our natural human instinct to cling to the comfort of the solutions we know and are familiar with. That said, it's still possible to take a page from *The Fifth Discipline* and create your own minilearning organizations. (For more on implementing learning organization concepts, see the *Getting Results Through Learning* website, especially the Individual Learning Strategies section.)

Learning on the job may include on-site training programs, project work, professional development funds, tuition reimbursement, or formal mentoring programs. (In fact, you may want to consider negotiating for professional development opportunities and support if not already company policy as part of your total compensation package when you start talking about salary.)

Or learning on the job might just be hanging out with those new Generation Y staffers who know the latest technology tools and are willing to share their knowledge, or those seasoned practitioners willing to coach you through your first budgeting adventure. These informal learning exchanges are perhaps one of the greatest benefits of working in our new four-generation workplace, so it only makes sense to take advantage of it whenever possible.

Your workplace is also a great place to learn by doing. Work projects give you an opportunity to develop new skills by working with experienced pros, and you'll get immediate and ongoing feedback on whether your skills are up to the task. Get proactive and volunteer for new initiatives based on what new knowledge or skill development they'll provide you. Or look into job rotation, which allows you to cross train and add additional skills to your portfolio.

Learn from the LIS Profession

It's often noted that one of the really great things about this profession is peoples' willingness to share knowledge. That means you're part of one of the world's biggest, friendliest learning communities.

There are all sorts of ways to tap into this broad and deep knowledge base. Find successful local practitioners who have done what you're interested in doing, take them to coffee or lunch, and ask them what the key skills are in their position—and how they learned theirs. Even if they can't take the time to meet in person, most will at least be willing to respond with an e-mail answer, albeit a brief one (and possibly a few weeks down the road). Be as specific as possible with your questions; "What should I do with my life?" is guaranteed to produce a glazed look and no useful answers.

In addition, enlist one of the most valuable and easily accessed learning tools of the professional community by signing up for the best blogs, electronic discussion groups, Twitter and RSS feeds in your areas of interest. To get a sense of who's most knowledgeable, most innovative, and/or most credible on a given topic, ask colleagues you respect who they follow, see whose stuff gets cited, linked to, or retweeted most often, check out who's writing for key publications or speaking at conferences or giving terrific webcasts or podcasts. Check out who your favorite bloggers have in their blogrolls and follow the links. Your goal is to identify and then begin to monitor a group of experts whose shared knowledge will help you increase your own.

In addition, you may want to consider signing up for online and regional courses, workshops, and one-day seminars through professional associations like ALA, SLA, PLA, the American Association of Law Libraries, the Library and Information Technology Association (LITA), or the Medical Library

Association (and their regional chapters). Check out classes offered by your state library (if your state has one) or library association, your regional bibliographic utilities or training organizations, or look into regionally delivered vendor training. Attend preconference workshops at state and national association conferences, where you can often also pick up vendor technology training sessions for free. In addition, if you're new to the profession, consider programs like SLA's First Five Years group or ALA's New Members' Round Table Mentoring Program.

Also, look for online tutorials and discussion groups (try, for example, Google groups or LinkedIn groups focused on your topic of interest), which can often be a great source of lessons learned and wise counsel. LinkedIn provides an especially wide range of professional groups whose members share questions, answers, and expertise. Additionally, consider relevant YouTube videos and industry podcasts or explore the amazing presentations at TEDx.

Learn in Grad School

Being in grad school is a terrific opportunity to learn—but it's up to you to set your own learning agenda in order to most effectively position yourself for maximum career opportunity. Every course you take provides two learning paths that should go forward side-by-side: the structured learning identified in the course syllabus, and the self-directed learning you identify for yourself.

For example, in a business research class, your learning agenda might include researching the telecommunications industry, trends in corporate information centers, or social entrepreneurship if these are areas of interest for you. In an information ethics class, you may decide to perfect your presentation or group leadership skills. In a knowledge management class, you may choose to research bioinformatics for your class project with an eye toward expanding your sci/tech expertise. Approach every course assignment asking *what do I want to learn with this?* rather than *what do I have to do to get an A on this?* Align every paper, project, and class activity with your personal career agenda whenever possible, and you will be both learning the core LIS knowledge and positioning yourself for your postgraduation career.

Learn after Grad School

Many MLIS programs are beginning to realize that continuing professional education/development is not only a critical need among practitioners, but can also be a lovely source of additional revenue for the schools. So, for example, schools such as Simmons Graduate School of Library and Information Science, the iSchool at Drexel College of Information Science and Technology, the San Jose State University School of Library and Information Science, and the University of Wisconsin-Madison School of Library & Information Studies are now actively promoting their online CPE courses to the entire profession, regardless of whether participants happen to be alumni.

Alternatively, consider community colleges, training DVDs, books for be-ginners, online tutorials, or the offerings of private training companies not affiliated with the LIS world. Depending on how LIS-centric the topic is that you need to master, these can be inexpensive and efficient learning options.

Learn from a Mentor

For many of the skills you want to develop, especially the people-related ones, a mentor who will coach you through your learning path can be invaluable. As noted in Chapter 4, although some organizations have formal mentoring programs, the informal ones you seek out and structure yourself can be just as helpful, and sometimes more so. Keep in mind that the responsibility for making a mentoring relationship work will rest with you; in other words, you'll need to identify what types of advice or learning you seek, how often you'd like to meet (although this will be decided by your mentor's availabil-ity), etc. And most importantly, you'll need to be willing to follow through on any learning assignments your mentor recommends.

How do you choose a mentor? There are many considerations, but per-haps the most important is chemistry. In her article "How to Choose and Work with a Mentor," Pamela Ryckman says, "if the mix of personalities isn't right, find someone new." Anyone who's been in this awkward situation will vouch for the wisdom of Ryckman's advice.

Read Books!

There are a number of publishers who focus primarily on helping the LIS profession keep up with new knowledge, for example, Libraries Unlimited, Information Today, Neal-Schuman, ALA Editions, and Chandos. This book is an example of a professional development book whose aim is to help you begin or advance your career. But there are others that deal with such topics as technology advances, programming for emerging populations, taxonomy-building, user experience, competitive intelligence, social media, gaming in the library, and hundreds of other topics that probably weren't covered in grad school but are now either a hot job opportunity or a new responsibility that just landed on your desk.

Learn from Your Own Professional Community

Lastly, don't forget that your network of professional colleagues is an incred-ibly valuable, informal, and readily available source of knowledge and ex-pertise. As you go through your career, you'll build relationships with fellow students, coworkers, association colleagues, fellow panelists at professional conferences, and myriad other connecting points. This community of col-leagues is not only one of the most rewarding aspects of having a long career, it also offers a rich source of advice, counsel, and insight.

In fact, a recent book on learning outside the academy and a terrific resource on the topic of self-directed group learning is Michelle Boule's *Mob Rule Learning: Camps, Unconferences, and Trashing the Talking Head.*

Boule (a former *Library Journal* Shaker and Mover) suggests that it's time for individuals in the profession to start creating their own knowledge ecosystems, and then proceeds to provide clear instructions on just how that can be done, and where to find these types of learning opportunities. Unconference, anyone?

There are many more ways to expand your knowledge and skills, depending on what criteria you need to meet. If you are able to focus on the learning itself and don't need a credential or credit to document it, then consider the least expensive options first, including informal learning.

Finding Your Learning Path

One of the most important career skills you can develop is an understanding of how you most effectively learn. This translates into how you can master and apply new knowledge as quickly and painlessly as possible. The challenge is how to learn rapidly, effectively, and on demand. The solution is to understand the approaches to mastering new material that best align with the way *your individual* brain processes and absorbs information.

The classic work in this area is Howard Gardner's *Frames of Mind: The Theory of Multiple Intelligences,* published initially in 1983 and updated in 2006 with new content and a new title, *Multiple Intelligences: New Horizons in Theory and Practice.* According to Gardner, intelligence may manifest itself as linguistic, musical, logical-mathematical, spatial, bodily-kinesthetic, and personal (internal or outward-facing), although as with all intelligence and learning types, we all exist on a continuum rather than as an absolute. Nevertheless, understanding in which direction you tend to lean among Gardner's framework can provide one clue to understanding which environments or approaches are most likely to enhance your learning efforts.

Learning styles build on Gardner's ground-breaking work by explaining that just as there are many types of intelligences, so are there many ways for people to process, absorb, and master new information. Although there are many approaches to learning styles, generally, you'll want to figure out which type you are within three main categories: senses, reasoning types, and learning environments. (For a quick online test of where you fit within the spectrum and how that might suggest your most effective learning approaches, see *What's YOUR Learning Style?*)

Understanding your personal learning style will help you shape how you most effectively structure your learning approach. For example, have you found as a student that you learn most easily by taping a lecture and then reviewing it by playing it back multiple times? Or have you found that drawing concept maps with different-colored pens helps you quickly master a key lesson? Or perhaps you've discovered that reading, highlighting, and re-reading sections of a text or manual don't help with retention nearly as well as listening to instructions? Your answers will help you understand which (or how many) of today's new learning opportunities, e.g., podcasts, videos, webinars, workshops, etc., will work for you, and why.

If you're not sure which of these approaches best describes how you learn most comfortably (and quickly), try each of them out and then assess the results. This can be via a formal approach, for example, a classroom setting, or an informal one, perhaps where you're teaching yourself a new language or a technology tool. Your goal can be not only to learn the knowledge or skill itself, but also to learn through experimentation the most effective techniques and processes for improving your time to mastery, as the training pros say.

To quote futurist Alvin Toffler, "The illiterate of the 21st century will not be those who cannot read and write, but those who cannot learn, unlearn, and relearn." And in the LIS profession, those who can learn most quickly and effectively will have the greatest number of career opportunities to pursue.

Resources

Starred titles are mentioned in the chapter.

Associations

*Note:*In general, all LIS and LIS-related associations have strong education and professional development mandates as part of their missions. Therefore, be sure to check the websites of any associations in your area of interest to see what sorts of education programs they offer, many of which may be available to you online. In addition, many of the major divisions or special interest groups within specific associations provide continuing education programs for their members and others, so be sure to explore that possibility as well.

Following are examples of the education offerings of the major LIS professional associations.

**American Library Association—Allied Professional Association (ALA-APA)
http://ala-apa.org
ALA-APA provides services to librarians and other library workers in two primary areas: certification programs for paraprofessionals and library technicians/assistants and library supervisory staff (post-MLS), and direct support of comparable worth and pay equity initiatives, and other activities designed to improve the salaries and status of librarians and other library workers. Publishes the monthly *Library Worklife: HR E-News for Today's Leaders.*

**Center of Research and Education (CORE) / Medical Library Association (MLA)
http://mlanet.org/core/
The CORE site aggregates links to MLA's educational clearinghouse, web-based courses, an online bootcamp for new health sciences librarians,

courses offered at MLA annual meetings, association webcasts and teleconferences, independent educational opportunities, and the MLA mentoring database, among other resources.

**Clearinghouse for Professional Development / Library and Information Technology Association (LITA)
www.ala.org/lita/professional/clearinghouse
An example of a selective but useful aggregation of professional development tools from one of the most active ALA divisions, including links to relevant certification and related technical training; conferences and forums; courses, workshops, and other professional development programs; desktop applications; internet/intranet technology; standards; and website development tools.

**Click University / Special Library Association (SLA)
www.sla.org/content/learn/aboutclicku/index.cfm
Click (standing for Continuous Learning to Improve Career Knowledge) University is SLA's online learning community, offering courses and certificates in such topics as getting the most out of LinkedIn, content rights management, and leadership training. In addition, SLA offers premium programs, for example, certificate programs in copyright management, competitive intelligence, and knowledge management.

**Education / American Association of Law Libraries (AALL)
www.aallnet.org/main-menu/Education
AALL offers its members a wide range of learning opportunities, including workshops and programs at the annual conference, webinars on various topics (e.g., Introduction to Legal Project Management), AALL2Go (continuing education programs, current and archived webinars, audio and video recordings), a Leadership Academy, a Management Institute, and CPE program grants.

**e-Learning@PLA / Public Library Association (PLA)
www.ala.org/ala/mgrps/divs/pla/onlinelearning/index.cfm
Webinars, self-directed online workbooks, symposiums, and virtual conferences are among the learning opportunities provided through the Public Library Association's online learning program. PLA also offers a week-long Results Boot Camp designed to provide "the management training and skills you didn't get in library school," and Turning the Page, a free public library advocacy training course. In addition, it's an approved provider of the Certified Public Library Administrator (CPLA) management courses.

**First Five Years Advisory Council / Special Library Association (SLA)
www.sla.org/content/membership/firstfive.cfm
The council is charged with developing "learning and networking opportunities to attract and retain new information professionals." Check out its Facebook and LinkedIn pages to follow group activities.

**Mentoring Program / New Members' Round Table (NMRT)

www.ala.org/nmrt/initiatives/nmrtmentguide/nmrtmentoring
Part of NMRT's mission is to provide a wide variety of programs to assist, encourage, and educate people who are new to the profession, and one way it supports that mission is the NMRT mentoring program. New LIS professionals should consider this annual, structured October–July program; applications are due at the end of September for each year.

Office for Human Resource Development & Recruitment (HRDR) / ALA

www.ala.org/ala/aboutala/offices/hrdr/index.cfm
HRDR has as its mission "to facilitate the development of librarianship as a profession." To accomplish this purpose, HRDR focuses on education and learning programs; recruitment of a diverse workforce; and establishing policies and practices in the areas of management and human resources that best serve the needs of libraries and their employees. This is the central, coordinating entity for the multiple education initiatives ALA supports.

Additional LIS Education Providers

Amigos Library Services

www.amigos.org/
Offers training courses on an array of topics important to libraries via both online and face-to-face delivery. Sample topics include OCLC training, Internet skills, preservation, imaging, reference, technical services, management, and technology.

Lyrasis

www.lyrasis.org/
One of the largest regional bibliographic utilities, Lyrasis offers a wide range of classes and courses related to professional development for LIS professionals. (Among their top 20 "Hot Classes": Introducing RDA, Practical Approaches to Information Literacy, Demystifying Serial MARC Records, and Web Tools for Reference Librarians).

TechSoup

http://home.techsoup.org/pages/default.aspx
TechSoup provides nonprofits and libraries with technology that empowers them to fulfill their missions and serve their communities. In addition to providing technology products and information geared specifically to the unique challenges faced by nonprofits and libraries, TechSoup also offers free training webinars, other learning events, and a deep collection of training articles.

WebJunction

www.webjunction.org/
A 2003 spinoff from the OCLC training group, Web Junction provides learning services (resources and programs, webinars, etc.) for both library staff and library organizations. *Note*: The courses related to

WebJunction's Competency Index are no longer available to individuals, and are instead only accessible to members sponsored by their state library.

LIS Graduate Programs Offering Online Professional Development Options

Clarion University of Pennsylvania
www.clarion.edu/libsci
Offers a 15-graduate-credit certificate of advanced studies program "designed to provide the post-master's student an opportunity to expand and update professional skills and competencies through a structured pattern of continuing education."

**The iSchool at Drexel College of Information Science and Technology Professional Development
www.ischool.drexel.edu/CS/SpecialPrograms/ProfessionalDevelopment
Offers postgraduate for-credit courses, certificates, and post-master's specialist programs.

**San Jose State University
http://slisweb.sjsu.edu/certificate/
Offers online post-master's certificate in Library and Information Science within five areas of specialization: digital archives and records management, digital services and emerging technologies, information intermediation and instruction, web programming and information architecture, and youth services.

**Simmons Graduate School of Library and Information Science
www.simmons.edu/gslis/careers/continuing-education/
Offers over 70 workshops annually, as half-day or one-day onsite programs (at the Simmons campuses) as well as asynchronous online workshops that take place over a month.

University of Arizona
http://sirls.arizona.edu/programs/digIn
Offers the Digital Information Management Graduate Certificate Program (DigIn), consisting of six 14-week graduate-level courses taken within a three-year period.

University of Illinois, Urbana-Champaign
www.lis.illinois.edu/academics/programs/cas
Offers a certificate in advanced study with various choices for specialization, including digital libraries and biological informatics.

University of South Carolina
www.libsci.sc.edu/ce/pangoldfa2011/pangold.htm
In partnership with other regional LIS organizations providing CE courses, offers multiple online synchronous workshops.

University of Toronto
www.institute.ischool.utoronto.ca/
Offers professional development courses and certificate programs on such topics as records management fundamentals and engaging adult learners: strategies for information professionals.

University of Wisconsin–Madison School of Library & Information Studies
www.slis.wisc.edu/continueed.htm
Offers continuing education unit (CEU) courses, most online and asynchronous, that generally last six to eight weeks.

Print Resources

**Boule, Michelle. *Mob Rule Learning: Camps, Unconferences, and Trashing the Talking Head.* Information Today, 2011. 224p. ISBN 0910 965927.
Heard someone mention an unconference and wondered what the heck they were talking about? *Library Journal* Mover and Shaker Michelle Boule explains what they are, why they may be a large part of the future of LIS professional development, and how to organize your very own nontraditional, self-directed group "knowledge ecosystem." Includes case studies, interviews, and examples of how other people have used these approaches successfully.

Dweck, Carol. *Mindset: The New Psychology of Success.* Ballantine Books, 2007. 288p. ISBN 0345472322.
Do you have a fixed mindset or a growth mindset? If the latter, according to the author, you see yourself as an ever-changing work in progress—and an eager and effective learner. While affirming the importance to career resiliency of a growth mindset, Dweck also coaches readers on how to move from a fixed to a growth mindset (lest you find yourself among the former).

**Gardner, Howard. *Multiple Intelligences: New Horizons in Theory and Practice.* Basic Books, 2006. 320p. ISBN 0465047688.
The classic work on the seven intelligences: linguistic, musical, logical-mathematical, spatial, bodily-kinesthetic, internal personal, and outward-facing personal. Gardner's work was ground-breaking when first introduced, and many have built upon his theories to further understand how learning takes place. An excellent resource for understanding how to structure your learning processes, techniques, and environment to learn most easily and quickly; also discusses multiple intelligences in the workplace.

Knowles, Malcolm S., Richard A. Swanson, and Elwood F. Holton III. *The Adult Learner: The Definitive Classic in Adult Education and Human Resource Development,* 7th ed. Butterworth-Heinemann, 2011. 416p. ISBN 1856178110.

Prior to his death in 1997, Knowles had long been recognized as the most authoritative voice on the special characteristics of adult learners. Although the focus of this book, continued and updated by co-authors Swanson and Holton, is on how corporate trainers can most effectively structure their organizational training programs, its information is applicable for anyone working with adult learners, or wishing to more clearly understand their own adult-learner characteristics and motivators.

**Senge, Peter. *The Fifth Discipline: The Art & Practice of The Learning Organization,* rev ed. Crown Business, 2006. 445p. ISBN 0385517254.
Senge identifies and explores the five disciplines that enable companies to learn from the knowledge they gather both internally and externally: (1) personal mastery (clarifying personal vision, focusing energy, recognizing and accepting reality); (2) shared vision (transforming the vision of individuals into a shared, collaborative vision); (3) mental models (identifying existing internal pictures and understanding how those conceptual frames drive actions); (4) team learning (creating safe, nonjudgmental team environments for sharing knowledge and learning from failures); and (5) systems thinking (understanding and implementing the previous four disciplines in a cross-disciplinary, integrated framework). These principles apply equally well when creating a learning professional.

Zachary, Lois J. and Lory A. Fischler. *The Mentee's Guide: Making Mentoring Work for You.* Jossey-Bass, 2009. 176p. ISBN 0470343583.
Part of a trilogy of best-selling books on mentoring (*The Mentor's Guide* and *Creating a Mentoring Culture* round out the series) *The Mentee's Guide* covers such topics as choosing a mentor, setting appropriate goals, mentoring etiquette, and creating effective mentoring relationships. Useful for both formal and informal mentoring situations.

Publishers

Note: In addition to the specific books listed previously, you'll also want to be aware of the primary publishers in the LIS profession. Some of them publish both reference and professional books, others focus specifically on how to perform the wide range of professional responsibilities found throughout the LIS universe. The publishers who specialize in books potentially relevant to your career development include the following.

**ALA Editions
www.ala.org/ala/aboutala/offices/publishing/index.cfm
See especially the eCourses series related to several of the publications.

**Chandos Publishing
www.woodheadpublishing.com/en/ChandosHome.aspx

**InformationToday
http://books.infotoday.com/

See especially the Accidental series of books, designed for those who find themselves in an unanticipated professional role and need to master key information quickly.

Libraries Unlimited
www.abc-clio.com/aboutus/Default.aspx?id=60300
See especially the Crash Course series, created for individuals working in libraries of all sizes who need basic, how-to information on various service-specific topics.

Neal-Schuman
www.neal-schuman.com/
See especially the How-to-Do-It titles, which focus on practical application rather than conceptual overviews or theory.

Online Resources

The Fine Art of Failing
http://infonista.com/2010/the-fine-art-of-failing/
You pretty much can't grow if you can't deal positively with failure; this blog post identifies the five things you can take away from any failure that will convert it to a successful learning experience.

**Getting Results through Learning
www.humtech.com/opm/grtl/index.htm
From the Human Resource Development Council, this website provides a conceptual overview of learning organizations, information about organizational learning strategies and individual learning strategies, examples of key concepts, relevant links, and reference materials.

**"How to Choose and Work with a Mentor"
www.nytimes.com/2010/09/02/business/smallbusiness/02sbiz.html?pagewanted=all
Part of the *New York Times*'s online Small Business Guide, this article by Pamela Ryckman provides insights on mentoring by dozens of businesspeople who have been involved in both sides of the process.

**Job Outlook: The Candidate Skills/Qualities Employers Want
www.naceweb.org/s10262011/candidate_skills_employer_qualities/
Results from a 2011 survey of employers by the National Association of Colleges and Employers (NACE) as to their preferred employee skills and qualities.

Learning-Style Inventory
http://pss.uvm.edu/pss162/learning_styles.html
David Kolb did the initial developmental work related to learning styles, and this overview of his learning styles inventory provides a useful and insightful introduction to his ideas. Kolb's learning styles inventory is supplemented here with references to multiple intelligence theory and checklists to help you identify your own intelligence categories.

Learning-Styles-Online.com

www.learning-styles-online.com
An easy-to-understand overview of various learning styles with links to more in-depth information on each.

"Retaining Knowledge and Driving Innovation"

http://findarticles.com/p/articles/mi_m0FWE/is_7_13/ai_n45031891/
October–November 2009 *Information Outlook* column by Debbie Schachter that lays out how "informal training and development can enable information professionals to help their organizations be more innovative during lean times" Her key points are equally applicable, however, to informal professional development for career sustainability.

"Sit With the Kids"

www.rethinkinginformationwork.com/column-archives/sit-with-the-kids/
What happens when an executive is given a choice to sit with "the suits," that is, the executive management team, or "the kids," the recent college grads who know all the coolest stuff.

**TEDx

www.ted.com/tedx
Based on the original concept of ideas worth spreading, TEDx provides "communities, organizations and individuals the opportunity to stimulate dialogue through TED-like experiences at the local level." The outcome is some amazing learning events, many of interest to LIS professionals (check the site for presentations of interest).

**What's YOUR Learning Style?

http://people.usd.edu/~bwjames/tut/learning-style/
An online learning-style quiz that will help you determine where you fall on the learning-style spectrum. A resource made available from a University of South Dakota instructor, this site will also help you understand how to use your learning style most effectively to master new information.

Social Networks—LIS-Related Groups

Note: Many social network sites have groups of extraordinary professional-development value to LIS students and professionals, places where questions, answers, information, and career insights are freely exchanged and members can learn in a supportive, collaborative environment. Two of the largest aggregations of potentially relevant groups are found within Google groups and LinkedIn; see the following for ways to explore their professional development resources.

**Google Groups

http://groups.google.com/
Search on your topic of interest in the "Search for a group" search box, but be ready to narrow that topic down; a search on "libraries" brought up about 4,300 hits.

**LinkedIn Groups
www.linkedin.com/home
From the home page, choose "Groups" from the drop-down search box menu, then enter your topic of choice. Following is a representative selection of some of the most active (and therefore, usually most informative) groups:

- Buslib-l
- Code4lib
- Corporate Librarians
- Digital Asset Management
- Digital Book World
- Digital Libraries
- eBooks in Libraries
- Historians, Librarians and Archivists
- Information, Knowledge & Content Management Specialists
- Job Skills for Future Library Careers
- Librarians in the Job Market
- LIS Career Options (subgroup of ALA LinkedIn group)
- Metadata Management
- SLA First Five Years
- Society of American Archivists
- Strategic and Competitive Intelligence Professionals (SCIP)
- Taxonomy Community of Practice

6
Building Your
Professional Network

Chapter Highlights

- What Is a Professional Network?

- Building and Sustaining Your Professional Community

- Introverted? You Can Still Build a Network

- Still a Student? Start Building Your Network in Grad School

- Networking Strategy

- Benefits of a Professional Network

In your career-building arsenal, few things are as effective as creating a broad and deep network of professional connections. However, networking has understandably gotten a bad name, assumed by many to be just an obnoxious way to exploit friends, colleagues, and transitory, business-card acquaintances.

Consider this alternate frame: a network is your professional family, a community of colleagues who support you, share (and request) knowledge and contacts with/from you, and help you move toward your goals over a span of decades. When it comes to your career, your network enables you to extend your reach and expand your opportunities, while also providing a really cool group of individuals to hang out with at conferences.

In addition, as we've seen, having a strong, wide-ranging network of people who know you and your work is one of the best ways to connect with invisible job opportunities. In ALA's *Network Your Way into a Job*, Miranda Wax makes a strong case for the value of personal connections to help open up access to jobs well beyond those found among the standard LIS job lists.

What Is a Professional Network?

A professional network is the group of people with whom you've established a sustained (if often very loose) relationship of some sort. That connection is usually based on some type of commonality—shared friends, interests, experiences, employers, and so on. But it might also be that you're both members of a certain organization, that you both served on a conference committee, that you're alumni of the same graduate program, or that a mutual friend said you ought to connect on a professional issue. The reasons for establishing a relationship are as numerous and varied as those relationships themselves—and as indicative of a rich and rewarding career.

We're not talking rolodex networking here—we're talking the trust that begins to build when you have an opportunity to say, "how can I help?" to a coworker, or a fellow committee member, or a classmate, about the lifelong friendships that evolve out of shared professional challenges and efforts, about the goodwill that grows from your willingness to share knowledge, expertise, and credit for accomplishments.

When you seek to build a professional community by asking "how can I help you?" rather than "how can you help me?" you create relationships whose foundation is giving rather than taking. The goodwill and trust that builds from this is not only invaluable and intrinsically rewarding at the deepest human levels, it also becomes extraordinarily helpful when you need to expand career options. The people you know also know lots of other people—and if you've been a caring and responsive colleague, they'll probably be willing to help connect you with names, job opportunities, or potential projects.

Building and Sustaining Your
Professional Community

So how do you start building a professional network or community if you haven't been already? If networks are about building relationships, then growing a network is about identifying and nurturing connecting points, or the links between you and another person. It's actually easier than it seems; in fact, any time you meet someone new, whether in person or virtually, you have an opportunity to build your network. (This really *is* simply an opportunity because with every interaction with a new person, you get to decide whether you want to include that particular individual in your professional community—and it's okay if the answer is no.) The ways you can do this could be the following.

Face to Face

Connecting with someone in person can be an especially effective way to jumpstart your network-building efforts. Shared experiences are always a starting point—for example, having worked on the same community project, been on a professional panel presentation together, worked on some sort of volunteer program or local initiative together, been students in the same grad program. These types of in-person experiences can create a bond of shared stories (okay, sometimes war stories!) that may form the basis of delightful and rewarding lifelong relationships.

Connecting with groups of people, for example, at local association meetings or national conferences, can also be a highly effective way of building your network face-to-face. But what if a roomful of strangers leaves you tongue-tied at best? Consider the how-to classic, *The Fine Art of Small Talk. How to Start a Conversation, Keep it Going, Build Networking Skills—and Leave a Positive Impression,* by Debra Fine, for its practical, actionable conversational tips.

Fine's work is a great starting point for preparing for any upcoming conferences, where you'll be faced with numerous network-building opportunities (or opportunities to sit at the back of the room and hope no one notices you). For strategies on how to reach out at conferences, check out "Professional Networking at Conferences" by Jacqueline Ayala; "Tips and Suggestions to Get the Most Out of Internet Librarian" (or any conference) by Librarian by Day blogger Bobbi Newman; and Stephen Abram's "Tips for First-Time Conference Attendance," all of which offer strategies for not only meeting people but also for building valuable network connections from those meetings. (Insider tip: make sure to take business cards to pass out! You can create basic and inexpensive business card from several popular online vendors, such as Vistaprint.com and MOO.com.)

Virtual

More and more frequently, people find themselves building relationships virtually, getting to know people via e-mail, conference calls, virtual committee meetings, online courses, and so on.

Other virtual professional connections can be established through such venues as association forums, special interest listservs such as *Buslib-l,* and online LIS courses' virtual team projects (a very valuable indicator of whether you'd ever want to work with someone again!), among other avenues.

The growth of social media sites as professional networking venues, however, has emerged as one of the easiest and most effective ways to build a highly valuable, easily maintained, extensive virtual network. Services like LinkedIn and Facebook are specifically set up to enable you to publicly provide enough information about yourself that other people will be able to quickly determine your relevant connecting points—for example, you may have attended the same school or worked at one point for the same employer, you may share an interest in taxonomy-building or body surfing, you may both have been volunteers for Habitat for Humanity, and so on. Social media tools allow you to quickly determine with whom you want to network (and why), join groups relevant to your professional interests or personal passions, and see updates about what's going on in the lives of those in your network so that you can reach out and congratulate them on their achievements or offer to help with an impending job search.

A great starting point for how to use the various social media tools for career networking is Miriam Salpeter's *Social Networking for Career Success: Using Online Tools to Create a Personal Brand.* It explores all of the major social media options—LinkedIn, Twitter, Facebook—plus a number of other social media approaches (blogging, social bookmarks, etc.) in terms of how each can be most effectively used as a networking tool.

LinkedIn especially is becoming a standard platform for establishing and maintaining a robust professional network, because, quite frankly, it's simply so easy to use once you've done the initial work to establish your profile. After that, you can just start reaching out to connect with others and joining relevant groups. (For more on how to request connections, see "Asking to Connect on LinkedIn—Words to Use.")

As you go through your career (or graduate program) you're likely to meet people (perhaps at conferences, through professional development courses, at local community happenings, or through myriad other events) with whom you strike up a connection that builds into a relationship of shared stories or experiences. Your goal is to find ways to continue to nurture and strengthen those connections, so that the bond between you remains resilient, even if you end up connecting only occasionally or from a distance.

Sustaining Your Network

The reality is that almost no one I know (including myself) has as much time as we'd like to consistently stay in contact with the people in our professional community, so coming up with a few strategies for staying connected on the fly can help. For example, consider

- meeting up over coffee (or cocktails) after work,
- sending quarterly e-mails to colleagues just to see how they're doing and letting them know what's up with you,
- forwarding on information of interest (perhaps an online article or blog post) with a note that you're thinking of them,
- using conference attendance as a great opportunity to connect with virtual colleagues so you can meet face-to-face, and

- joining social media sites so you can receive automatic updates on friends and colleagues as they change jobs, get promotions, or undertake new career paths (be sure to send a congratulatory note!).

And although it would be ideal if we could nurture our professional relationships in person or with a handwritten note or phone call, the reality is that generally, for most purposes, an e-mail is just fine.

Introverted? You Can Still Build a Network

Although there aren't any official statistics on how many LIS professionals fall into the introvert category, enough LIS students and colleagues self-identify as introverts that sometimes it's helpful to have information specifically on networking for those for whom reaching out to others doesn't come easily. Fortunately, there are some terrific resources on this topic.

LIS professional Marcy Phelps, founder and owner of Colorado-based Phelps Research, was concerned that her introversion—and aversion to networking—was going to keep her from building her independent research business. So she set about learning everything she could about how to how to network effectively despite being an introvert. The result? Her wildly popular blog, *Power Networking for Introverts,* which describes strategies and tactics for those of us who, shall we say, need all the encouragement we can get.

Another great resource here, for introverts and others, is Devora Zack's *Networking for People Who Hate Networking: A Field Guide for Introverts, the Overwhelmed, and the Underconnected,* which is especially strong on networking in business/organization environments.

Still a Student? Start Building Your Network in Grad School

Grad school offers a rich opportunity to start building your community of professional friendships and connections, a resource that'll be critical to opening up career options after your graduate. For example, consider the following ways to make the most of your student networking opportunities.

Classmates

Classmates offer an easy, built-in opportunity to build relationships with people who you already have something in common with: shared career goals, shared class experiences, and often the shared challenge of juggling school and work (read: exhaustion!). If you make connections with classmates who are pursuing your same degree, you'll probably end up in the same profession, and these people will be invaluable contacts for you at their various employers. (You will be invaluable to them, as well.)

Faculty

Get to know your teachers and let them get to know you. Let them know what type of work you'll be looking for when you graduate, and ask them for advice and feedback. Let them know if you enjoyed their course or found an assignment especially useful—like anybody else, teachers like to know their hard work and efforts are appreciated, and this is a great way to cement your connection.

Then when you graduate, stay in touch. Your teachers can be a great source of referrals, contacts, and references. And in return, you can offer to be a guest speaker in one of their classes to share your new professional expertise.

Guest Speakers

Whenever one of your classes has a guest speaker, pay special attention. If the speaker works in a field or job that might possibly be of interest to you, make sure to establish a connection by asking thoughtful questions in class and then introducing yourself after class, letting them know that you appreciated their taking the time to share their expertise with the class. Follow up with a written or e-mailed thank-you note, perhaps mentioning the comments you found to be especially useful or insightful.

When you're ready to do some information interviews to learn more about specific career paths, these individuals are likely to be willing to spend time with you, sharing their experiences and recommendations—and just possibly their knowledge of potential job openings.

Others You've Reached Out To

If you use your assignments to connect with professionals (for interviews, class research, group projects), you'll probably come across people that you admire, enjoy, or find especially helpful. Stay in touch with these people with an occasional e-mail update or offer to spring for a cup of coffee so you can catch up on their careers, and let them know how your degree work is progressing. Again, these individuals can be the source of career insights, contacts, and possibly job openings.

Student Professional Associations

Many of the LIS professional associations offer greatly reduced student membership fees. Participating in these groups will provide you with an opportunity not only to build relationships with fellow student members but also with members of the national organization, who will see you as a highly engaged professional-in-training. Most professionals are happy to help students find their way in their careers, and are usually generous with sharing their time, expertise, and connections. Consider college to be a target-rich environment for building your network.

Networking Strategy

From a career-building perspective, it would seem to make sense to focus your networking efforts on individuals who share your professional space—in other words, people with whom you have much in common in terms of professional interests and experience. These would be considered strong ties or connections. In fact, however, you want to grow a network of both strong and weak ties, weak ties being those individuals with whom you connect but who are outside of your normal professional sphere. Why? Because this gives you access to a much wider and diverse range of potential job opportunities than if you are only operating within the same group of connections that those in your network possess.

In "How to Build Your Network," authors Brian Uzzi and Shannon Dunlap made an effective case for this approach in a 2005 *Harvard Business Review* article. Based on "The Strength of Weak Ties," an article reporting on original research on social networks undertaken by Mark Granovetter of Johns Hopkins University in 2004, Uzzi and Dunlap examine how information—and connections—flow based on the nature of those connections. (Most notably, they identify Paul Revere as an information broker.) Key take-away: if you consider your career from a broader perspective than your current work situation, it becomes evident that having multiple connections in diverse professional (and personal) communities increases exponentially the potential for finding job opportunities out of the mainstream.

Also, the more non-LIS connections you have, the more likely it is that for many of those connections, you'll be the only person they know who has your information skills. That means that you'll likely be the person who comes to mind when they're asked for a recommendation or referral by one of their *other* connections in need of information expertise.

Benefits of a Professional Network

As you build your career over the years or decades, a professional network often evolves into less of what others can do to help you and more about all of the ways that you can help others build their careers. But early on, a robust professional network or community of colleagues can be an invaluable resource for helping you create the career path that's right for you. For example, an extensive professional network can help you in the following ways.

Identify and Connect with More Job Opportunities

Bottom line: The more people you know and who know what you can do, the more potential jobs or projects you're likely to hear about (or be recommended for). If a large number of colleagues know you're interested in a certain type of work or a specific job, that translates into a large number of people who can potentially help you with contacts, information, referrals, and advice. In sports as in life, the best defense is a good offense; in terms of your career, having a solid professional network is like having a great team backing up your career moves, ready to help you move the ball forward.

Get Smarter, Faster, by Tapping into Your Network

Being able to master new information rapidly is critical in the LIS field, yet there's only so much time in a given day as opposed to an endless flow of new tools, technologies, and processes to stay on top of. No matter how quickly you can learn, you'll be able to move faster and with greater agility throughout your career if you're able to able to tap your friends and colleagues for their coaching, tutoring, or mentoring to learn from their skills and expertise. Find out who in your professional community knows what, or how to do what, to get smarter faster. And then, of course, reciprocate with your own knowledge.

Find Answers at the Point of Need

Just as you can turn to your network for learning, those same individuals can often come up with answers when what you need is a quick piece of information. You may know tons about alternative medicine, Mary Ellen may know all about small business start-ups, Marcy may be an expert in local market research resources, and Scott may be nationally recognized for his social media smarts. Having a broad base of knowledge, which you get with a diverse network of colleagues, means that your friends know things you don't (and vice versa). A quick e-mail or phone call to the right colleague lets you extend the reach of your knowledge on demand, from sources you know and trust.

It Makes Career Transitions Easier

When you're bridging into a new field or career, it's helpful to have connections who can help ease the way into your new direction. The more diverse your network, the likelier it is that someone will be able to help you cross the bridge into that new industry - and opportunity.

Career Karma Rocks

Lastly, when you have a large network of professional colleagues, the likelihood is that you'll be able to help a lot of friends and colleagues reach their career goals. More connections just automatically lead to more career opportunities—for those you care about as well as for yourself. If the basis of your approach to building a network is to seek ways to help others, you'll find that career karma will bring many, many more opportunities heading back your direction.

Resources

Starred titles are mentioned in the chapter.

Print Resources

Ferrazzi, Keith and Tahl Raz. *Never Eat Alone—And Other Secrets to Success, One Relationship at a Time.* Crown Business, 2005. 309p. ISBN 0385512058.
    Never Eat Alone established Ferrazzi as a master networker with a focus on authentic, empathetic relationships; his follow-up book, *Who's Got Your Back* (Crown Business, 2009), expands on that concept to describe the importance of creating your own inner circle of trusted individuals (sort of a super network) to help sustain you through the ups and downs of your career.

**Fine, Debra. *The Fine Art of Small Talk: How to Start a Conversation, Keep it Going, Build Networking Skills—and Leave a Positive Impression!* Hyperion, 2005. 224p. ISBN 1401302262.
    Fine uses examples, exercises, and how-to encouragement to help readers feel more comfortable talking to strangers. Although not all of her ice-breaker lines will resonate, they provide ideas that you'll be able to adapt to your own style and interests. A great resource for those of us who blanch at the thought of walking into a roomful of strangers.

Laney, Marti Olsen. *The Introvert Advantage: How to Thrive in an Extrovert World.* Workman Publishing Company, 2002. ISBN 0761123695.
    Being an introvert doesn't doom you to the constrained career of a shrinking violet; instead, Laney makes clear, you have some distinct strengths and advantages to call on. The chapters in the book's three sections—characteristics of an introvert, being an introvert in an extrovert world, and creating a life that works for your personality—highlight the many ways to make being an introvert your strongest asset. For networking, see especially the chapters on socializing and working.

Lowndes, Leil. *How to Talk to Anyone: 92 Little Tricks for Big Success in Relationships.* McGraw-Hill, 2003. 368p. ISBN 007141858X.
    Similar to *Fine Art of Small Talk,* Lowndes's book provides practical, easily used tips for talking to people, key to your networking efforts at conferences, professional meetings, and other on-the-fly interactions with strangers.

Mackay, Harvey. *Dig Your Well Before You're Thirsty.* Currency Books, 1999. 336p. ISBN 385485468.
    MacKay was a networking guru before networking was cool—so his viewpoint is both broader and much less technology-based than most

of the more recent "how to network" books. *Dig Your Well* is completely focused on business success, so less touchy-feely than many other books on networking.

Misner, Ivan and Michelle R. Donovan. *The 29% Solution: 52 Weekly Networking Success Strategies.* Greenleaf Book Group Press, 2008. 286p. ISBN 1929774540.
  Although Misner and Donovan are focused on networking more as a business (rather than career) development tool, their timelined, workbook structure works especially well for those looking for a step-by-step, week-by-week action plan.

Randel, Jim. *The Skinny on Networking: Maximizing the Power of Numbers.* Rand Media Co., 2010. 156p. ISBN 0984441816.
  Looking for a quick and entertaining read on networking tactics that still covers all the bases? Randel's *The Skinny on Networking* (part of his multi-book Skinny On . . . series) is short, practical, and readable over a long-ish lunch hour.

**Salpeter, Miriam. *Social Networking for Career Success.* LearningExpress, 2011. 368p. ISBN 1576857824.
  One of the best books on using the major social media tools—for example, LinkedIn, Twitter, Facebook, Quora—plus other social media approaches (blogging, social bookmarks, etc.) to establish and sustain both a professional network and long-term career advantage.

Schaffer, Neal. *Windmill Networking: Understanding, Leveraging & Maximizing LinkedIn: An Unofficial, Step-by-Step Guide to Implementing Your LinkedIn Brand—Social Networking in a Web 2.0 World.* Book-Surge Publishing, 2009. 382p. ISBN 1439247056.
  Wondering how to make the most of that LinkedIn profile you created and then promptly forgot about a couple of years ago? *Windmill Networking* provides step-by-step guidance for how to use your LinkedIn presence to extend (or start building) your professional network. One of the best books on using LinkedIn strategically.

**Zack, Devora. *Networking for People Who Hate Networking: A Field Guide for Introverts, the Overwhelmed, and the Underconnected.* Berrett-Koehler, 2010. 192p. ISBN 1605095222.
  Focusing primarily on networking at business events, Zack proposes a process-based approach for navigating networking situations. Casual in tone and engagingly written.

Online Resources

**Asking to Connect on LinkedIn—Words to Use
  http://infonista.com/2011/asking-to-connect-on-linkedin-don%E2%80%99t-default-to-the-defaults/
  One of the important aspects of networking on LinkedIn is reaching out and establishing links to others. Although the LinkedIn system

provides you with default request language, it's much better to tailor your request to the individual you're reaching out to. This blog post gives examples of wording you can adapt for your own circumstances.

**Buslib-l

http://lists.nau.edu/cgi-bin/wa?A0=BUSLIB-L

One of the most active electronic discussion groups, Buslib-l is an excellent example of a highly active network of LIS professionals who share questions, information, and professional support.

How to Be an Effective Networker

www.careercenter.sjsu.edu/students/launch/networking/networking.html

From the San Jose State University Career Center, this is a brief, practical overview of networking tactics, especially useful for MLIS students in any program.

**"How to Build Your Network"

www.kellogg.northwestern.edu/faculty/uzzi/ftp/uzzi's research_papers/uzzi_dunlap%20hbr.pdf

This article, written by Brian Uzzi and Shannon Dunlap and published in the December 2005 *Harvard Business Review,* is a fascinating exploration of how information—and connections—flow based on the nature of those connections (for example, the authors call Paul Revere an information broker). The authors feel that "networks deliver three unique advantages: private information, access to diverse skill sets, and power." And from a career development perspective, they also often deliver job opportunities, knowledge shared among colleagues, and a highly effective way to showcase your professional persona.

How to Network Effectively

www.inc.com/guides/2010/08/how-to-network-effectively.html

A methodical, well-organized overview of how to think strategically about the various aspects of your network, and how to gain the most benefit from each of those aspects. Includes techniques for getting the most from LinkedIn as a networking tool.

Job Search Resources: How Do I Network

www.getajob.ala.org/?cat=14

Ten articles and interviews about networking as a career-development and job-hunting strategy. Part of ALA's "'Get a Job!' Toolkit for Getting a Job in a Tough Economy" resource.

"Networking for the Busy Information Professional: Fostering Relationships Despite Everyday Obstacles"

http://lisjobs.com/career_trends/?p=489

Written by Lori Gluckman Winterfeldt, this encouraging article lines out "ways to develop relationships without feeling stressed, uncomfortable, and pressured to choose between meeting your responsibilities and growing your professional network." Winterfeldt has provided lots of good ideas and thoughtful insights in a short amount of space.

**Network Your Way into a Job
www.atyourlibrary.org/career/network-your-way-job
A brief but useful guide to using networking techniques in support of your library-focused job-hunting efforts.

**Power Networking for Introverts
www.introvertscannetwork.com/
From independent information professional Marcy Phelps, this "blog by an introvert for introverts" has been wildly popular with LIS students and practitioners as well as others outside the profession. The focus is on tips, techniques, and coping strategies that enable introverts to network effectively and (relatively) painlessly.

**Professional Networking at Conferences
http://blog.webjunctionworks.org/index.php/2007/12/12/weekly-tips-pro
fessional-networking-at-conferences/
From guest blogger Jacqueline Ayala, with the basic premise that "Networking on the Web is undoubtedly fundamental to being an active member of the library community, but nothing beats the in-person connections we make with our colleagues at conferences." Ayala asserts that careful planning is key to gaining the most value from attending a conference, and she provides pointers for how to do just that.

Promoting Your Professional Development: The Value of Being Proactive
http://lisjobs.com/career_trends/?s=networking
An article by Penny Scott written for *Info Career Trends* in 2009, this excellent piece discusses Scott's decision to create a promotion binder to trace her career development. As part of that tracing, Scott identifies ways that she built her professional network, and the outcomes of those efforts. A wonderful, no-hype exploration of networking as a part of a broader career development process.

**"The Strength of Weak Ties"
http://smg.media.mit.edu/library/Granovetter.WeakTies.pdf
From the May 1973 *American Journal of Sociology,* this article by Mark S. Granovetter is the basis on which much of the subsequent research on networking was built. Granovetter looked at why weak ties, or connections to people outside your normal sphere of influence/engagement, can prove to be a highly effective way of opening up additional career opportunities as well as extending your access to knowledge and insights outside your normal sphere of influence.

**Tips and Suggestions to Get the Most Out of Internet Librarian
http://librarianbyday.net/2010/10/20/tips-and-suggestions-to-get-the-
most-out-of-internet-librarian-il2010/
From Librarian by Day blogger Bobbi Newman, this post offers great advice for networking at (and surviving) any conference.

**Tips for First-Time Conference Attendance
http://sla-phl.org/blog/2011/03/30/tips-for-first-time-conference-attendees/
From former SLA president Stephen Abram and including tips from current SLA president Deb Hunt, the focus of this blog post is on tips for

first-time SLA conference attendees. However, they work equally well for any conference attendance.

Vistaprint

www.vistaprint.com

If you have business cards furnished by your employer, terrific. But if you don't, or if you're a student yet to be employed, it's important that you have your own personal business cards to hand out at professional meetings, conferences, and any other events where you're likely to meet people you don't know. Vistaprint is one company that creates professional-looking business cards online easily and inexpensively (as in, really, really cheap); another popular option is MOO (http://us.moo.com).

7
Establishing Your Professional Brand

Chapter Highlights

- Key Characteristics of a Professional Brand
- Career Branding, Social Media, and Introverts
- Building Your Brand in Grad School
- Why Your Professional Brand Is *Really* Important to Your Career

---

In the marketing world, a brand comprises the collective characteristics that the market attributes to a given product or service. A professional brand is similar, in that it's how the world views who you are, what you can contribute, and how you contribute. Although in the old days of LIS careers most of us never give much thought to having (or building) a professional brand, now it has become one of the most important aspects of ensuring that you'll have the types of professional opportunities you'd like over the course of your career.

It's especially important to pay attention to your professional brand because the reality is that you have one *whether or not you actively manage it.* As Harvard Business School professor Laura Morgan Roberts noted in *Creating a Positive Professional Image,* you must realize that if you aren't managing your own professional image, someone else is. People are constantly observing your behavior and forming theories about your competence, character, and commitment, which are rapidly disseminated throughout your workplace. It is only wise to add your voice in framing others' theories about who you are and what you can accomplish.

Think of these people: Secretary of State Hillary Clinton, antiapartheid activist and former president of South Africa Nelson Mandela, and media entrepreneur Oprah Winfrey. Each of these people has a very specific brand. That is, they are known to the world for very specific values, passions, skills, and professional competencies. When you thought of them, you probably also had a set of expectations regarding how they might (or do) behave in their various roles and circumstances.

So it is with your own professional brand. A professional brand isn't about creating a phony persona or pretending to be someone you're not. Instead, it's about showcasing the best of who you are and the unique value you provide. Your professional brand highlights the strengths that you want to be known for, and takes the initiative to shape others' assumptions about your ability to contribute.

Key Characteristics of a Professional Brand

There are many opinions about what attributes constitute a professional brand, but one way to think about brand characteristics is laid out by authors David McNally and Karl D. Speak in *Be Your Own Brand*. They identify the big three characteristics as competencies, standards, and style:

- *Competencies.* Not only what you're good at, but what you want to be *known* for being good at. What work are you passionate about doing? (If you're a decent manager, but you hate managing people, you don't want to build your brand around management competencies.)
- *Standards.* How do you perform your competencies? Are you known for always beating deadlines, bringing creative thinking to a project, paying attention to all the details, or ensuring the smooth running of team projects? Are you a perfectionist? What level of performance should others expect of you?
- *Style.* How do you communicate and interact with others? Think about your relations with classmates, coworkers, bosses, customers, etc. Are you generally more casual in your interactions or more formal? A high-visibility contributor or a more reflective, quiet participant? Do you gravitate toward leadership roles, or prefer to be more of a team player? Are you someone who uses humor (when appropriate) to lighten the mood? These are the attributes you would showcase as part of your professional brand.

Every day, you have multiple ways to demonstrate or express your brand by choosing how you present yourself to and interact with the profession at large and the world around you. For example, consider these brand elements:

- *Your words.* What you say—and how you say it—provides one of the first sets of indicators of how you approach the world. Are your words kind and interested, or cold and distant? Is your voice confident and strong, or hesitant and wavering? Is your contribution to the conversation arrogant and self-absorbed or do you encourage others to share their experiences through your questions?

- *The way you dress.* I'll admit it, my ideal work wardrobe involves a T-shirt, a pair of well-worn jeans, and no shoes—fine for those days when I'm working at home. But when you're in a professional situation, it's important that you dress in a manner that will reassure your employer/client/customer/interviewer that he or she can trust your professional judgment. How that translates into wardrobe choices depends on the professional environment you aspire to, but generally speaking, you want to dress like the person whose trust you are trying to earn. If you want others to take you seriously as a professional, you have to be seen to take yourself seriously in that role first. My favorite quote summing up this reality: "Maybe appearances shouldn't count, and maybe jerks with no sense of style shouldn't be allowed to pass judgments based solely on how someone is dressed, but it happens every day" (Robin Fisher Roffer, *Make a Name for Yourself*).

- *Your participation.* One of the ways you build both connections *and* a positive professional reputation is by engaging in professional-level activities (not necessarily within the LIS community). So consider what projects or volunteer work you might take on that reflects or demonstrates the professional characteristics you want to be known for—for example, a commitment to community development, innovative pilot programs, a leadership ability to bridge and motivate diverse groups, event management smarts, and so on.

- *Your public communications.* Social media—including professional online discussion forums as well as sites like Facebook and LinkedIn—can have a huge impact on how the profession (and potential employers) perceive you. (See "Are Any of These Behaviors Damaging Your Personal Brand" to make sure you're not dooming your job prospects.) In fact, there are people I've never met but would never consider hiring or recommending simply because of the many snarky things I've seen them say online. But also consider the strong positive impact of a great blog post, a well-written article, a helpful or insightful presentation at your state's library conference. All of these are public communications, and all contribute to establishing the professional reputation or brand that will help grow (or torpedo) your career.

- *The attitude you convey.* Yep, we all have off days, but in general, it helps your professional brand to be a positive person. Not phony or smarmy, but simply more often than not positive rather than negative. It's exhausting to work with a toxic, complaining coworker, so to the extent possible, you want to be known as the person who's easy to work with and a supportive, enthusiastic team member. No whining. Well, at least not very often.

Even if you're just beginning your career, you'll have many opportunities to start building your professional brand. What do you want that brand to say about you? For starters, you might want to focus on developing a reputation for being

- easy to work with—emotionally steady, flexible, resilient;
- a strong and positive team participant, whether as a leader or team member (there was a reason for all those group projects in grad school!);
- someone whose judgment can be trusted;
- reliable; and
- confident in your own skills and knowledge, but also respectful of others' expertise.

If you develop a brand based on—or reputation for—these characteristics when you're starting out in your career, you'll find your coworkers, bosses, and former colleagues will be much likelier to want to help you move your career forward. (It's always easier to recommend someone who you know is going to be a great employee and coworker.)

Career Branding, Social Media, and Introverts

Establishing a strong career brand by showcasing your professional strengths makes it a lot easier to open up the types of professional opportunities you might aspire to. However, if you're an introvert (as so many in the LIS profession, including me, classify themselves), the prospect of having to tell others about yourself can be challenging, if not downright daunting.

This is the challenge Nancy Ancowitz takes on in her wonderful, wise, and empathetic book *Self-Promotion for Introverts: The Quiet Guide to Getting Ahead,* noting that "While the inward-facing nature of introverts can be a source of strength, if we neglect to reach outward, we miss out on the richness that human interaction can bring—not to mention the career advancement associated with our increased visibility." Focusing on strategy (shifting negative self-talk to strengths self-talk, creating do-able approaches to networking, public speaking, job interviewing, etc.) as well as tactics (what to say in specific situations), Ancowitz makes a convincing case that introverts can successfully develop a positive professional brand in what often feels like a world full of extroverts.

The really good news? We are increasingly living and communicating in an online environment, which is ideal for those of us who prefer to think through our ideas before sharing them with the rest of the world.

In fact, social media sites like LinkedIn, Facebook, and Twitter offer an invaluable opportunity to engage with our professional community on an ongoing basis without actually having to *talk* to it. Other alternatives include blogging (individual, group, or guest), creating a personal website on a topic of interest to you, or becoming active in one or more of your professional associations' online communities.

How important is your online presence? Very. First, as noted, experts estimate that 90 percent of hiring managers will use a search engine to check you out before making a decision as to whether or not to interview you. You want them to find excellent examples of your professional expertise — and a killer LinkedIn profile—at the very least. Second, as Kirsten Dixson, coauthor of *Career Distinction* points out, "Building your personal brand online gets you noticed in the real world." And in her excellent *Social Networking for Career Success: Using Tools to Create a Personal Brand,* Miriam Salpeter suggests that we "[p]icture the modern job seeker as a magnet, constantly attracting opportunities by using social media to raise his or her profile in a way that draws in people—and jobs."

Start easing into that outward reach Ancowitz recommends by using online tools to let the world—and potential employers—know how terrific you are. To quote Harry Beckwith in *You, Inc.,* "You must not merely answer what makes you different, but how what you do makes a difference for others."

Building Your Brand in Grad School

Still working on your MLIS? Grad school is the perfect place to start building your professional brand. (In fact, now might be a great time to read one of the basic how-to books, such as Wilson and Blumenthal's *Managing Brand You,* about building your professional brand.)

While you're in school, classmates, faculty, guest speakers, administrators, assignment contacts, and others are constantly forming an impression of who you are and what type of person you would be to work with. This means that every day, through your interactions, you're building your professional brand, for better or worse.

You've heard that old saying, actions speak louder than words? Well, when it comes to your professional brand, *both* of them shout pretty loudly. What are yours telling the world about you?

Keep in mind that those you come into contact with—whether face-to-face or online—will build their impression of you based on your behavior, your physical presentation, your attitude, your contributions and reliability as a collaborator and team member, and the engagement you bring to the classroom.

In addition, the volunteer projects you take on, the leadership opportunities you rise to, and your willingness to extend yourself to help and/or reach out to other students will establish who you are and the value you offer as a professional. This is the beginning of your professional brand among people who could well end up being your colleagues (or hiring managers).

Following are some of the easiest ways to ensure that you're building the kind of reputation that will make people want to work with you in the future.

Support Fellow Students

Word gets out quickly when someone develops a reputation as a backstabber. Play nice—when you help others succeed, they'll be much more interested in helping you succeed.

Be Reliable

Everybody drops a ball now and then, but if you consistently fail to meet deadlines, deliver papers on time, or show up prepared, you'll develop a reputation for being unreliable and immature—regardless of how smart or talented you are. Become the group project person everyone knows they can count on to deliver.

Avoid the Blame Game

Employers look for people who can step up and take responsibility, for both successes and failures. Students who always refuse to take responsibility for their actions when they don't go well, and instead blame others, lose the respect and trust of their classmates and faculty (word gets around). When things go wrong on a group project, first look for and implement solutions, then figure out what lessons you can learn for next time.

Give Credit for Others' or Team Efforts

A professional looks for ways to give credit to those who've earned it. Those obnoxious classmates who take credit for other team members' work or successes? They will quickly develop a reputation as a selfish, untrustworthy classmate—and coworker. That reputation eventually makes its way to faculty who might otherwise have recommended them to potential employers, not to mention fellow students who might have been the source of job possibilities.

Be Easy to Work With

You don't want to develop a reputation as the person who's temperamental, moody, arrogant, negative, or always taking offense at perceived slights. You want classmates (read: potential future colleagues) to *want* to work with you on team projects again, and eventually to recommend you to their new employers. If "great to work with" is part of your professional brand, *everyone* will try to find ways to work with you!

Always Remember to Say Thank You

Throughout your grad school experience, a lot of people will help you in various ways. Remembering to thank them, especially with a written note, is not just a professional courtesy, it's how you build a reputation as a conscientious and appreciative individual. Those who've received your thank you's will remember your extra effort, and are likely to feel positive about recommending you for future job opportunities.

Why Your Professional Brand Is *Really* Important to Your Career

Having a strong professional brand can help you build the career you want in a number of ways.

- *It provides stability in the midst of workplace and economic chaos.* You know the drill: pink slips are flying left and right, companies are changing direction (and staffing needs), entire industries are contracting (and job opportunities along with them). You may have made a decision that your current job (or employer) is a dead-end deal, and that it's time to head in a new direction. Having a strong professional brand lays the groundwork for you to land on your feet with a new employer if needed, because you've already built a reputation (which they can see online and/or hear about from others) that lets them know how valuable you are.

- *It helps shape how people are willing to let you contribute.* If you're new on the job, and no one really knows you, they won't know what to expect of you. Should they trust your judgment? Should they give you the important assignments or new opportunities? If you've built a track record—a brand—that lets them know you're smart, capable, and have high professional standards, you've gone a long way toward answering those questions for them.

- *It positions you in the path of opportunity.* If you've done a good job of building a reputation as a strong contributor, you're more likely to be mentioned by others when new opportunities arise.

It's impossible to tell where a new project may be developing, when a company may be taking a new direction that would be a perfect fit for your skills, or how a startup is going to need your expertise to take advantage of an expanding market segment. But if you've got a great brand that's visible to a lot of people, it's a lot likelier that your name will cross paths with those opportunities through people who can connect the dots for you.

Resources

Starred titles are mentioned in the chapter.

Print Resources

**Ancowitz, Nancy. *Self-Promotion for Introverts: The Quiet Guide to Getting Ahead.* McGraw-Hill, 2009. 288p. IBSN 007159129X.

Ancowitz writes from the heart: she is an introvert, yet is also a successful consultant, writer, and speaker. Her book draws on stories from well-known business, sports, and entertainment figures, everyday clients, and her own experiences to lay out a life approach that will help introverts find the career success their efforts merit, but in a way that recognizes how they interact with the world.

**Arruda, William and Kirsten Dixson. *Career Distinction: Stand Out by Building Your Brand.* Wiley, 2007. 224p. ISBN 0470128186.

Organized by three broad themes: unearth your unique promise of value, communicate your brand to your target audience, manage your brand environment. Key statement: "What makes you unique, makes you successful." Lots of solid how-to advice, resources, and cool quotes.

**Beckwith, Harry and Christine Clifford Beckwith. *You, Inc.: The Art of Selling Yourself.* Business Plus, 2007. 336p. ISBN 0446578215.

Best-selling business author Harry Beckwith's expertise is how to use communication to sell, and here he turns his focus to helping you sell yourself via your career brand. The book is packed with brief, concise points (roughly two pages long) that each conclude with a pithy action statement. Consider this career-branding bootcamp.

Brogan, Chris and Julien Smith. *Trust Agents: Using the Web to Build Influence, Improve Reputation, and Build Trust,* rev. and updated. John Wiley & Sons, 2010. 302p. ISBN 0470635495.

Brogan's best-selling book focuses more on business-related online brand-building, but his concepts have relevance as well for personal, professional brand-building. His thinking related to transparency, social capital, and media is especially compelling.

Cain, Susan. *Quiet: The Power of Introverts in a World That Can't Stop Talking.* Crown, 2012. 352p. ISBN 0307352145.

A student recommended this book, and a question about it on the LinkedIn LIS Career Options group has so far elicited a rousing 50-plus comments about how to create a thriving, resilient career while dealing with the challenges of being an introvert in what often seems like an extrovert world. A terrific resource for those of us who *are* introverts, or work with them, are raising them, married to them, and so on.

Kaputa, Catherine. *You Are a Brand! How Smart People Brand Themselves.* Nicholas Brealey Publishing, 2010. 208p. ISBN 0891062130.

Winner of multiple career book awards, this book is particularly strong on tactics and tools. Many of Kaputa's ideas are unique to this book, and yet once she's suggested them, seem like common sense (e.g., include testimonial quotes on your resume). Key concept: a strong personal brand raises the perception of your value among others, and consequently your earning power.

**McNally, David and Karl D. Speak. *Be Your Own Brand: A Breakthrough Formula for Standing Out from the Crowd,* 2nd ed. Berrett-Koehler Publishers, 2011. 168p. ISBN 1605098108.
One of the more reflective, thoughtful, and methodical of the branding books. Key statement: "The 'right way' to go about building a strong personal brand is to make sure your brand resonates and is relevant, in the most distinctive way possible, for those people with whom you want to build strong relationships on a long-term basis." Useful graphics clarify a number of the key concepts.

**Roffer, Robin Fisher. *Make a Name for Yourself: Eight Steps Every Woman Needs to Create a Personal Brand Strategy for Success.* Crown Business, 2002. 224p. ISBN 9780767904926.
A marketer by profession, Roffer was one of the early entrants in the personal branding arena. Her book is written for women because, she asserts, they usually have the toughest time drawing positive attention to themselves. As a marketer, Roffer's approach to personal branding is a bit, ah, flashier than most of us might feel comfortable with (and the book's recommendations are pre–social mediasphere); nevertheless, she makes many very helpful and still-valid points.

**Salpeter, Miriam. *Social Networking for Career Success: Using Tools to Create a Personal Brand.* Learning Express, 2011. 368p. ISBN 1576857824.
One of the best books on using the major social media tools—for example, LinkedIn, Twitter, Facebook, Quora—plus other social media approaches (blogging, social bookmarks, etc.) to establish and sustain both a professional network and long-term career advantage. Salpeter also focuses on how these same tools can be equally effective in showcasing your brand to a broad but targeted audience.

Schwabel, Dan. *Me 2.0, Revised and Updated Edition: 4 Steps to Building Your Future.* Kaplan, 2010. 288p. ISBN 9781607147121.
Successfully following his own advice, Schwabel has become a personal-branding guru. Strong coverage of social media tools and channels, and how to leverage your brand strengths for increased career opportunities. Although the strong focus on blatant self-promotion can be a bit off-putting, the book is nevertheless jammed with actionable advice and tactics (and exclamation points).

Van Yoder, Steven. *Get Slightly Famous: Become a Celebrity in Your Field and Attract More Business with Less Effort,* 2nd ed. CreateSpace, 2007. 330p. ISBN 145375671X.
Van Yoder's approach is delightfully realistic for most of us—we're not aiming to become a rock star, we'd just like to get a little more visibility for our professional contributions. Covers all the basics of brand-building, including identifying your niche, working with the

various media channels, and creating an online presence. Of special interest to LIS professionals is Chapter 10, "Info-Products: Create Multiple Income Streams."

Vetter, Simon. *Stand Out! Branding Strategies for Business Professionals.* July Publishing, 2005. 200p. ISBN 097043037X.
Stand Out! is noteworthy for its use of business experts' personal stories as examples of successful branding strategies. Although most of these are drawn from the fields of professional speaking, training, and personal coaching, many of the strategies and tactics used can be adapted for information professionals.

**Wilson, Jerry S. and Ira Blumenthal. *Managing Brand You: 7 Steps to Creating Your Most Successful Self.* AMACOM, 2008. 256p. ISBN 0814410685.
Wilson is the Senior Vice President and Chief Customer and Commercial Officer for Coca-Cola and Blumenthal a nationally recognized brand consultant—which is to say they know a lot about building a brand. In *Managing Brand You,* they focus that knowledge on how to identify your unique identity, then how to create, execute, and monitor a strategy for showcasing that unique identity. Methodical and actionable, albeit with a strong focus on corporate environments.

Online Resources

"Advocating for Yourself"
www.allbusiness.com/professional-services/librarians/16704533–1.html
Originally published in SLA's September 2011 *Information Outlook,* this article by former SLA president Stephen Abram lays out practical strategies for marketing your professional skills to people who often underestimate the value information professionals are able to contribute. A good reminder that we need to continue to seize control of how we're perceived by the non-LIS world.

**Are Any of these Behaviors Damaging Your Personal Brand?
http://infonista.com/2011/what-was-i-thinking-how-to-protect-your-online-professional-brand/
Top 10 ways to derail your online professional reputation. When 90 percent of hiring managers are now routinely checking out applicants for their online presence, it's critical to avoid damaging behaviors that will give potential employers a reason to doubt your professional judgment.

Build Your Professional Brand on LinkedIn
http://careerinsiderbusiness.ca/2011/build-your-professional-brand-on-linkedin/
From Career Insider Business, a blog focused on and often written by college students, this post provides a useful, basic student's approach to using LinkedIn to establish professional credibility.

**Creating a Positive Professional Image
http://hbswk.hbs.edu/item/4860.html
Interview with Harvard Business School professor Laura Morgan Roberts on the most important elements of creating a strong professional brand. See especially her comments about building credibility and maintaining authenticity.

How to Ruin (or Build) Your Personal Brand
http://davefleet.com/2010/05/ruin-build-personal-brand/
This no-holds-barred post is divided into three brief sections: (1) how to ruin your personal brand; (2) how to build your personal brand; and (3) things you can do today. A quick and concise action plan from Dave Fleet, a communications/PR/social media guy.

Librarian or Information Professional?
http://libwig.wordpress.com/2011/07/28/alignment-within-the-profession/
One of the more thoughtful discussions about a key professional branding question for the LIS profession—what to call ourselves. The writer, a law librarian, explores the pros and cons of self-identifying as librarian or information professional.

"LinkedIn: Everything I Ever Wanted to Tell You, But Was Too Shy/Modest/Embarrassed to Say . . . "
www.liscareer.com/dority_linkedin.htm
LIS article on how and why LinkedIn can be an invaluable tool for stealth self-promotion for introverts uncomfortable with more active professional promotion activities.

"Manage Your Brand as a Librarian"
http://practicallibrarian.blogspot.com/2011/05/manage-your-brand-as-librarian.html
From Practical Librarian Mary Kelly, this is the first of three posts on the importance of establishing and actively managing one's professional reputation or brand as a librarian. Because it's focused on traditional libraries, it has special relevance for those in traditional library settings who feel the professional brand issue doesn't apply to them. Especially valuable is her advice about complaining online.

100 Personal Branding Tactics Using Social Media
www.chrisbrogan. com/100- personal- branding-tactics-using-social-media/
From *Trust Agent* author Chris Brogan, this post is a bit out of date (2008) in terms of specific tools to use, but the key concepts and action items still hold.

One Minute Commercial
http: //slisweb.sjsu.edu/resources/career_development/networking_commercial.htm
Ah, the dreaded elevator speech. An essential part of networking is being able to tell strangers who you are and what you do, especially if you are

in job-hunting mode. Although designed for MLIS students, this brief guide will help anyone work through creating their own self-introduction. See especially the One Minute Commercial template.

Personal Branding Blog—Dan Schwabel

www.personalbrandingblog.com/
From the author of *Me 2.0* (see previously), Schwabel's blog is heavy on hype for his various coaching products, but also includes useful posts on how to build a professional brand that serves your career goals.

Reinventing Your Personal Brand

http://blogs.hbr.org/cs/2010/11/how_to_reinvent_your_personal.html
This *Harvard Business Review* blog post by strategy consultant Dorie Clark provides concrete solutions to the question of what to do about your professional brand when you've just reinvented yourself in a new career. This information may not seem pressing right now for you, but if we're actually going to be changing careers anywhere near as often as experts predict, these tips will come in very handy.

Students: Getting Started on LinkedIn

http://learn.linkedin.com/students/step-1/
LinkedIn is one of the most effective tools for building an easily maintained professional brand platform. This tutorial focuses on how students can use LinkedIn for career-building in general, as well as for establishing and promoting a professional brand. LinkedIn provides similar guides for Small Business, New Users, Job Seekers, and Entrepreneurs, all of whom can benefit from establishing a strong professional reputation.

Using LinkedIn for Branding and Networking: Getting-Started Basics

http://infonista.com/2011/using-linkedin-for-branding-and-networking-getting-started-basics/
A quick run-through of the action items needed to establish at least a basic LinkedIn presence. Since this is likely the first place hiring managers will check you out, it's important to make sure that you've shaped the information you want them to see, that is, your professional brand.

"Your Virtual Brand"

http://americanlibrariesmagazine.org/columns/your-virtual-brand
From LIS thought leader Meredith Farkas, this American Libraries column explores the importance of building "a strong and positive personal brand online." Covering both the why and how to, this article should be must-reading for every LIS student and practitioner.

8
Managing

Good managers are the workplace's unsung heroes—they not only contribute directly to helping the organization achieve its strategic goals, they can also create work environments that enable their staff to contribute at their highest level, ensuring a job experience that's both rewarding and enjoyable for all concerned.

What if you aspire to become a manager, or you've actually just become one, and feel unprepared? Happily, management has been one of the most-studied areas of human endeavor ever, so there is a wide range of resources to help you succeed.

What Is Management?

According to *Business: The Ultimate Resource,* a manager is someone who "identifies and achieves organization objectives through the deployment of appropriate resources." Those resources may be in the form of activities, capital, information, and/or people, but "it is the capability to harness resources that largely distinguishes a manager from a non-manager."

143

Or, from another perspective, the late legendary management expert Peter F. Drucker asserted in *Managing for the Future: The 1990's and Beyond* (1993) that "[a] manager's task is to make the strengths of people effective and their weakness irrelevant—and that applies fully as much to the manager's boss as it applies to the manager's subordinates." And, lest you underestimate the importance of good management skills, Drucker had pointed out 20 years earlier in *Management: Tasks, Responsibilities, Practices* (1973) that "[t]he worker's effectiveness is determined largely by the way he is being managed."

The activities involved in management differ from organization to organization (including library to library), but tend to include such tasks as planning, prioritizing, budgeting, scheduling, ensuring staff accountability for performance goals, and dealing with personnel issues. Very few individuals who move into managerial roles have received formal training for their new responsibilities, especially when it comes to managing people effectively. Although most LIS students take a basic management course during their graduate program, other than that, pretty much every newly promoted manager is doing the best he or she can while equipped with the barest minimum of relevant knowledge.

Additionally, the organizations, circumstances, and people relations needing to be managed increase in complexity daily. As Joan Giesecke and Beth McNeil note in the introduction to the second edition of *Fundamentals of Library Supervision,*

> Management used to be simple. The manager or supervisor told employees what to do and employees did what they were told. That world does not exist today. Today's managers, supervisors, team leaders, project managers, and unit heads face a more complex environment. Managers need to balance production goals with concern for people issues in a continually changing setting. The workplace and the workforce are different. Managers may now find themselves overseeing four generations of staff, each with its own characteristics and needs. Each group responds best to a different management style. Additionally, more women are in management roles, bringing a different perspective to the administration of organizations. (vii)

The good news is that there is a wide range of resources to call on to learn how to become a better manager, so if this is one of your career goals, there are ways to gain the knowledge that will help you succeed. Some of them are intended for managers in any situation, while others are specific to library settings.

Management Insights

Among the classic management resources are any works by Peter F. Drucker, but especially *Managing the Nonprofit Organization: Principles and Practices,* which draws from his *The Effective Executive* and *Managing for Results.* Although the book is intended more for traditional nonprofits than for libraries, its coverage of areas such as measuring performance when there's no bottom line and working with volunteers and board members have direct relevance to library circumstances.

At the other end of the spectrum, but useful as an easy-to-understand introduction to the day-to-day aspects of a manager's role, consider Bob Nelson and Peter Economy's *Managing for Dummies.* It has the usual light-hearted approach of the series, but also offers a seriously useful overview of the key managerial responsibilities: creating a cohesive and high-performing team, hiring, goal-setting, staff development, delegating, communication, performance evaluations, budgeting, and so on.

Another excellent management title that will help you bring out the best in your staff is Marcus Buckingham and Curt Coffman's *First, Break All the Rules: What the World's Greatest Managers Do Differently.* Based on a massive study of managers at all levels undertaken with the goal of iden- tifying the most effective practices, the book describes how effective manag- ers (and organizations) focus on bringing out individuals' strengths rather than investing time and energy in attempting to fix their weaknesses. That's a major simplification of a complex and detailed concept, but the authors make the valid point that companies frequently hire people for positions that end up highlighting their weaknesses rather than their strengths, then wonder why they're failing in their jobs.

When it comes to library-focused management titles, the LIS profes- sion's publishers (and authors!) have done an admirable job of stepping up to the challenge. Among the management overview guides in addition to *Fundamentals of Library Supervision,* there is the second edition of *A Man- agement Strategy for Achieving Excellence,* by Ruth F. Metz, and Richard Moniz's *Practical and Effective Management of Libraries: Integrating Case Studies, General Management Theory and Self Understanding,* a slim vol- ume that provides a basic overview of key management concepts. More tacti- cal in nature are Carol Smallwood's edited contributions from practitioners, *Library Management Tips That Work* (nearly 50 in all) and John L. Huber's *Lean Library Management: Eleven Strategies for Reducing Costs and Im- proving Customer Service,* which combines a recent business trend, that is, lean management, with librarianship.

But what about people skills? Anyone who's suffered through the pain of working for a bad boss understands clearly the need for managers to have strong people skills, but the reality is that like parents, managers are pretty much having to make it up as they go along; very few get the coaching neces- sary to bring out the best in their direct reports (or themselves). Although the books by Buckingham on strengths and Goleman on emotional intel- ligence are both highly useful for improving outcomes in this area, there are a number of LIS-specific resources to call on as well. For example, Catherine Hakala-Ausperk's *Be a Great Boss: One Year to Success* lays out a step-by-step, week-by-week plan for developing effective people manage- ment skills (the ones that will not only cause your staff to trust and respect you but also want to give you their best efforts).

James McKinley and Vicki Williamson focus as well on the people side of things in *The ART of People Management in Libraries: Tips for Managing Your Most Vital Resource* (ART in this case translating into Attention, Results, and Techniques). For the practical side of people management, a good basic introductory handbook for HR responsibilities is Mary J. Stanley's *Managing Library Employees: A How-to-Do-It Manual.* Although its templates, checklists, forms, and other helpful tools (and information) are intended for HR managers, many smaller libraries incorporate this responsibility into departmental managers' roles—if that's the case for you, Stanley's book will be a great help.

Several books also address the special management circumstances of specific types of libraries. For example, although intended as an MLIS textbook, the fifth edition of Betty J. Morris's classic *Administering the School Library Media Center* nevertheless provides insights into management and technology leadership strategies that would be valuable to those new to this role. Claire Gatrell Stephens and Patricia Franklin's more tactical *Library 101: A Handbook for the School Library Media Specialist* will help you understand not only how to manage the library itself but also the relationships—clerical help, volunteers, teachers, administrators—that come with it. And the fourth edition of Blanche Woolls's *The School Library Media Manager* continues to serve as the go-to resource for addressing traditional management topics within the unique circumstances specific to school libraries.

Smaller public libraries are the focus of Jane Pearlmutter and Paul Nelson's *Small Public Library Management,* which covers managerial tasks such as budgeting, workflow and delegation, community outreach initiatives, and similar activities. Similarly, *Running a Small Library: A How-to-Do-It Manual,* edited by John Moorman, provides practical advice especially valuable to those who find themselves suddenly managing a small library of any type without having had any previous experience doing so (a scenario much likelier to happen in the more than 7,000 small libraries across the country serving populations of 25,000 or less than in our larger public libraries).

For those aspiring to (or in) academic management roles, a very helpful resource is *Middle Management in Academic and Public Libraries.* Edited by Tom Diamond, this compendium of contributed insights from 20 academic and public library middle managers provides advice and counsel within the broad categories of "managing [in general] and managing people," "creating a leadership development program," "managing cross-collaborations," and "developing managerial skills."

Lastly, *Assessing Information Needs: Managing Transformative Library Services* by Robert J. Grover, Roger C. Greer, and John Agada is somewhat unique among LIS management titles in that its management frame is outward-facing. That is, the authors consider community analysis as the prioritizing factor of any library's mission, and explore both how to undertake community analysis and then how to integrate the results into the library's mission and services. Although this would initially seem like a managing framework bestsuited to public libraries, the customer-focused concepts, processes, and resulting actions Grover, Greer, and Agada lay out could be applicable to any type of library, including school, academic, and special.

Key Management Challenges

The basic management challenge is how to create and sustain an environment that enables your staff to perform at their highest level in support of your organization's strategic goals. Naturally, that's easier said than done under the best of circumstances; given today's economic environment, there are a number of other issues confronting managers in libraries as well as in every other type of organization. Specifically, today's managers are being asked to

- help their staff (and organizations) navigate an unprecedented amount of change;
- create a high-performing workplace while doing more with less; and
- find ways to help four generations of employees overcome differences in age, experience, knowledge, and professional expectations in order to perform at a consistently high level.

Although none of these issues is unique to libraries or information organizations, the combination of budget cuts, reductions in staff, and the unexpected nonretirement of many older librarians heightens their impact from a management standpoint.

Helping Staff Navigate Change in a Positive Way

In his classic work *Leading Change,* Harvard Business School professor John Kotter provided leaders of organizations with an eight-step program to help them lead those organizations through the myriad obstacles that push back against change—not least of which is staff resistance. In his follow-up work, *The Heart of Change: Real-Life Stories of How People Change Their Organizations,* Kotter and coauthor Dan S. Cohen delved further into the factors that enable employees to accept and help implement organizational change. Their finding? Only by telling a compelling story—by engaging the emotions of their employees—would leaders be able to effect sustainable change.

However, although organization leaders must be the driving energy and vision for any major change, it generally falls to managers to *execute* that change. No easy task. Even though our changing profession circumstances demand flexibility, adaptability, and an openness to trying new ways of working, all of our human instincts lean most often in the exact opposite direction, that is, toward order, stability, and predictability.

The challenge for managers is that while they're likely experiencing the same change resistance issues themselves, it's up to them to model change-agent behavior, to set the team expectations through their own attitude and evidence of positive commitment. Two recent books may prove useful to you when approaching this challenge. The first is *Switch: How to Change Things When Change is Hard* by brothers Dan Heath and Chip Heath. *Switch* does a great job of both exploring how and why we're hardwired to resist change, and then laying out strategies to help circumvent that hardwiring. This may help you deal with your own change resistance issues while providing ways to help your staff overcome theirs as well. The second book is Daniel Pink's *Drive: The Surprising Truth About What Motivates Us,* which will help you understand how to elicit the performance and commitment you need by working with your staff members' individual internal drivers. Surprisingly (and, during a time of budget cuts, fortunately), the primary motivator is not money.

For library-specific change management guidance, consider Tinker Massey's *Managing Change and People in Libraries,* which explores management theory, how people react to change and the stress it produces, and how to implement positive change strategies that minimize the damage to staff morale. Another good resource is *The Challenge of Library Management: Leading with Emotional Engagement* by Wyoma vanDuinkerken and Pixey Anne Mosley. vanDuinkerken and Mosley approach leading change in libraries from the perspective of understanding and addressing the emotional, cultural, and political issues inherent in any change process. Although ostensibly aimed at an audience of library leaders, this book can be equally valuable for the managers who will be tasked with implementing the change initiative.

Still insightful and helpful even though a bit out of date now is Susan Carol Curzon's *Managing Change: A How-to-Do-It Manual for Libraries.* Similar in concept to other Neal-Schuman How-to-Do-It guides, this title provides step-by-step coaching on how to help both your organization and your direct reports successfully (and with as little stress as possible) navigate the change process.

Creating a High-Performance Workplace While Doing More with Less

Reductions in professional staff through layoffs or attrition, contracting acquisitions budgets, cutbacks in professional development funds—these and other circumstances can have an understandably discouraging effect on staff. Yet for managers, it's important to keep your team performing at a high level for both the well-being of the organization *and* the well-being of your individual team members. Nobody can perform well in a toxic, demoralized workplace.

Calling again on Daniel Pink and *Drive,* more than 40 years of research into human motivation has indicated that people are motivated by three things:

- autonomy, or the ability to direct our own lives
- mastery, or the engagement that comes from learning and creating new things
- purpose, or working for a cause greater than ourselves

Money is always nice, and raises always help, but in the current (and foreseeable) economic climate, both may be in short supply. What other options do you have to boost staff morale and encourage high levels of performance? As a manager, you can work to create an environment that provides your staff with the greatest opportunity to connect with these three motivating factors. Can you offer more self-direction, more flexibility in scheduling, more in-house learning opportunities? In what ways can you encourage personal initiative, and create a safe environment for trying new ideas on a small scale and "failing smart"? (A terrific book on this topic is *Little Bets: How Breakthrough Ideas Emerge from Small Discoveries* by Peter Sims.)

Managing a team tasked with doing more with less will require your best people management—and people motivation—skills. If you're not sure about your managerial ability to turn your department into a high-performing, cohesive team, you may want to read Patrick Lencioni's best-selling *The Five Dysfunctions of a Team: A Leadership Fable* and his follow-up book, *Overcoming the Five Dysfunctions of a Team: A Field Guide for Leaders, Managers, and Facilitators.* These books will help you not only understand the dysfunctions (absence of trust, fear of conflict, lack of commitment, avoidance of accountability, and inattention to results), but also be able to successfully resolve them.

Your strongest asset in the success of your team, however, will be you. Your own positive attitude and efforts to create an engaged, motivation-friendly work environment will have a tremendous impact on your staff's willingness to engage and contribute at their highest levels. True, there will be some staffers who are determined to be disgruntled, but your management energy and engagement will go most productively to those who are looking for a reason to stay engaged, or to re-engage. They will be the core and strength of your high-performing team.

Managing the Four-Generation Workplace

From the Millennials (those born during the 1980s and early 1990s) to the nonretiring baby boomers, workplaces across the country are now struggling with how to create an environment that enables teams and departments whose staffers have wildly divergent experiences, expectations, and work ethics to still work together in a positive and productive manner. To say this is a challenge is to vastly understate its potentially devastating impacts if organizations can't figure this out.

On the other hand, if done successfully, the multigenerational workplace can offer substantial benefits to those at both ends of the spectrum as well as those in between.

For those new to the workplace, the four-generation workplace provides

- an opportunity to learn how organizations work from those who know the ropes;
- an opportunity to improve their skills by working with experienced practitioners;
- a potential opportunity to connect with career mentors, formal or informal; and
- an opportunity to learn how to share their expertise in a way others can appreciate (and learn from).

For older workers, hanging out with "the kids" can provide

- an opportunity to learn new technologies on the job from people they work with, which will help keep their skills up to date;
- an opportunity to rethink how they've always done things, and consider alternative approaches;
- the potential opportunity to mentor younger staffers, formally or informally; and
- an opportunity to update their cultural knowledge, attitudes, and ability to connect with the kids in their personal lives.

The benefits for managers may include the following:

- Every generation has its blind spots; four generations brainstorming together helps you cover more bases.
- Having multiple generations of workers can give you better insight into potential constituencies or markets.
- Younger staffers will be less risk averse, older ones can help them fail smart, i.e., learn lessons fast.
- For those organizations successful in creating positive multigenerational workplaces, that success is likely to translate into higher productivity, more innovative initiatives, and greater competitive strength.

Since the major disrupting force here (80 million strong) is the arrival of the Millennials in the workforce, it's important to understand how they differ from the employees who have preceded them. Happily, this demographic group is now the focal point of a tremendous amount of sociodemo-graphic research, so there are some great resources available to help you understand generational differences.

One of the best sources of detailed insights is the Pew Resource Center's *Millennials: A Portrait of Generation Next,* which characterizes this generation as "confident, self-expressive, liberal, upbeat, and receptive to new ideas and new ways of living." *Managing the Millennials: Discover the Core Competencies for Managing Today's Workforce* by Espinoza, Ukleja, and Rusch addresses first the characteristics of Millennials as employ-ees then the management strategies that will help you bring out their best contributions. Michelle Manafee and Heidi Gautschi's engaging *Dancing with Digital Natives: Staying in Step with the Generation That's Trans-forming the Way Business is Done* draws on the experiences and insights of some 20 contributors to sketch out not only how digital natives will change the work environments for all of us, but also how to help them bring their best stuff. And to understand the Millennial perspective, check out Gen-Y author Jason Ryan Dorsey's fascinating and smart *Y-Size Your Business: How Gen Y Employees Can Save You Money and Grow Your Business.* Ac-knowledging the validity of some of the more challenging characteristics of his fellow Gen-Y workers, Dorsey provides over 50 strategies for motivat-ing them to engage and contribute at the high levels of which they're capable.

Few career roles are as challenging as managing people, but also few can have as great an impact on the success of both organizations and the individuals you manage. A good manager is as much a coach as a boss, and understands that "the ability to harness resources" is, in fact, the ability to motivate, challenge, support, and enable each team member to contribute at his or her highest level. Can it be stressful? Absolutely. But can it also be incredibly rewarding while also opening up additional career opportunities? Again, absolutely.

Resources

Starred titles are mentioned in the chapter.

Associations

Note: Following are management-development offerings of the major LIS professional organizations, however, you should always check with all associations of which you're a member to determine whether they have man-agement courses of interest. Keep in mind also that almost all professional associations also publish their own journals, e-newsletters, or print newslet-ters for members only, and these publications often address management topics.

Certified Public Library Administrator Program / ALA-APA
   http://ala-apa.org/certification/
   A collection of nine competency courses, of which seven must be fulfilled to complete the CPLA certification. The competency courses are: budget

and finance, management of technology, organization and personnel administration, planning and management of buildings, current issues, marketing, fundraising/grantsmanship, politics and networking, and serving diverse populations.

Leadership & Management Resources / ALA Online Learning

www.ala.org/ala/onlinelearning/management/leadership.cfm

Among the online fee-based learning opportunities ALA offers is Management Issues for Library Leaders, providing webinars, workshops, and multi-week courses on topics such as leadership and management, budgeting, building and facilities, human resources and staff development, and outcome measurement, among others.

Library Leadership & Management Association (LLAMA)

www.ala.org/llama/

A division of ALA, LLAMA provides continuing education opportunities (webinars) for members on multiple management and leadership topics; a selected number of webinar recordings are available for purchase.

Management Institute / American Association of Law Libraries (AALL)

www.aallnet.org/main-menu/Education/management-institute

Held every other year, the AALL Management Institute covers building and nurturing a professional network; developing effective communication skills; negotiating and handling difficult situations; developing a strategic plan; taking on project management; and championing the library's role within the institution and building partnerships. Open to AALL members only.

Management—Services / SLA Information Portals

www.sla.org/content/resources/infoportals/index.cfm

For SLA members only, this aggregation of links on management-related content includes topics such as benchmarking in information centers/libraries, disaster planning, information audits, library costs and budgets, records management, and starting and managing a special library, among others. Currency of the materials varies, but most of the content is still relevant.

Workshops and Seminars / Canadian Library Association (CLA)

www.cla.ca/AM/Template.cfm?Section=Workshops_and_Seminars1& Template=/CM/HTMLDisplay.cfm&ContentID=10010

CLA offers over 25 professional site-based workshops annually, many of which address library/information center management issues.

Print Resources

**Buckingham, Marcus and Curt Coffman. *First, Break All the Rules: What the World's Greatest Managers Do Differently.* Simon & Schuster, 1999. 256p. ISBN 0684852861.

Written for managers and company executives, this landmark work was based on extensive research by the Gallup Organization into the behavior of managers and the approaches they used to achieve success for their companies. One of the central findings (greatly simplified here) was that most people have inherent strengths and weaknesses, and managers (as well as the individuals themselves) tend to invest inordinate (and ineffective) effort into fixing their weaknesses (which will probably only improve to a point of not quite as bad) rather than building their strengths to excellence. The book explores how smart managers have succeeded by understanding, identifying, and hiring for specific strengths relative to the jobs in question.

Cialdini, Robert B. *Influence: Science and Practice,* 5th ed. Prentice Hall, 272p. ISBN 0205609996.
The classic work on persuasive influence, Cialdini's book focuses on how people are persuaded to undertake a preferred action (for most of Cialdini's readers, how to influence someone to buy something). It also, however, functions as a fascinating guide to social psychology, and potentially how to influence groups of people (read: team members and workplace colleagues) to understand and agree with your viewpoint.

Curtis, Joan C. *Managing Sticky Situations at Work: Communication Secrets for Success in the Workplace.* Praeger, 2009. 213p. ISBN 0313362785.
Although the sticky situations described in this guide draw their examples and scenarios from settings like health care, retail, information technology, and small businesses, the author's solutions are equally applicable to library environments. Curtis's Just Say it Right model gives you the specific coaching (and language) you need to confidently handle the 26 sticky situations described.

**Curzon, Susan Carol. *Managing Change: A How-to-Do-It Manual for Libraries,* rev. ed. Neal Schuman, 2005. 129p. ISBN 1555705537.
In this updated edition of Curzon's 1989 title on this topic, she has kept the strengths of the original work (practical guidance on conceptualizing and planning for change, managing staff responses and resistance, and execution and assessment steps) while adding a series of change scenarios or mini-case studies that demonstrate how to manage specific (and common) types of library changes. The combination results in a book that is a realistic, practical, how-to-do-it guide.

**Dorsey, Jason Ryan. *Y-Size Your Business: How Gen Y Employees Can Save You Money and Grow Your Business.* Wiley, 2009. 240p. ISBN 0470505567.
Consider *Y-Size Your Business* to be an insider's guide to the generation that's going to be in charge of our future. Acknowledging the validity of some of the more challenging characteristics of his fellow Gen-Y workers with insight and humor, Dorsey provides some 50 practical strategies for motivating them to engage and contribute at the high levels of which they're capable.

**Drucker, Peter. *Management: Tasks, Responsibilities, Practices.* Harper Paperbacks, 1973. 864p. ISBN 0887306152.
Drucker's aim in this management classic is "to equip the manager with the understanding, the thinking, the knowledge and the skills for

today's and also tomorrow's jobs." Drucker pretty much single-handedly developed modern management thinking; here he describes the management practices that have proven effective among the hundreds of companies for whom he had consulted, and does so in ways as accessible to LIS professionals as MBA types. Other equally useful books by Drucker include *Managing for Results* (Collins, 1993) *The Practice of Management* (Harper Paperbacks, 2006), *The Effective Executive: The Definitive Guide to Getting the Right Things Done,* rev. ed. (Harper Paperbacks, 2006).

**Drucker, Peter. *Managing the Nonprofit Organization: Principles and Practices.* Harper Paperbacks, 2006. 256p. ISBN 0060851147.
First published in 1990, this classic work focuses on both leading and managing nonprofit organizations within five broad categories: the role of the leader; strategies for marketing, innovation, and fund development; managing for performance (how to define and measure it); managing people and relationships (staff, board, volunteers, community); and developing yourself as a person, executive, and leader. The book is interspersed with interviews of major nonprofit leaders. Although written for managers and leaders of traditional nonprofits, many of Drucker's key points will also resonate with library managers and leaders.

**Espinoza, Chip, Mick Ukleja and Craig Rusch. *Managing the Millenials: Discover the Core Competencies for Managing Today's Workforce.* Wiley, 2010. 172p. ISBN 0470563931.
One of the better guides for managers of multiple generations in the workplace, *Managing the Millennials* will help managers understand the unique characteristics of their young staffers and elicit their best contributions.

**Giesecke, Joan and Beth McNeil. *Fundamentals of Library Supervision,* 2nd ed. American Library Association, 2010. 199p. ISBN 9780838910160.
Part of the ALA Fundamentals series, this is a down-to-earth, actionable, comprehensive handbook aimed at those new to supervising others and trying to quickly learn the ropes in an increasingly complex work environment. The authors use the narrative model of two new supervisors (one new to the library, the other promoted from within) to demonstrate different perspectives and approaches, and supplement with examples and strategies. The first chapter's overview of trends in today's library workplace and their impact on supervision and management is a terrific lead-off to the rest of the book's key points.

Goleman, Daniel. *Working with Emotional Intelligence.* Bantam, 2000. 400p. ISBN 0553378589.
When Goleman published his landmark *Emotional Intelligence: Why It Can Matter More Than IQ* in 1995, he launched a veritable cottage industry in publishing EQ-related books. This book focuses on EQ's 12 self-mastery competencies and 13 key relationship skills to help you understand how you can contribute to—or create—a more positive and

high-performing workplace (and career). Recommended for both individuals exploring their own style of workplace participation as well as for managers seeking to create healthy and productive work environments.

Gordon, Rachel Singer. *The Accidental Library Manager*. Information Today, 2004. 362p. ISBN 1573872105.
Very few individuals—including librarians—are prepared or trained in any depth to assume management roles in their organizations. Yet for most professionals, this is the road to greater responsibility and opportunity. The *Accidental Library Manager* steps in to fill that gap by offering concrete, proven advice for aspiring and/or accidental managers, as well as insights from library staff on what management characteristics they value most.

Gravett, Linda and Robin Throckmorton. *Bridging the Generation Gap: How to Get Radio Babies, Boomers, Gen Xers, and Gen Yers to Work Together and Achieve More*. Career Press, 2007. 222p. ISBN 156414898X.
How to manage and/or work effectively and happily in the four- or five-generation workplace is quickly becoming one of the most important considerations for organizations trying to elicit the unique strengths of each generation while mitigating intergenerational conflict. Because this is a first-time occurrence, just about no one knows for sure how to achieve this sort of balance. Gravett and Throckmorton have, however, done a good job of identifying the issues and suggesting useful approaches. Although intended for managers and business owners, *Bridging the Generation Gap* is also useful for individuals working as part of those generations, helping them understand how to work more effectively and positively with those whose life experiences and expectation are literally decades from their own.

**Grover, Robert J., Roger C. Greer, and John Agada. *Assessing Information Needs: Managing Transformative Library Services*. Libraries Unlimited, 2010. 212p. ISBN 1591587972.
The transformative library services referred to in the title are based on the increasing trend toward using community needs analysis as the data foundation on which the library's services are then built. This entails a management shift on many levels, from the activity of data gathering and analysis itself to rethinking approaches and processes for program planning, collection development, outreach efforts, marketing, and more. The book's practical guidance regarding data gathering and analysis can be applied to all types of libraries—school, public, academic, and special—and will be especially helpful to managers inexperienced with data-driven decision-making.

Growing Schools: Librarians as Professional Developers. Debbie Abilock, Kristin Fontichiaro, and Violet H. Harada, eds. Libraries Unlimited, 2012. 250p. ISBN 1610690419.
School librarians certainly have the professional skills to take a more central management role in their organizations, but often lack the opportunity to step forward. As pointed out in this excellent contributed

work with a strong practical focus, staff development is just that key management opportunity. Chapters reflect the diverse but valuable experiences of librarians in K–12 public and private schools, district and regional librarians, and academic libraries throughout the United States and Canada as they've taken on professional development roles in their organizations.

**Hakala-Ausperk, Catherine. *Be a Great Boss: One Year to Success.* ALA Editions, 2011. 252p. ISBN 9780838910689.

Intended as a self-study guide for those new to management, *Be a Great Boss* lays out 52 modules or lessons within monthly topics, for example, "Attitude," "Success with Stakeholders," "Staffing," "Communication," and so on. The guide is set up as a workbook, that is, the author lays out information, worksheets, and exercises with the suggestion that you work on one weekly lesson, for example, The Art of Negotiating, for one hour each week. Hakala-Ausperk brings humor, empathy, and credibility to her writing; highly recommended for both those new to managing and those who feel their management skills may be a bit rusty.

Hallam, Arlita W. and Teresa R. Dalston. *Managing Budgets and Finance: A How-to-Do-It Manual for Librarians and Information Professionals.* Neal-Schuman, 2005. 230p. ISBN 9781555705190.

Most LIS grads are able to get through their program and the early stages of their careers without being subjected to the traumatizing task of putting together a budget—which is actually too bad. Budgeting is a central part of resource allocation and management, which is a central part of the management role. This step-by-step manual walks you through the budgeting and budget creation process, distinguishes among different types of budgets, and helps you understand how to track the results and create forecasts from them. Good coaching for a crucial management skill.

**Heath, Chip and Dan Heath. *Switch: How to Change Things When Change is Hard.* Broadway Books, 2010. 305p. ISBN 9780385528757.

It isn't just that people have a tough time making significant changes in their lives and organizations, argue the Heath brothers, it's that our brains are actually hardwired to put emotional obstacles (the emotional mind) in the path of the choices we can see logically (the rational mind) make good sense. Laying out the key aspects of this conflict, the Heaths then identify strategies for helping people overcome their resistance to change and instead create and commit to change processes that engage both minds. A key resource for managers struggling to both understand and overcome change resistance among their staff members (as well as within themselves).

**Huber, John J. *Lean Library Management: Eleven Strategies for Reducing Costs and Improving Customer Service.* Neal-Schuman, 2011. 175p. ISBN 9781555707323.

Drawing on concepts first tested in the Lean Manufacturing movement (where author Huber was a key player), *Lean Library Management* focuses on how to apply lean concepts and practices to library processes. Sample strategies: recognize that service performance is the key to customer retention; transform your change-resistant culture; understand how delivery service chains drive your library's performance; align your performance metrics with your delivery service chains. Although some may be put off by the strong business-operations mindset Huber espouses, his concepts especially make sense in the current do-more-with-less environment.

**Kotter, John P. *Leading Change*. Harvard Business Press, 1996. 208p. ISBN 0875847471.
One of the original explorations of how leaders can help their organizations successfully transition through change. Kotter is widely considered the expert on change leadership/management; in this work he provides an eight-step framework for leading change: establish a sense of urgency; create a guiding coalition; develop a vision and strategy; communicate the change vision; empower employees for broad-based action; generate short-term wins; consolidate gains and produce more change; and anchor new approaches in the culture. Written for those leading change, this work and Kotter and Dan S. Cohen's *The Heart of Change* (2002) can nevertheless provide valuable insights as well for those charged with executing it, i.e., managers.

Laughlin, Sara and Ray W. Wilson. *The Quality Library: A Guide to Staff-Driven Improvement, Better Efficiency, and Happier Customers*. ALA Editions, 2008. 192p. ISBN 9780838909522.
The goal is continuous improvement driven by ongoing process evaluation and change (if merited). The focal point is twofold: improving service to the customer while improving productivity (read: reducing inefficiencies) of those customer-focused activities. Based on the mantra that you can't manage what you can't measure, *The Quality Library* also provides worksheets and other aids to help staff document the results of improvement-driven changes.

**Lencioni, Patrick. *The Five Dysfunctions of a Team: A Leadership Fable*. Jossey-Bass, 2002. 229p. ISBN 0787960756.
Lencioni uses a fictional story as the basis for his lesson about how teams consistently derail themselves (and often, their organizations): through absence of trust, fear of conflict, lack of commitment, avoidance of accountability, and failure to pay attention to and learn from results. Lencioni's follow-up title, *Overcoming the Five Dysfunctions of a Team* (2005), uses tools, exercises, and case studies to provide more specific coaching on how to address those five dysfunctions.

***Library Management Tips That Work*. Carol Smallwood, ed. ALA Editions, 2011. 208p. ISBN 9780838911.
Just short of 50 contributions grouped within the broad categories of "The Manager Role," "Running a Library," "Information Technology," "Staff," and "Public Relations" make up this compendium. Many of the contributions are library-specific (public, school, academic), while others address topics of relevance across all working environments

(e.g., "Why a Wiki? How Wikis Help Get Work Done"). The strength of this collection is that all of the contributions are by practitioners who have first-hand experience with the topics they're writing about.

**Manafy, Michelle and Heidi Gautschi. *Dancing with Digital Natives: Staying in Step with the Generation that's Transforming the Way Business is Done.* CyberAge Books, 2011. 408p. ISBN 9780910965.
One of the best books on how to understand, communicate with, and bring out the best in your "digital native" staff, also known as Gen-Ys and Millennials. The authors, both well-known and respected in the business information and communications technology worlds, have gone beyond their own research and experience to draw on the expertise of roughly twenty contributors, writing chapters within the broad categories of "The Digital Native Goes to Work," "Marketing and Selling to the Digital Native," "Entertaining the Digital Native" (favorite quote: "The Digital Natives *Are* the Entertainment!"), and "Educating the Digital Native." Interesting, critical, and well-researched insights.

**Massey, Tinker. *Managing Change in People and Libraries.* Chandos Publishing, 2009. 108p. ISBN 9781843344278.
The key strength of Massey's book is its acknowledgement of the stress produced among staff when change is in play. Massie does a good job of addressing this issue, and identifies ways to diffuse that stress and instead focus on positive motivation and team productivity.

**McKinlay, James and Vicki Williamson. *The ART of People Management in Libraries: Tips for Managing Your Most Vital Resource.* Chandos Publishing, 2010. 312p. ISBN 9781843344230.
Based on recent trends in people management theory and practice, *ART* explores how to apply that knowledge within library settings, especially academic and research libraries. The authors approach the topic through a systems-thinking framework, then lay out a step-by-step plan for implementing their recommendations. The ART in the title refers to Attention (things to pay attention to), Results (initiatives that help to achieve desired results), and Techniques (ways to apply the authors' concepts).

**Metz, Ruth F. *Coaching in the Library: A Management Strategy for Achieving Excellence,* 2nd ed. ALA Editions, 2011. 112p. ISBN 0838910378.
One of the key findings about managing Gen-Y/Millennial staffers is that they seek out professional feedback and coaching to a degree not seen among the other generations. That alone makes *Coaching in the Library* a valuable resource for those not accustomed to this role. The book provides library-specific coaching examples and scenario samplers to buttress its chapter concepts (e.g., coaching individuals, coaching teams, coaching and organization effectiveness), plus sample forms and tables (for example, "Ten Performance Factors") readers can use to implement Metz's recommendations. An extremely thorough and encouraging book for those who may find themselves in coaching situations.

**Middle Management in Academic and Public Libraries.* Tom Diamond, ed. Libraries Unlimited, 2011. 233p. ISBN 1598846892.

Middle management is one of the most challenging organizational roles there is, but also one of the most important. How can you effectively navigate from a position notorious for all the accountability, none of the authority? Diamond and his contributors, all of whom have been there, done that, coach readers through this challenge with practical advice on the key management issues (see especially the chapter "Caught in the Middle: Managing Competing Expectations").

**Moniz, Richard J. *Practical and Effective Management of Libraries: Integrating Case Studies, General Management Theory and Self Understanding.* Neal-Schuman, 2010. 158p. ISBN 9781843345787.

Moniz introduces the basic concepts of classic management theory then demonstrates their implementation within library settings through case studies. Topical coverage includes tools to develop strategic thinking and decision-making skills, approaches for motivating staff members, and communicating effectively, among other subjects. A solid overview of management thinking and how to successfully apply it.

**Morris, Betty J. *Administering the School Library Media Center,* 5th ed. Libraries Unlimited, 2010. 580p. ISBN 9781591586890.

Used as the textbook for many school library management courses, the fifth edition of Morris's comprehensive overview of running a school library media center is also a practical resource to be able to check in with when day-to-day operations raise questions outside your expertise. Sample chapters include "Functions of the School Library Media Center," "Developing a School Library Media Center Program," "The Media Center Budget," and "Staff." In addition to including the latest standards and addressing the new technologies and their most effective uses, the book provides extensive and updated bibliographies for each chapter.

**Nelson, Bob and Peter Economy. *Managing for Dummies,* 3rd ed. 384p. ISBN 0470618132.

One of the better books in the "for Dummies" series, this basic tour of what's involved in managing people and teams outlines what key roles a manager is responsible for and how to successfully perform those roles. While it doesn't go into great depth in any of the 15 management tasks it identifies (for example, hiring, goal-setting, coaching and mentoring, delegating), the book does provide a solid starting point for understanding how to manage effectively and wisely.

Patterson, Kerry, et al. *Crucial Conversation: Tools for Talking When Stakes are High,* 2nd ed. McGraw-Hill, 2011. 288p. ISBN 0071771328.

One of the most important tools managers have for creating a high-performing team or department is the ability to communicate effectively at the point of need. Most of us, however, struggle with what the right words might be to address a specific issue or conflict. *Crucial Conversation*s is based on the concept of dialog, or how meaning flows between two or more participants in a conversation, and creating environments that enable that flow. Important and highly useful guidance.

**Pearlmutter, Jane and Paul Nelson. *Small Public Library Management.* ALA Editions, 2011. 176p. IBSN 9780838910856.

Managers of small public libraries are often close to being a one-man band, performing multiple roles and juggling a wide range of responsibilities. Pearlmutter and Nelson offer a practical how-to handbook to help managers in small public libraries cover the basics: budget preparation, collection development/weeding, creating community outreach initiatives, and so on. A helpful resource for those wondering where to start.

**Pink, Daniel. *Drive: The Surprising Truth about What Motivates Us.* Riverhead Books, 2009. 242p. ISBN 9781594488849.

A fascinating and engaging exploration (based on years of research) of the key drivers that motivate people to perform at their highest levels of value and participation. Those three drivers are: autonomy, or the ability to direct our own lives; mastery, or the engagement that comes from learning and creating new things; and purpose, or working for a cause greater than ourselves. Important insights for managers attempting to motivate staff members during stressful times.

***Running a Small Library: A How-to-Do-It Manual.* John Moorman, ed. Neal-Schuman, 2006. 300p. ISBN 9781555705497.

Whether your small library is a school, public, academic, or corporate library, Moorman's goal is to help librarians, paraprofessionals, and volunteers understand what needs to be done and how to do it in an environment of minimal resources. Covers programming, outreach, cataloging, and circulation among other topics, and concludes with a resource section that includes not only library-management-specific items like furniture, automation, and book and periodical vendors, but also the listservs, discussion groups, and professional organizations that can serve as a lifeline for an isolated librarian.

**Sims, Peter. *Little Bets: How Breakthrough Ideas Emerge from Small Discoveries.* Free Press, 2011. 224p. ISBN 1439170428.

People, teams, and organizations that never fail aren't perfect—they're just not taking the risks necessary to innovate, grow, and learn. The smarter approach, according to Sims, is to try a lot of small-scale, creative ideas, quickly learn from the results, and then move forward armed with new knowledge of what works, what doesn't, and why. Although ostensibly intended for entrepreneurs, this message is applicable for all organizations (and individuals).

Singer, Paula M. with Gail Griffith. *Succession Planning in the Library: Developing Leaders, Managing Change.* ALA Editions, 2010. 160p. ISBN 9780838910368.

Succession planning can be a challenging activity for the best organizations, given that it necessarily deals with organizational change, people's aspirations and expectations, and assessments of core competencies (or lack thereof) relevant to management roles. Singer draws on her HR consulting background to help organizations (and managers) assess their current administrative structure, identify core competencies for key management positions, and prepare for potential future vacancies. One of the most valuable aspects of this book is its focus on the importance of supporting professional development for all staff, and especially for those demonstrating leadership potential.

Staff Development: A Practical Guide, 4th ed. Carol Zsulya, Andrea Stewart, and Carlette Washington-Hoagland, eds. ALA Editions, 2012. 152p. IBSN 9780838911495.

An initiative of ALA's Library Leadership & Management Association (LLAMA), the fourth edition of this guide is even more timely as professional development budgets are being cut back. *Staff Development* provides the tools and guidance needed for libraries to build their own training programs. Topics include strategies for staff development, how to measure the effectiveness of that training (what has changed for the better?), needs assessment and goal setting, and the effective use of instructional design concepts, among others.

**Stanley, Mary J. *Managing Library Employees: A How-to-Do-It Manual.* Neal-Schuman, 2008. 247p. ISBN 9781555706289.

Consider this your HR resource if your library doesn't have an actual HR person; covers basic but important issues like how to write a job description, what questions to ask in an interview, how to develop a staff training program, how to recognize and reward outstanding employees, and so on. A well-organized, easy to use, very practical resource.

**Stephens, Claire Gatrell and Patricia Franklin. *Library 101: A Handbook for the School Library Media Specialist.* Libraries Unlimited, 2007. 248p. ISBN 9781591583240.

An introductory handbook for those new to their position, *Library 101* provides the basics about the school library media specialist role, library organization (including a walk-through of the Dewey Decimal system), circulation policies and mechanics, and similar day-to-day administrative topics. The coverage of television production is especially useful, as is the guidance on how to successfully manage relationships with teachers, administrators, and clerical help, both paid and volunteer.

**vanDuinkerken, Wyoma and Pixey Anne Mosley. *The Challenge of Library Management: Leading with Emotional Engagement.* ALA Editions, 2011. 184p. ISBN 9780838911020.

The challenge referred to in the title is change management, whether it be changes to staff, space, mission, or other disruptors to existing circumstances. The book targets library leaders (i.e., at the director/ dean level), but it's equally valuable for mid-level managers tasked with moving the troops through the change process in a positive, supportive way. The chapter on "Managerial Baggage" is especially helpful, as it identifies those attitudes and past experiences that may unconsciously compromise managers' own abilities to embrace change, and therefore their ability to help others do the same.

Willis, Mark R. *Dealing with Difficult People in the Library,* 2nd ed. ALA Editions, 2012. 224p. ISBN 9780838911143.
The first edition (1999) of Willis's helpful guidebook was hailed for offering "concrete solutions to handling the myriad number of problems connected with difficult people." In the intervening years, the problems associated with difficult people in public libraries have only increased in number and intensity, so this second edition is a much-needed tool to help managers be proactive and prepared. Among the topics covered: using communications techniques to control difficult situations, creating guidelines for addressing situations like patron cell phone abuse and viewing pornography on the library's computers, and dealing positively with mentally ill and/or homeless patrons. Especially useful: staff training suggestions and sample policies.

**Woolls, Blanche. *The School Library Media Manager,* 4th ed. Libraries Unlimited, 2008. 296p. ISBN 9781591586487.
Whereas Morris's *Administering the School Library Media Center* has the comprehensiveness and theory-plus-practice approach of a textbook, the fourth edition of *The School Library Media Manager* is intended to provide more tactical advice and coaching for new and midcareer school library media managers. That advice is delivered in clear, accessible language, and covers such topics as collection development, facilities management, personnel, technology, collaborating with teachers, proposal writing, and accepting leadership responsibilities, among others.

Online Resources

The Bad Apple Syndrome
http://knowledgetoday.wharton.upenn.edu/2011/11/the-bad-apple-syndrome/
From the Knowledge@Wharton Today blog, this post discusses a *Wall Street Journal* article on the contagious, damaging impact of one toxic employee on the rest of his or her colleagues, and the importance of responding quickly and emphatically as a manager. The Knowledge@Wharton blog, from the University of Pennsylvania's Wharton School of Business, is a terrific (and free) source of current best practices and thinking in business, management, and leadership.

Colloqia Archives (San Jose State University School of Library & Information Science [SJSU SLIS])
http://slisweb.sjsu.edu/slis/colloquia/colloquia.htm
SJSU SLIS offers several free online colloquia every semester, on topics ranging from career development to technology and policy issues to management and leadership subjects. Check the colloquia index for archives of management-related webinars of interest.

Library and Information Center Management, 7th ed. Book Companion Site

www.abc-clio.com/BookCompanion.aspx?id=2147498060

A companion site to Stueart and Moran's classic textbook, this collection of management resources includes general and budget case studies, management exercises, examples, and web links. A great update for students who have used *Library and Information Center Management* in a grad school management course, or an equally useful stand-alone set of resources for brushing up on management topics.

Library Media Center Management

www.sldirectory.com/libsf/resf/manage.html

For school librarians, this site comprises links to publicly available policy manuals and other management tools plus a collection of ideas for new media specialists. The materials have been contributed by actual school library media centers.

Links for Librarians

www.ilsa.lib.ia.us/liblinks.htm

Integrates the former Links for Iowa Librarians with the former Links for Library Management page, to produce a delightfully eclectic but also very useful group of links to library management resources scattered throughout the web.

Lyrasis Classes and Events

www.lyrasis.org/Classes-and-Events/Catalog.aspx

Search on "management" to see all management-related offerings, such as Volunteer Management, Library Management, and Management 101: What is Management? Access to Lyrasis courses is through library/institutional membership.

**Millennials: A Portrait of Generation Next

http://pewresearch.org/millennials/

From the Pew Research Center, the subtitle of this fascinating report on the Millennial generation should provide encouragement for our future: "Confident. Connected. Open to Change."

Moving Into Management (Infopeople Workshop)

http://infopeople.org/training/past/2008/moving

This workshop was offered by the California-based Infopeople in February 2008, and the workshop materials have remained publicly available for review. The posted content includes the agenda, Power-Point presentation, bibliography, exercises, and handouts. An excellent collection of resources for those moving into management roles for the first time.

Special Libraries Management Handbook: The Basics

www.libsci.sc.edu/bob/class/clis724/SpecialLibrariesHandbook/INDEX.htm

With chapters (essentially lengthy papers) written by students in Professor Robert V. William's Special Libraries and Information Centers courses at the University of South Carolina College of Library and

Information Science between 1999 and 2007, this is an eclectic but well-done collection of topics related to managing a special library, with many of the pieces having broader applicability (example: "A Bad Boss: How to Handle").

To Be a Better Boss, Know Your Default Settings
http://blogs.hbr.org/hill-lineback/2011/02/to-be-a-better-boss-know-your.html
From the excellent (and free) *Harvard Business Review (HBR)* blogs, this post points out the importance of self-knowledge to understanding how you personally can be the most effective boss, given your individual preconceived preferences, or default settings. An insightful article, and typical of the quality of all of the free *HBR* blogs.

Web Junction
www.webjunction.org
WebJunction training is now accessible only through state libraries that have signed up as members, but it does continue to provide free webinars on a variety of subjects, including management topics. Check the website or sign up for their RSS feed to find webinars of interest. Fee-based training and webinars (accessible through your state agency if it is a member) include such management topics as budget and finance, community relations, facilities management, funding, marketing, organizational and personnel management, project management, and staff training and development, among others.

9
Leading

Who would have thought that when William Shakespeare wrote in *Twelfth Night* "Be not afraid of greatness: some are born great, some achieve greatness, and some have greatness thrust upon them," we would still be trying to understand how greatness—that is, leadership—could be taught to those in the latter two categories?

Or when American political pamphleteer Thomas Paine uttered that famous directive (and popular bumper sticker) "Lead, follow, or get out of the way," that over 200 years later, individuals, groups, and organizations would still be wrestling with how to most effective identify and achieve their goals?

For one has only to have worked for a brief amount of time in any organization to realize that leadership is an art not easily mastered, but one whose effective performance is critical not only to the success of the organization but also to the well-being of those who work there.

Definition of Leadership

What is leadership? As defined by *Business: The Ultimate Resource*, leadership is "the capacity to establish direction and to influence and align others toward a common goal, motivating and committing them to action and making them responsible for their performance." This concise and clear definition certainly captures the main points, but also substantially underplays the astounding complexity of challenges facing leaders in all organizations today.

However, it does have the major advantage of not constraining leadership roles to those who head up organizations, but instead allows for leadership activities to be undertaken throughout the organization, by anyone. In today's transitioning libraries and organizations (transitioning to what, none of us are sure at this point), the ability to instill some aspects of leadership, including self-leadership, among employees may be one of the most important tasks of the organization's recognized leader, whether that be director, dean, or chief executive officer (CEO).

What distinguishes leadership from other activities? The classic definition comes from management guru Peter F. Drucker, who famously stated that "Management is doing things right; leadership is doing the right things." So leadership, then, is about operating at a level of strategy, whereas management is about execution. Leadership is about seeing the big picture, both inside and outside of the organization, and setting priorities that best position the organization within those twin frameworks. Management, on the other hand, is about executing those priorities in a way that most effectively utilizes the available resources (while still maintaining a positive, engaged, high-performing team environment). Or, as author and businessman Max De Pree put it, "Management has a lot to do with answers. Leadership is a function of questions. And the first question for a leader always is: 'Who do we intend to be?' Not 'What are we going to do?' but 'Who do we intend to be?'"

Are management and leadership ever combined in one role or individual? Often. And equally as often, leadership arises from the middle, where the individual in question may have no formal authority but instead possesses an innate ability to inspire, motivate, and achieve outstanding results from those around him or her. (For a delightful and insightful book on this topic, see *"Leading from the Middle," and Other Contrarian Essays on Library Leadership* by John Lubans Jr.)

Becoming a Leader—The Outside Perspective

The commonly accepted characteristics of leaders have changed over the years, from the command-and-control authoritarian style to a broader focus that includes the ability to identify the strategic priorities that will frame the organization's efforts and goals, create and communicate a compelling vision, and establish an organizational mission that inspires and enlists commitment from others. Successful leaders today are likely to have exceptional people skills in order to elicit the highest levels of performance not only from their managers but also from the teams that report to those managers.

In addition, leaders are likely to be able and willing to take (informed) risks to take advantage of or create strategic opportunities for the organization (for example, the library director who conceives of or supports an innovative new community outreach program despite uncertainty about its success).

Because leadership is such a critical but not easily defined concept, many business experts have weighed in with both definitions of what effective leadership consists of as well as how individuals can become better leaders. Some of the best-known and most highly regarded works on leadership come from a handful of writers: Warren Bennis, James M. Kouzes and Barry Z. Posner, and John C. Maxwell. Although they aren't writing about the LIS profession or information organizations specifically, their insights often readily transfer from the business world to LIS environments.

Warren Bennis's classic work, *On Becoming a Leader,* makes the case that effective leaders are not born that way, but rather are individuals who learn to hone their potential leadership skills to a point of excellence. First published in 1989 and now in its fourth edition, *On Becoming a Leader* lays out Bennis's three necessary elements of leadership: (1) a guiding vision that determines the direction of organizational efforts and its means of execution; (2) a passion for accomplishing the stated vision so compelling that it motivates and inspires followers; and (3) personal integrity, born of self-knowledge. (Integrity is also one of the four elements Bennis identifies as requisite for trust-building, along with consistency, congruity, and reliability.) For readers who would like more coaching on the author's leadership concepts, Bennis has also written *Learning to Lead: A Workbook on Becoming a Leader,* which guides you through mastering his six competencies (mastering the context, knowing yourself, creating a powerful vision, communicating with meaning, maintaining trust through integrity, and realizing intention through action).

The Leadership Challenge, by James M. Kouzes and Barry Z. Posner, is more strongly based on research and case studies than is Bennis's work, but similarly suggests that leadership is a learned—and learnable—art. With the goal of "getting extraordinary things done in organizations," the fourth edition of this systematic book identifies and walks readers through the five practices and ten commitments of exemplary leadership, with explanations of how to master and incorporate those practices and commitments into a leadership mindset. (An example of a practice would be Model the Way, while this practice's commitments would include [1] clarifying values by finding your voice and affirming shared details and [2] setting the example by aligning actions with shared values.) Like Bennis, the authors have produced a guide, *The Leadership Challenge Workbook,* for individuals interested in delving deeper into and mastering their key concepts.

John C. Maxwell is a veritable cottage industry of leadership books, all of which are designed, as with the previous authors', to empower you to develop your inner leader. In one of his most popular books, *The 5 Levels of Leadership: Proven Steps to Maximize Your Potential,* Maxwell presents a useful and interesting five-point take on *why* people follow leaders. The first four reasons are *position* (basically people follow you because the position you hold means they have to), *permission* (people so trust or admire you that they follow you because they want to, rather than have to); *production* (your contributions to the organization cause people to feel good about following you); and *people development* (the good things you've done for others previously has caused them to be willing to follow your lead). In Maxwell's conceptualization, the fifth level is *pinnacle,* where people enthusiastically and confidently follow you because of who you are and what you represent.

Needless to say, Maxwell's goal is to help you achieve the fifth level of leadership, and the book does a good job of coaching you through the process necessary to get there. Additional useful works from Maxwell include *The 21 Irrefutable Laws of Leadership: Follow Them and People Will Follow You,* which describes, chapter-by-chapter, the 21 laws that once understood and mastered, will enable you to become an effective leader, and *Developing the Leader within You.* Also, one of his most interesting and valuable books, from my perspective, is his take on the challenge of leading from the middle, *The 360-Degree Leader: Developing Your Influence from Anywhere in the Organization.*

In addition to these four authors, several other writers have addressed the leadership issue from a particular perspective. For example, Daniel Goleman, known for his landmark *Emotional Intelligence* (see "Resources," Chapter 4) wrote *Primal Leadership: Learning to Lead with Emotional Intelligence* to address the application of emotional intelligence to leadership situations. Goleman's central thesis is that exceptionally effective leaders are able to use emotional intelligence skills (e.g., empathy, emotional resonance with others) to elicit the highest levels of performance from their organizations.

Tom Rath, author of *Strengthsfinder 2.0* (see "Resources," Chapter 4) has cowritten with Barry Conchie *Strengths-Based Leadership: Great Leaders, Teams, and Why People Follow.* Based on interviews with 50,000 leaders, they identify not only the four leadership domains necessary for balanced leadership teams (strategic thinking, relationship building, influencing, and executing), but also the four most important leadership characteristics to their followers (trust, compassion, stability, and hope).

In addition, organizational change expert John P. Kotter looks at leadership within the prism of his own discipline in *Leading Change,* which explores how more than 100 companies attempted to change in order to become more competitive (some successfully, some not). Given that many libraries and information organizations are struggling simply to survive if not become more competitive, Kotter's eight-step approach for leaders seeking to overcoming obstacles to change (establish a sense of urgency, create the guiding coalition, develop a vision and strategy, communicate the change vision, empower others to act, create short-term wins, consolidate gains, institutionalize new approaches) have relevance to every organization.

Becoming a Leader—The LIS Perspective

The LIS profession, potentially facing an upcoming and unprecedented level of attrition among its leadership (if those rumors of impending retirements actually do ever come true), has also been focusing a spotlight on leadership skills, more specifically what they are and how to develop them in ourselves or in potential leaders coming up through the ranks.

Not only are there a number of useful books available on the topic of LIS leadership, many LIS professional organizations have also been proactively working to address this issue. A number of associations, including ALA, ALA's Library Leadership and Management Association (LLAMA), SLA, various state libraries and state library associations, some of the MLIS programs, and other professional groups have been or are now stepping forward to offer leadership institutes, workshops, webinars, and mentoring programs.

Although several of these programs are listed in the Resources section of this chapter, if you are interested in developing your own leadership skills or those of individuals who work for you, you'll first want to check out options at your own organization (which may have a professional development program in place). If, however, your employer doesn't offer any leadership training, check with your state library or state library association for programs, coaching, or mentorship programs. Next stop: your professional memberships (leadership development programs are often listed under "Education," "Professional Development," or some combination thereof). Another avenue may be the graduate programs that offer online continuing professional development courses (see Chapter 5 for a list).

Another option, however, is to look for leadership training programs outside the profession, for example, with an organization you volunteer with or through a local college's professional studies or career enrichment programs. Although leadership of LIS organizations does have its unique challenges, in general, leadership concepts and skills are fairly transferable.

In addition to these leadership development approaches, the LIS profession also has a number of excellent books to call on for guidance. Several of these books are applicable to any type of library or information organization, while others are specific to either a certain library setting or a certain aspect of leadership.

Leadership: The Challenge for the Information Professionals by Sue Roberts and Jennifer Rowley is perhaps the best starting point for exploring leadership concepts as they apply to LIS organizations, for a couple of reasons. First, it incorporates leadership concepts and insights applicable no matter where you are in an organization, whether just starting out, responsible for organizational performance, or somewhere in between. Second, it encompasses all types of information organizations, including corporate information environments.

Another excellent resource on this topic is *Leadership Basics for Librarians and Information Professionals* by Edward G. Evans and Patricia

Layzell Ward. With a strong basis in LIS leadership research, the book is intended for those who would aspire to leadership roles in the coming years. Its three-part organization (Background, Developing Leadership Skills, and The Experience of Leadership) is meant to first introduce leadership concepts to readers, then coach them through developing their leadership skills, and finally explain the real-life challenges to be expected and how to deal with those challenges. This last section is especially useful for making clear to those inexperienced in leadership roles that the road can be rocky under the best of circumstances.

Written primarily for those doing staff development, Robert D. Stueart and Maureen Sullivan's *Developing Library Leaders: A How-to-Do-It Manual for Coaching, Team Building, and Mentoring Library Staff* focuses on five aspects of leadership—influencing and persuading others, building and leading groups and teams, project management, coaching, and mentoring. Preceding these overviews is a lead-off exploration of key leadership theories and their applicability to information services as well as the leader's roles and responsibilities. A concluding chapter addresses succession planning and development, a topic that is usually missed by other leadership books. Although following the standard How-to-Do-It series model with short chapters and a focus on concise, actionable information, there is enough theory here to provide a good starting point for individuals, organization leaders, and succession planning teams.

Lastly, *Interpersonal Skills, Theory and Practice: The Librarian's Guide to Becoming a Leader* by well-known LIS leader Brooke E. Sheldon draws on the emotional intelligence concepts developed originally by Daniel Goleman and places them within the context of the LIS profession and library organizations. As is pointed out by every business leadership writer cited previously, strong interpersonal skills are critical to the ability to lead; Sheldon here explores how those skills can and should be woven throughout such typical leadership challenges as team-building, organizational change, and conflict resolution.

Gender/Gen-Y Frames and Leadership

Two areas that hold special relevance to the issue of leadership in LIS environments are women's leadership styles (because of the preponderance of women in the profession) and the potential or demonstrated leadership attributes of Gen-Y/Millennial LIS professionals, because studies show their approaches to work in general differ fairly substantially from those of the generations preceding them.

Women and Leadership

Although no LIS-specific resources exist yet on this topic, there are a number of well-known works on women's leadership styles in general that apply equally well to LIS settings. The seminal book on this topic is Sally Helgesen's 1995 classic, *The Female Advantage: Women's Ways of Leadership,* the first examination of the different ways that men and women approach work—and leadership. Studying four nationally recognized female leaders of corporations and nonprofits, Helgesen found that although different from their male counterparts, women leaders had unique strengths that enabled them to create highly collaborative, creative, and successful organizations when they had the authority to do so. (Helgesen recently updated her research and recommendations in *Female Vision: Women's Real Power at Work.*)

Another title, *Enlightened Power: How Women are Transforming the Practice of Leadership,* brings together essays from 40 male and female leaders, leadership experts, academics, and entrepreneurs that address key issues related to women's transitions into leadership roles. The topics covered are quite diverse, but do a good job of touching on many of the issues that challenge women unused to or uncomfortable with being in positions of power.

Related to that discomfort, one of the areas of greatest concern when it comes to women leaders is a psychological response called The Imposter Syndrome. Valerie Young, author of *The Secret Thoughts of Successful Women: Why Capable People Suffer from the Impostor Syndrome and How to Thrive in Spite of It,* recalls reading a column by a highly successful, nationally respected female journalist who "admitted to being plagued throughout her professional career by a constant fear of 'screwing up.'" It's a feeling that accompanies each new project or promotion, along the lines of *They just don't realize I have no clue what I'm doing, and this time I'm going to really mess it up and everyone will know I'm in way over my head.* Women seem much more prone to this debilitating self-doubt than men, although men can experience it as well. But especially when coaching women for leadership roles, the Imposter Syndrome is something that needs to be acknowledged and addressed.

Why is improving women's leadership skills so critical to the profession? Because increasing, LIS leaders deploy their leadership strengths in two directions: internally, within their organizations, and externally, to library boards, chief executive officers, provosts, funding agencies, and other groups that hold power over their organizations. Given the overwhelming numbers of women in the profession, it's imperative that they have the tools and knowledge necessary to become confident, articulate, and politically savvy power players and advocates for their organizations.

Gen-Y and Leadership

Most of the research that's been done so far on Gen-Y/Millennial characteristics has focused on their attributes as employees and new hires. But two works have explored what to expect from this fascinating demographic cohort as they move into leadership roles. The first, *Millennial Leaders: Success Stories from Today's Most Brilliant Generation & Leaders* by Bea Fields and others, brings together the stories of numerous successful Millennial leaders plus insights of those who have studied their leadership characteristics and likely approaches to leadership. In addition, the authors provide more than 100 strategies and tips for Millennials who hope to move into leadership roles.

A second title on the same topic is Lisa Orrell's *Millennials into Leadership: The Ultimate Guide for Gen Y's Aspiring to Be Effective, Respected, Young Leaders at Work.* Aimed at Gen-Y workers who intend to move into positions of leadership within their organizations, *Millennials into Leadership* also provides insights into how this generation's unique characteristics are likely to translate into equally unique styles of leading. Although the author's self-promotion can be a bit much, the insights are nevertheless useful and actionable.

Similar to developing women's strengths in LIS leadership, helping Millennials excel in LIS leadership roles will have great importance to the future of the profession, so the bettter we can understand how to develop their leadership skills to a point of excellence, the better for all of us.

Resources

Starred titles are mentioned in the chapter.

Associations

Note: Following are leadership-development offerings of the major LIS professional organizations, however, you should always check with all associations of which you're a member to determine whether they have leadership courses of interest. Keep in mind also that almost all professional associations also publish their own journals, e-newsletters, or print newsletters for members only, and these publications often address leadership topics. In addition, some major state library associations offer their own leadership training programs, such as the Texas Library Association's TALL Texans Leadership Institute.

Advanced Leadership Institute for Senior Academic Librarians / Association of College and Research Libraries (ACRL)
www.gse.harvard.edu/ppe/programs/higher-education/portfolio/leadership-academic-librarians.html
From ACRL and the Harvard Graduate School of Education, this annual institute focuses on three areas: planning, organizational strategy and change, and transformational learning. Aimed at those who must "think strategically about emerging student and faculty needs, changing expectations of library staff, new technologies, and long-range plans for the library."

**Emerging Leaders Program / ALA
www.ala.org/ala/educationcareers/leadership/emergingleaders/index.cfm
ALA's leadership development program. Provides support for those new to the profession (and under 35 years old) who would like to learn more about ALA and potential leadership roles within the organization and the profession. Check the website for application criteria.

Leadership Academy / American Association of Law Libraries (AALL)
www.aallnet.org/main-menu/Education/leadership-academy
Held every other year, the AALL Leadership Academy is "an intensive learning experience aimed at growing and developing leadership skills." Offering assessments, interactive discussions, small group activities, and mini-presentations, the event is open to AALL members only, with applications accepted from April 1 to June 30.

**Leadership and Management Division (LMD)
http://lmd.sla.org/
Membership includes information professionals working across the entire spectrum of information organizations, from seasoned senior managers to new information professionals interested in leadership and management concepts. A division of SLA, LMD's focus includes guidance on developing the soft competencies (e.g., navigating organizational culture, interpersonal relationships) as well as creative innovation and leadership smarts.

**Leadership & Management Resources / ALA Online Learning
www.ala.org/ala/onlinelearning/management/leadership.cfm
Among the online fee-based learning opportunities ALA offers is Management Issues for Library Leaders, providing webinars, workshops, and multi-week courses on topics such as leadership and management, budgeting, building and facilities, human resources and staff development, and outcome measurement, among others.

**Leadership Summit / Special Library Association (SLA)
www.sla.org/content/resources/leadcenter/LeadershipSummit
The annual gathering of chapter, division, and caucus planners and leaders to share best-practice information as well as leadership and management insights for the association.

**Library Leadership & Management Association (LLAMA)
www.ala.org/llama/
Per its mission statement, LLAMA exists to "nurture current and future library leaders, and to develop and promote outstanding leadership and management practices." A division of ALA, LLAMA is an extremely active and effective division, and includes eight special interest divisions of its own as well as several discussion groups. Continuing education activities in support of management and leadership include occasional webinars, and sponsorship of numerous relevant presentations at ALA conferences. An important resource for those considering LIS management or leadership roles.

Northern Exposure to Leadership (NELI) / Canadian Library Association (CLA)
www.ls.ualberta.ca/neli/
This annual institute, affiliated with the University of Alberta Libraries and "by and for Canada's library leaders," is designed to help LIS professionals who aspire to leadership roles "develop, strengthen, and evolve

their leadership potential" to better equip themselves for leadership roles in Canada's libraries and/or information service organizations.

Research Library Leadership Fellows Program / Association of Research Libraries (ARL)
www.arl.org/leadership/rllf/index.shtml
ARL's executive leadership program is designed and sponsored by ARL member libraries and intended to offer an opportunity for development of future senior-level leaders in large research libraries. Per its mission statement, ARL's program "exposes and engages library staff who have the desire and potential for leadership at ARL libraries to themes and institutions that will enhance their preparedness." ARL also partners with an outside provider to provide leadership and management skills training events.

Print Resources

**Bennis, Warren. *On Becoming a Leader,* 2nd ed. Perseus Books Group, 2003. 256p. ISBN 0738208175.
A classic work, *On Becoming a Leader* identifies the key characteristics of a leader, including a guiding vision, passion, integrity, self-knowledge, trust, and daring. This wide-ranging book considers the roles and responsibilities of leaders, their impact for good or ill, and the author's research-based assertion that effective leaders are made, not born, and can be found at all levels of the organization. Bennis has also created an accompanying workbook (*Learning to Lead: A Workbook on Becoming a Leader*) should you want more hands-on coaching.

Bryant, Adam. *The Corner Office: Indispensable and Unexpected Lessons from CEOs on How to Lead and Succeed.* Times Books, 2011. 272p. ISBN 0805093060.
Bryant (who writes the Corner Office column for the Sunday *New York Times* Business section) interviewed more than 75 business CEOs and executives from businesses large, small, and in between to create a collection of best-in-class advice on organizational leadership. The interviews are engagingly written, conversational, and packed with lessons learned. Notes Bryant: "The qualities these executives share: Passionate curiosity. Battle-hardened confidence. Team smarts. A simple mindset. Fearlessness."

Cialdini, Robert B. *Influence: Science and Practice,* 5th ed. Prentice Hall, 2008. 272p. ISBN 0205609996.
The classic work on persuasive influence, Cialdini's book focuses on how people are persuaded to undertake a preferred action (for most of Cialdini's readers, how to influence someone to buy something). It also, however, functions as a fascinating guide to social psychology, and potentially how to influence groups of people (read: team members and workplace colleagues) to understand and agree with your viewpoint. Recommended as a resource for both managers and leaders.

Collins, Jim. *Good to Great: Why Some Companies Make the Leap . . . and Others Don't.* HarperBusiness, 2001. 300p. ISBN 0066620996.

Based on exhaustive research on the topic of corporate success or lack thereof, Collins identified 11 companies (out of approximately 1,400 that he considered) that were able to make the leap to greatness. Collins calls the strategic circumstances common to the 11 the Hedgehog Concept, that is, they had a product or service that enabled them to outshine competitors, that drove the companies' economic engine, and about which the company was passionate. Collins explores the central role leaders play in this success, and the attributes that enable them to do so. Although this best-selling business title is now over a decade old, its key leadership points are still relevant.

Covey, Stephen M. R. *The Speed of Trust: The One Thing That Changes Everything.* Free Press, 2008. 384p. ISBN 1847392717.

The son of *Seven Habits of Highly Effective People* author Stephen R. Covey, the author stakes out his own area of expertise here. According to Covey (son), trust is the key factor in succeeding as a leader (and especially now with the failure of trust in so many institutions). The 13 behaviors of trust-inspiring leaders: talk straight, demonstrate respect, create transparency, right wrongs, show loyalty, deliver results, get better, confront reality, clarify expectations, practice accountability, listen first, keep commitments, and extend trust. Although these seem like common sense, they are unfortunately less common among leaders than one would hope, a fact that makes this an inspiring read.

Crowley, John D. *Developing a Vision: Strategic Planning for the School Librarian in the 21st Century,* 2nd ed. Libraries Unlimited, 2011. 162p. ISBN 9781591588917.

Strategic planning is one of those topics that may be touched on in grad school, but is rarely developed as a skill to the level needed by school library leaders. This book remedies that lack by lining out in great detail the why, who (i.e., the team members involved), and how of this key leadership activity for school library media specialists.

**Enlightened Power: How Women are Transforming the Practice of Leadership.* Lin Coughlin and Ellen Wingard, eds. Jossey-Bass, 2011. 576p. ISBN 1118085876.

Insights from 40 men and women (mostly women) who hold or have held high-visibility leadership positions or have studied the characteristics of women leaders. Thirty essays are organized within the broad categories of "Reimagining Power," "Paths of Power," and "A New Power in the World." An especially relevant resource for women who are moving into LIS leadership positions and feel uncertain about their new role.

**Evans, Edward G. and Patricia Layzell Ward. *Leadership Basics for Librarians and Information Professionals.* Scarecrow Press, 2007. 256p. ISBN 0810852292.

Based on findings from a 2004–2005 survey, this insightful and practical guide to LIS leadership best-practices looks at the challenges likely to be faced in the coming years and offers strategies for addressing them. The book's three sections provide background on LIS leadership issues, explore the development of leadership skills, and then offer real-world insights gleaned from survey respondents and interviews with LIS professionals in leadership roles. The focus on actionable information is carried through with additional readings, tips called out in text boxes, term definitions, checklists, exercises, and other supplementary materials.

**Fields, Bea, et al. *Millennial Leaders: Success Stories from Today's Most Brilliant Generation & Leaders,* 2nd ed. Writers of the Round Table Press, 2008. 324p. ISBN 0981454518.
True, it's a bit challenging to get beyond the off-putting hype of the title, but if you can, these 25 profiles of Millennial high-achievers deliver some interesting insights about values, aspirations, measures of success, and other generation-specific characteristics of this particular group of individuals. The authors also provide leadership coaching tips for aspiring Millennial leaders, which may be helpful if you're a Gen Y staffer considering how to develop your leadership skills.

**Goleman, Daniel, Richard Boyatzis, and Annie McKee. *Primal Leadership: Realizing the Power of Emotional Intelligence.* Harvard Business School Press, 2004. 336p. ISBN 1591391849.
Goleman is the author of *Emotional Intelligence,* the original work on how emotional literacy trumps straight smarts. This work, based on interviews with 4,000 executives, applies that concept to leadership, while identifying and elaborating on the six leadership styles—visionary, coaching, affiliative, democratic, pacesetting, commanding—and the circumstances under which each is most effective. A fascinating and insightful resource.

**Helgesen, Sally. *The Female Advantage: Women's Ways of Leadership.* Doubleday Currency, 1995. 272p. ISBN 0385419112.
Originally published in 1990, Helgesen's *Female Advantage* was the first work to examine the difference between male and female styles of leadership and assert that women's approaches, though different, could be equally successful, and often advantageous. She notes that women leaders tend to create organizational environments that support creativity, collaboration and cooperation, and shared decision-making power. She recently updated her research with *The Female Vision: Women's Real Power at Work* (Berrett-Koehler Publishers, 2010), which explores the different ways men and women see things, the different things they see or notice, and how both approaches are necessary for organizations to flourish.

Kotter, John P. *Leading Change.* Harvard Business Press, 1996. 208p. ISBN 0875847471.
One of the original explorations of how leaders can help their organizations successfully transition through change. Kotter is widely considered

the expert on change leadership/management; in this work he provides an eight-step framework for leading change, beginning with establishing a sense of urgency and concluding with the critical final step of anchoring new approaches in the culture.

**Kouzes, James M. and Barry Z. Posner. *The Leadership Challenge,* 4th ed. Jossey-Bass, 2008. 416p. ISBN 0787984922.

First published over twenty years ago, *The Leadership Challenge* lays out in accessible language the five practices and 10 commitments that readers—not necessarily CEOs—have come to rely on for growing their leadership skills. The book's key points and recommendations are meant to be immediately applicable, furthering the authors' premise that "leadership is everyone's business." Similar to Bennis, the authors have also created an accompanying guide (*The Leadership Challenge Workbook*) for more hands-on coaching.

**Law, Jonathan. *Business: The Ultimate Resource,* 3rd ed. A&C Black, 2011. 1760p. ISBN 140812811X.

Like an MBA in a box, the third edition of *Business* follows the format of previous editions: hundreds of articles by topic thought leaders under the broad heading of Best Practices; a Management Library comprising overviews of important business books; a section devoted to profiles of 50 key business thinkers and management giants (both historical and contemporary) and the ideas for which they are known; a dictionary of key business and management terms; and over 200 pages of business information sources, organized by topic (example: accounting, intellectual property, learning organization). Extensively cross-referenced, this reference book is a key resource for LIS professionals who need to become familiar with the business world and its vocabulary.

**Lubans, John, Jr. *"Leading from the Middle," and Other Contrarian Essays on Library Leadership.* Libraries Unlimited, 2010. 298p. ISBN 9781598845778.

A collection of delightful but also pragmatic essays on library leadership from one who has practiced it in numerous roles. The 36 chapters are organized under the broad categories of Leadership, Leading from the Middle, Teamwork, Empowerment, Followship; Leaders, Bosses, Challenges, Values; Coaching, Self-Management, Collaboration, Communication; and Techniques and Tools, Productivity, Climate. Lubans makes a strong case for the importance of strong followers—who lead from the middle—as being key to effective, successful leadership. Sample essay title: "'I'm So Low I Can't Get High': The Low Morale Syndrome and What to Do about It."

The Many Faces of School Library Leadership. Sharon Coatney, ed. Libraries Unlimited, 2010. 147p. ISBN 9781591588931.

Ten chapter-length essays on various aspects of school library leadership from such well-known experts as Ken Haycock ("Leadership from the Middle: Building Influence for Change"), Deb Levitov ("The School

Librarian as an Advocacy Leader"), Jody Howard ("The Teacher-Librarian as a Curriculum Leader"), and Blanche Woolls ("Leadership and Your Professional School Library Association"). Additional leadership topics include staff development, technology, literacy, intellectual freedom, and being a learning leader. Extensive resource lists conclude each chapter.

**Maxwell, John C. *The 5 Levels of Leadership: Proven Steps to Maximize Your Potential.* Center Street, 2011. 304p. ISBN 159995365X.

This best-seller on leadership identifies five levels of leadership: (1) Position—People follow because they have to; (2) Permission—People follow because they want to; (3) Production—People follow because of what you have done for the organization; (4) People Development—People follow because of what you have done for them personally; and (5) Pinnacle—People follow because of who you are and what you represent. Naturally, Maxwell provides in-depth information on each level, but the goal is to understand your own leadership profile and learn how to progress to the fifth level. Maxwell has also authored several equally popular leadership books, including *Developing the Leader Within You* (Thomas Nelson, 1993), *The 21 Irrefutable Laws of Leadership: Follow Them and People Will Follow You* (Thomas Nelson, 1998), and *The 360 Degree Leader: Developing Your Influence from Anywhere in the Organization* (Thomas Nelson, 2005).

**Orrell, Lisa. *Millennials into Leadership: The Ultimate Guide for Gen Y's Aspiring to Be Effective, Respected, Young Leaders at Work.* Intelligent Women Publishing, 2009. 170p. ISBN 1936214008.

Written from the perspective that even an entry-level position can be experienced as a leadership role, *Millennials into Leadership* provides an interesting perspective on leadership coaching for Gen Y staffers. Orrell is a self-described branding expert and her self-promotional abilities are evident throughout. However, some of her points are quite interesting, for example her discussion of conflicts between Gen X and Gen Y staffers as being similar to sibling rivalries. A lot of hype, but worth perusing within the context of how you personally would coach Millennials aspiring to leadership roles, or, if you're a Millennial aspiring to leadership opportunities, how you might start building your career in that direction.

**Rath, Tom and Barry Conchie. *Strengths-Based Leadership.* Gallup Press, 2009. 216p. ISBN 1595620257.

Building on the original strengths books, *First, Break All the Rules: What the World's Greatest Managers Do Differently* (Simon & Schuster, 1999) and *Now, Discover Your Strengths* (Free Press, 2001), this book is similarly based on astoundingly extensive Gallup research on leadership (including responses from both leaders and followers). Their findings: the three things that the most effective leaders consistently do are: (1) consistently invest in their strengths; (2) surround themselves with the right people and then maximize their team; and (3) understand their followers' needs.

**Roberts, Sue and Jennifer Rowley. *Leadership: The Challenge for the Information Profession*. Neal-Schuman, 2008. 256p. ISBN 978156046091.
A thoughtful exploration of the role of leadership across all LIS environments, and at all levels within an organization. Building on the "Leadership and Management" chapter in their previous work, *Managing Information Services* (Library Association Publishing, 2004), the authors successfully blend an overview of leadership theory with actionable, step-by-step coaching supplemented by case studies, chapter summaries, review questions, and reflection points. Recommended for students as well as practitioners.

**Sheldon, Brooke E. *Interpersonal Skills, Theory and Practice: The Librarian's Guide to Becoming a Leader*. Libraries Unlimited, 2010. 96p. ISBN 9781591587446.
Interpersonal skills is one of those professional skills that MLIS grad programs rarely have time to touch on, but as Sheldon here points out, they are critical to the success of both your career and LIS organizations. Drawing on the concepts first popularized by Daniel Goleman in *Emotional Intelligence* (see "Resources," Chapter 4), she identifies not only how emotional intelligence and strong interpersonal skills can be deployed in the service of leadership goals, but also how you can develop these skills.

**Stueart, Robert D. and Maureen Sullivan. *Developing Library Leaders: A How-to-Do-It Manual for Coaching, Team Building, and Mentoring Library Staff*. Neal-Schuman, 2010. 106p. ISBN 9781555707255.
How-to guide for those aspiring to leadership roles or attempting to develop leadership capabilities among staff. Action items are placed within the context of leadership theory; topics covered include coaching, team building, project leadership, mentoring library staff, and roles and responsibilities of leaders, among others.

Wincentsen-Lowe, Dawn. *Mid-Career Library and Information Professionals: A Leadership Primer*. Neal-Schuman, 2010. 260p. ISBN 9781843346098.
By the time you're a mid-career LIS professional, you've probably had an opportunity to observe (or experience) excellent leaders as well as those, ah, less so. So if now is the time for you to consider moving into a leadership role yourself, this is a terrific place to start. The author offers not only practical advice from herself and others, but also the encouragement needed to instill confidence in those hesitant about making this important career move.

**Young, Valerie. *The Secret Thoughts of Successful Women: Why Capable People Suffer from the Impostor Syndrome and How to Thrive in Spite of It*. Crown Business, 2011. 304p. ISBN 0307452719.
If you've ever thought "I don't deserve this success," "I'm not really smart enough to do this and I'm going to be found out," "I'm a fraud—it's all just been good luck," or some other variation of these self-diminishing statements, you're probably in the grip of the impostor syndrome (especially if you're also a woman in a leadership role). Young's insightful

book not only explains where this devastating self-doubt comes from, but also how to successfully counter it. Favorite quote, from Bertrand Russell: "The whole problem with the world is that fools and fanatics are always so certain of themselves, and wiser people so full of doubts."

Online Resources

Gen Y Leaders—The "Me" Generation or the "We" Generation?
www.tanveernaseer.com/the-truth-about-gen-y-leaders/
From business coach Tanveer Naseer's blog, this research-based analysis of Gen Y attitudes suggests that they have high levels of commitment to self-development and innovation, and also scored higher than other generation on the characteristics that signified effective leadership capabilities.

The Imposter Syndrome: Or How I Learned to Get Over My Panic Attack, Love My Promotion, and Make My To-Do List
http://lisjobs.com/rethinking/?p=50
From the *Rethinking Information Work* blog, this post addresses a phenomenon often experienced by women who are promoted to positions of leadership or authority. The Imposter Syndrome is a feeling that despite your promotions and increasing levels of responsibility, you're actually a fake and/or incapable of doing high-level work and people will discover at any moment that in truth you've no idea what you're doing.

Is Gen Y Prepared for Leadership?
http://blog.clomedia.com/2011/04/are-gen-y-prepared-for-leadership/
From the *Chief Learning Officer* blog, this post presents a fascinating take on the different approach Millennials may take to leadership, based on their more collaborative approach to work. Suggests author Ladan Nikravan: "Millennial leaders motivate by enabling others to be leaders . . . Members of Gen Y know the strengths of those they lead and seek to make use of those skills to develop the individual and team. A Gen Y leader delegates to people to work together to reach their goals because collaboration is thriving and use of leaders is being questioned."

John Maxwell on Leadership
http://johnmaxwellonleadership.com/
Blog from the author of *The 5 Levels of Leadership: Proven Steps to Maximize Your Potential* and *The 21 Indispensable Qualities of a Leader*. Somewhat self-promotional, but reading through his archives can produce some insightful posts.

Lead Change Group: Helping Leaders Grow Leaders
http://leadchangegroup.com/blog/
A group blog created by a nonprofit leadership development community promoting character-based leadership. Although the topics and quality of the posts vary, this is a good resource for connecting with values-based leadership concepts, which tend to resonate with LIS professionals.

Leadership for New Librarians

www.liscareer.com/sloan_leadership.htm

From the LIScareer.com Career Strategies for Librarians blog, this post by Susan Sloan is a wonderful overview of ten ways for new (or seasoned) librarians to become leaders. Although written in 2005, every word Sloan wrote still rings true.

Next Generation Experience: Leadership and the New Information Professional

http://lmd.sla.org/2011/09/next-generation-experience-leadership-and-the-new-information-professional/

From SLA's Leadership and Management Division blog, this post by Lisa Chow provides smart tactics in answer to the question, How do you develop or gain leadership skills when you're not in a leadership position?

SmartBrief on Leadership

www.smartbrief.com/leadership/index.jsp

Daily e newsletter that aggregates leadership articles and blog posts from around the web. An easy and useful way to keep up with recent developments and new thinking related to leadership.

10
Going the Independent Route

```
┌─────────────────────────────────────────────────────────┐
│                    Chapter Highlights                      │
│                                                            │
│   • Types of Independent Work                              │
│                                                            │
│   • Is Being an Independent for You?                       │
│                                                            │
│   • Ways to Approach Independent Work                      │
│                                                            │
│   • Questions to Consider before You Leap                  │
│                                                            │
│   • Creating Additional Revenue Streams                    │
│                                                            │
│   • From Solo to Small Business (and Everything in Between)│
└─────────────────────────────────────────────────────────┘
```

If I were to become an independent, what kind of work would I do? Although you may be in a job you love right now, at some point you may find yourself wanting to consider this option.

Or maybe you're thinking about adding a second revenue stream in addition to your day job. Or wanting to develop a new career path into which you'll eventually transition. If you've got information skills (or are willing to learn them), there are all sorts of ways to turn that knowledge into income.

Types of Independent Work

Basically, all of the types of work that LIS professionals do for employers (libraries, businesses, bibliographic utilities, nonprofits, etc.) can fairly easily become types of contract project work that you can do as an independent.

For example, if you've been laid off from your job as a corporate librarian, you might want to consider approaching your former employer to do competitive intelligence research on a contract basis. (In this age of downsizing, staff may go away, but the business needs they were meeting rarely do, a fact that many organizations belatedly realize.)

Consider some of these options for independent or project work:

- meta-tagging online content elements
- taxonomy-building
- doing competitive intelligence
- researching and writing white papers
- analyzing and summarizing key industry trends
- creating records management architectures
- digitizing archival materials

Or consider deploying your transferable skills into independent opportunities. For example, if you've developed an expertise in marketing your public library, this skill might be translated into a consulting business developing marketing plans for nonprofits and cultural institutions. Or you might want to consider a sideline in website development based on the outstanding work you did (and can point to) designing and implementing your academic library's web portal. Have you really enjoyed your job as a bibliographic instruction librarian? Then consider the possibility of pursuing an independent or sideline path in a related field, for example as a K–12 tutor, online teacher, instructional designer, or creator of online product tutorials for businesses.

The independent path most frequently associated with LIS professionals is client-based research, and in fact that can be a great way to deploy your skills as an information professional. But it's only one of many, many options. In fact, independents have pursued careers as manuscript evaluators and consulting acquisitions editors, freelance book-talkers and/or storytellers, workshop and seminar presenters, adjunct faculty (classroom-based or online), library architecture consultants, organizational development consultants, writers (books, articles, and online content), and grant writers. Others have established sidelines as freelance legal researchers, set up and maintained specialized libraries for biomedicine start-ups, written position papers for nonprofits, cataloged private libraries for wealthy book-loving clients, specialized in local market research or materials patent searching, written research guides for virtual libraries, taken on systems and networking projects, provided research training to corporate departments, created an annual series of trend analysis reports for marketing companies, done provenance research to authenticate artworks, performed historical research, edited manuscripts for LIS publishers, and done contract cataloging—all based on their LIS professional skills.

LIS professionals with writing skills can also engage in project (or retainer) work researching and writing business white papers, client newsletters, business plans, grant proposals, content strategy, topical and targeted articles for websites, syndicated articles, and resource materials for business and nonprofit websites, as well as jumping into social media activities for clients.

Is Being an Independent for You?

Working independently or being an information entrepreneur isn't for everyone. As Mary Ellen Bates points out in the second edition of her classic independent information pro guide, *Building & Running a Successful Research Business,* "Running a successful business means not only having the research skills but also being able to think and act like an entrepreneur—to know how to price your services, anticipate changes in the economy and the information environment, market yourself and your business constantly, and develop new skills as your clients' needs change."

A number of good assessments are available to work through to determine if the life of an independent/entrepreneur is the right choice for you, such as Chapter 4 of *Building & Running a Successful Research Business,* "Are You a Potential Independent Info Pro," which looks at people skills, entrepreneurial skills, business skills, information skills, and where you can turn for help to buttress these skill areas. Susan Awe, in her *Entrepreneur's Sourcebook: Charting the Path to Small Business Success* (2nd ed.), suggests that entrepreneurs must possess "a compelling vision, a driving passion, versatility or flexibility in planning and changing plans, and confident execution . . . Additionally, curiosity is another necessary attribute, since curious people are creative or innovative—and questioning of current practices, procedures, and methods triggers innovation."

Additionally, the *Small Business Administration* (SBA) site has an Entrepreneurial Test of some 25 questions to help you assess whether this is a wise career choice for you (examples: Am I prepared to spend the time, money, and resources needed to get my business started? Why am I starting a business? What is my competition?) Another great source here is a *Harvard Business Review* blog post from Daniel Isenberg, "Should You Be an Entrepreneur? Take this Test," a set of 20 occasionally tongue-in-cheek questions to help you assess your personality fitness for the challenges of entrepreneurship.

Additionally, you may want to browse the resources on the website for the Association of Independent Information Professionals (AIIP), the primary organization for those offering independent information services.

Regardless of which assessment (or how many) you take, however, three critical characteristics for entrepreneurs are the ability to take risks, the ability to market yourself and your business, and a willingness to work long hours for minimal (if any) compensation, at least initially.

Ways to Approach Independent Work

As noted, the independent path can be as simple as performing the same type of work you did previously as an employee, but doing it instead on a contract or project basis. Or it can mean taking the more complex route of starting a new product or service business based on the expertise, contacts, and professional reputation you've built along the way as an LIS professional.

In addition, there are many different ways to pursue independent work. You can take on outside gigs (assuming this presents no conflict with your employer) as a supplement to your day job. Or you may decide to set up shop on your own, working as a "solopreneur" and offering your services as a freelance indexer to publishers around the country. You might work with a single client, for example, being a contract substitute librarian for one library district. Or you might work on multiple projects for multiple clients (juggling multiple deadlines, relying on your excellent project and time management skills).

If you prefer being part of a team, however, you might want to consider building a business that includes several employees. If you don't mind managing people, this option can extend your ability to handle multiple clients and projects simultaneously. Or, if you feel you enjoy the camaraderie of group projects but you'd rather not take on the management and overhead that employees involve, you may find that a great alternative is to instead pull together a loose network of information pros whose skills complement your own, then bring them together on an as-needed project basis. Assume your network can be local or virtual.

Another alternative if you'd like to try out project work is to sign up with a temp or contract project agency, such as LAC, that specializes in all types of LIS work. There are a number of benefits to this approach: it can provide more diversity in your work life, it can let you try out a number of different types of work (and potential employers/clients), and it means that someone else will be taking care of finding, landing, and managing the client (while you get to focus on the actual work).

The good news: no matter which way you'd like to structure your independent work, all of the choices are yours to make. That includes what skills you offer and to whom, what clients you pursue (or fire), how much or how little you charge, and at what rate you grow your business (depending, for example, on your revenue and lifestyle goals).

Questions to Consider before You Leap

Before considering the independent path, you'll want to thoroughly explore and answer the following questions.

What Product or Service Would You Offer?

This is the most important question, yet it's not as simple as it seems. Often the idea we have for what we're convinced would be a killer offering is much less compelling to our target market—and if we're really lucky, we find that out *before* we've invested much time or energy in it. So now is the time to start doing some serious market research. You want to know the answers to questions like

- How would you use this?
- What would you use instead to solve your challenge/issue/problem if you didn't have this?
- Would you consider this to be nice to have or need to have? (assume only need to have will result in you getting paid)
- How much would you expect to pay for a service/product like this?
- How often would you be likely to purchase it over the course of a year?

In Bates's chapter on "Who You Are and What You Do," she suggests you start off by asking yourself questions such as What subject(s) do I know best? and Who is willing to pay for information? (or your type of product/ service). She further suggests these five tips for defining your service and clients (substitute your product or service if not research):

- target professionals with a high need for strategic intelligence
- focus on clients who will provide repeat business
- get to know your prospective clients before you define your services
- offer something that you clients immediately see the value of
- don't limit your geographic range unnecessarily

One way to explore the viability of your potential market (and market offering) is to test them on a very small scale, perhaps just doing a couple of small-scale independent projects on the side while you continue with your day job. This is a variation on the business idea of rapid prototyping, that is, creating a bare-bones and inexpensive prototype or test of your idea before you invest too much time or money in pursuing it. You may discover that although your target market isn't so keen on your initial idea, it may be wildly enthusiastic about (and willing to pay for) a similar concept with a couple of changes made to your original offering.

Elaborating on the tendency of entrepreneurs to first develop their product or service (*I just know everyone is going to want this!*) then figure out whether there's a market for it (or not), Steven Gary Blank lays out an easily executed, common-sense approach to reversing that process. In his *The Four Steps to the Epiphany,* he points out that customer development should precede product or service development or at the very least go hand-in-hand in order to avoid investing time and money in a product/service offering that no one's going to want. Good advice.

How Would You Work?

For example, would you work from home or in a leased office space? Would you work a regular 9–5 day five days a week, or do four 10-hour days so you could have regular three-day weekends? Would you prefer to work for national clients (may entail business travel, although not necessarily) or local companies (often have smaller budgets, but easier to build a relationship with). If you decide you want to target local markets, a terrific resource is Marcy Phelps's *Research on Main Street: Using the Web to Find Local Business and Market Information,* which will help you gather the information you need to identify and segment your potential market (and competition).

Whether you decide to work from a home office or one outside your home, you'll want to familiarize yourself with the tax deductions available to you. The best series of books on tax and self-employment issues come from NOLO Press, and the one you should start with is Steven Fishman's *Working for Yourself: Law & Taxes for Independent Contractors, Freelancers & Consultants* (8th ed.), which explores the pros and cons of working for yourself, what type of business structure makes the most sense for you, the pluses and minuses of a home- versus outside-location office, and a host of other important considerations. Fishman's accompanying title, *Deduct It! Lower Your Small Business Taxes,* is an excellent overview not only of all of the business expenses you may legitimately deduct, but also how to do so in a way likely to avoid IRS concerns.

What Market Would You Target?

The choices here are many, but the two biggest questions are the following.

- *What type of market will you focus on?* Options here might include consumer-focused or business-focused companies (B2C versus B2B); start-ups versus established companies; the library and information services market or clients outside the LIS world; nonprofits or government agencies; industry specific (for example, the pharmaceuticals industry) or type-of-research specific (for example, patent research)?
- *Will you be a generalist or a specialist?* This decision can have a substantial impact on the viability of your business. For example, do you anticipate having your product or service be applicable across a broad range of organizations (which will offer a larger market opportunity) or will you instead be targeting a small niche market (which, while easier to market to and make a name for yourself in, will also be susceptible to market downturns)?

A major consideration with both of these options is whether you've already built up professional equity in a specific industry or area. A combination of professional expertise, your professional reputation, and your professional network, your professional equity (assuming it's positive) in a specific area makes it easier to gain traction for your independent work. People are more likely to know and trust your skills, you're more likely to understand their needs, and you've probably already built up a trust relationship with them. (This is one of the reasons it's generally easier to launch as an independent after you've worked at least several years as an employee somewhere, preferably for a large corporation where you've had an opportunity to establish lots of positive professional connections.)

What Would You Charge?

This question includes not only what amount you would charge (this usually computes to some sort of hourly rate, even though it may not be stated as such to your clients), but also whether you will, in fact, charge by the hour, by the project, or by some other criteria.

Several excellent resources can help you figure out how to approach pricing in a way that makes sense for you and your business. The first is Chapter 14 in *Building & Running a Successful Research Business,* "Setting Rates and Fees," which looks at how to set hourly fees, the pros and cons between doing a project on an hourly rate basis or a flat fee, estimating a project (one of the most challenging aspects of working as an independent!), and dealing with the money part of working with clients.

The second is by Alan Weiss, who has authored a multitude of useful books on how to thrive as a consultant. His book on pricing is *Value-Based Fees: How to Charge—and Get—What You're Worth.* A caveat: Weiss is expecting his readers to be in the $25,000 to $125,000 per-project range, but despite the fact that you're probably not starting out at that level, his ideas do have relevance and applicability to any independent. Lastly, another very practical resource is Laurie Lewis's *What to Charge: Pricing Strategies for Freelancers and Consultants.* Although the author is a freelance writer, her advice applies equally well to freelance researchers, indexers, user interface specialists, taxonomists, and so on.

How Would You Get Clients?

Ah, the dreaded *marketing* question! Even those who feel confident in their professional skills often feel completely intimidated by the idea of selling their services to potential clients. Nevertheless, the ability to land clients is critical to the sustainable success of your independent work. In fact, it's safe to assume that when you start out, at least 50 percent of your time will be focused on finding or creating client opportunities; that is, marketing and selling.

Services marketing is, to quote marketing guru Harry Beckwith, *Selling the Invisible.* Although published in 1997, this book is still considered the seminal work on how to sell services, which are, to his point, invisible or intangible. Perhaps equally valuable to independent information professionals, however, is Beckwith's more recent *You, Inc.: The Art of Selling Yourself,* which essentially says that what a client is buying is confidence in you: your judgment, your expertise, your ability to deliver as promised. Given that many independents are solo shops, this message—and Beckwith's approach to successfully selling your ability to clients—is especially relevant. (For hard-won insights on what does and doesn't work in marketing, see Bates's *Ten Mistakes New Independent Info Pros Make* in Chapter 21, "Marketing Do's and Don'ts.")

In addition to having an informative, polished, and professional-looking website, having a strong social media presence will help increase your "findability" and will also give potential clients a way to see how you conduct yourself, the issues you engage with, and your level of expertise before they hire you. So assume at the very minimum you've got a robust and compelling LinkedIn profile for yourself and possibly a company page. You may also find blogging a terrific way to establish your professional expertise. (Hesitant about blogging? Check out Handley's *Content Rules: How to Create Killer Blogs, Podcasts, Video, Ebooks, Webinars [and More] That Engage Customers and Ignite Your Business.*) And, depending on your circumstances (i.e., how much time you have to devote to social media marketing), you may also want to consider having a presence on Facebook, Twitter, and other social media venues.

Another approach to getting initial clients, depending on the type of work you do, is to consider exploring projects listed through freelance project sites like Elance.com or SimplyHired.com (use the search terms "freelance," "freelancer," "contract," and similar descriptors with your desired type of work). Because the fees paid through these types of sites are generally so low, I would suggest you only consider this option if you are simply trying to build a portfolio of clips or small client projects. My recommendation would be that if you need to build your portfolio, it makes more sense to do it as a volunteer with organizations that will also get you in front of potential real (and possibly ongoing) clients so you can demonstrate your expertise before you propose a working relationship.

For more ideas on marketing on a shoestring (the type of marketing most common for independents), John Jantsch's *Duct Tape Marketing: The World's Most Practical Small Business Marketing Guide* provides a practical, pragmatic roadmap for creating and executing an effective and sustainable marketing strategy. Another alternative is Jay Conrad Levinson's *Guerrilla Marketing* books (some of which are terrific, others less so). Perhaps the title of greatest value to independent information professionals is his *Guerrilla Marketing: Easy and Inexpensive Strategies for Making Big Profits from Your Small Business,* which takes a more, ah, aggressive stance toward marketing than does Jantsch, but it's a style that aligns with many entrepreneurs' approach to business, so worth checking out.

Those are just the *starter* questions! The good news is that there are excellent resources available to help you work through each of these and the myriad other issues to launching as an independent. (A quick peruse through *Building & Running a Successful Research Business* will give any independent information professional, regardless of the type of work you do, baseline guidance regarding what you need to think about before launching, and then how to handle the questions that will undoubtedly arise once you're up and running.) The reality-check news is that until you've thought all of these through and are confident that you've addressed each one, you're probably not ready to launch.

Creating Additional Revenue Streams

One of the most effective ways to create additional revenue streams is to develop a product or products based on the information-related service that you offer. Your mantra: create information once, repackage and resell it multiple times.

The difference between a service and a product is basically the level of engagement, interactivity, and control (by you) involved. For example, a service is more of a reactive relationship, where you wait to swing into action until a client has requested your engagement. Your work is tailored to the needs of the client, is generally on demand, and is delivered on the client's deadline.

A product, on the other hand, is typically something you have created based on your understanding of your market's need, and that you offer for sale or license to customers. Examples might include market research reports, workbooks and training guides, self-directed online tutorials, webinars, and e-books. When it comes to productizing your information expertise, your goal should be to develop a product once, then sell it to multiple purchasers for a set price. (Contrast this with a service, which usually entails creating information from scratch for a single user/client.)

One way to approach this is to ask yourself, what information/expertise do I have (or could I *easily* create) that I could package and turn into a product that someone would pay money for?

From Solo to Small Business (and Everything in Between)

One of the great things about being an information entrepreneur is the wide-open range of business choices it provides. For example, if you prefer to work solo, that can easily be done (as long as you don't mind being the only person on staff, which means you're pretty much responsible for everything!). Or as noted, you may decide to work as part of a loose network of information professionals who each have a different area of expertise, which means you can take on larger jobs than a solo might be comfortable with. Or, you may decide that you're goal is to build a company with multiple employees to establish a broader professional footprint (and possibly create a financial asset you'll be able to sell upon retirement).

Or you can just decide to start small via a low-maintenance sideline that you do now and then when the opportunity arises, with the possibility of ramping that sideline up when you have the time and/or interest. The great thing about independent work? All the choices are up to you!

Resources

Starred titles are mentioned in the chapter.

Government Resources

Service Corps of Retired Executives (SCORE)

www.score.org

A resource partner with the SBA, SCORE is a nonprofit association focused on "educating entrepreneurs and helping small businesses start, grow, and succeed nationwide." More than 13,000 SCORE network volunteers mentor small business owners on all aspects of starting, growing, and succeeding with their small businesses. Click on the Find a Chapter tab on the home page to see if there are SCORE volunteers in your area.

**Small Business Administration (SBA)

www.sba.gov

Under the Startup Basics section, check out the Entrepreneurial Test of 25 questions, which will help you evaluate your possible success in your own business. Other major sections cover business planning, financing, managing, marketing, employees, taxes, legal aspects, and business opportunities. You can also find online business forms, business plans, loan information, and many helpful publications. Some contents available in Spanish.

**Small Business Development Centers (SBDC)

www.sba.gov/content/small-business-development-centers-sbdcs

SBDCs are community-based partnerships primarily between the government and colleges/universities (and sometimes libraries and chambers of commerce), administered by the Small Business Administration. SBDCs are mandated to help local businesses grow and succeed, so provide counseling and information both in the local SBDC and online. Although few SBDCs have extensive experience with information-focused companies, they can still offer help with business plans, market research, and marketing strategies.

Associations

Note: The associations listed here are the ones that many independent information professionals belong to, but many other information organizations also have special-interest or discussion groups dedicated to their members who work independently, so be sure to check with your specific professional association to see if there are independent colleagues with whom you can connect. If you focus on specific industries, you may also want to consider joining the industry associations your target clients belong to as a way to gain visibility and stay abreast of key trends in their area.

American Society for Indexing (ASI)

www.asindexing.org

Professional association for those involved in indexing, abstracting, and database-building. Content-rich website offers a directory listing of indexers, links to resources of interest to indexers, articles, position papers about indexing, and information about ASI's special interest groups, which offer a range of specializations (business, psychology/sociology, sports/fitness, culinary, web, and science and medicine, among others). For career info, see So You Want to Be an Indexer in the Become an Indexer section.

APRA

www.aprahome.org

International organization for fundraisers who specialize in fundraising research, analytics, and relationship management. The research piece is donor prospecting, an area of opportunity for LIS professionals with research skills. APRA offers educational programs, networking opportunities, publications, and career resources (see Career Center in the left-hand menu). Formerly the Association of Prospect Researchers for Advancement.

**Association of Independent Information Professionals (AIIP)

www.aiip.org

The key resource for anyone considering a career as an independent information pro. AIIP is a very active, knowledge-rich organization whose members are legendary for their willingness to share best practices, business tips, product recommendations, and any other type of information that will help fellow members succeed. Membership in the organization brings access to the AIIP electronic discussion list, perhaps the most valuable learning tool available for independents, and a community of colleagues who will cheer your every success. Check the website for career information, publications, and information about the organization and its events.

Indexing Society of Canada (ISC)

www.indexers.ca/

Although the majority of its members specialize in indexing, ISC members also do "cataloguing, fact checking, glossary writing, HTML encoding, project management, teaching, thesaurus construction—and of course abstracting."

Patent Information Users Group (PIUG)

www.piug.org/

The organization for patent researchers, PIUG has "nearly 300 patent information professionals who do patent searching for corporations, over 100 patent information consultants, over 80 patent information professionals who do patent searching for law firms, and about 20 searchers based in academic institutions." This description provides a good indication of the diversity of patent research work, much of which is performed by independents.

Strategic and Competitive Intelligence Professionals (SCIP)
www.scip.org

Competitive intelligence (CI) is essentially researching what the competition is up to—a key element in business decision support. SCIP membership represents the very broad skills involved in CI, including LIS professionals, non-LIS business researchers, and subject specialists, among others. Members include independents as well as those employed by all types of organizations. Check the website under CI Resources for salary information, white papers, articles, career information, and several overviews of the CI process.

Print Resources

Periodicals

Connections
www.aiip.org

Connections is available to AIIP members only, but the current issue can be read by going to the AIIP website and selecting About > Newsletter. This will give you a good sense of current issues of interest to the membership. If you're an AIIP member, *Connections* is a wonderful source of insights from fellow independents.

eContent
www.econtentmag.com

From Information Today, Inc., *eContent* is a must-read for independents who focus on content development. Focusing on "the businesses of digital publishing, media, and marketing, targeting executives and decision-makers in these fast-changing markets," it's also a great resource for those whose clients include companies in these areas. Check the website for archived articles, resources, and the magazine's blog.

Entrepreneur
www.entrepreneur.com

This monthly magazine's coverage is often geared toward high-tech, high-money start-ups, but does regularly include articles on topics of interest to independents. The website has a wealth of resources on all phases of starting and running an entrepreneurial business (see especially the Guides section under the Startups tab).

Fast Company
www.fastcompany.com

Terrific resource for cutting-edge business trends and technology, innovative companies and thought leaders, and just way-cool ideas. Check out the blogs on the website for more in-depth stories and profiles.

Information Outlook
www.sla.org/content/Shop/Information/index.cfm

There's often substantial overlap between SLA members and independent information professionals, and that overlap shows up in many of the *Information Outlook* articles and profiles. Free to SLA members, this publication is a great resource on best practices for information pros.

Online
www.infotoday.com/online
Covers the information industry, its products and services, and current topics of interest to information professionals who rely to a substantial degree on online resources. See the website for articles from past issues and publication editor Marydee Ojala's *Online Insider* blog.

Searcher: The Magazine for Database Professionals
www.infotoday.com/searcher
The complement to *Online, Searcher*'s content is geared toward those who do professional-level database research. Coverage includes "online news, searching tips and techniques, reviews of search-aid software and database documentation," interviews with industry thought lead ers, and editorials. The website provides selective access to past issues' articles. A must-read for business researchers.

Books

**Awe, Susan C. *The Entrepreneur's Information Sourcebook: Charting the Path to Small Business Success,* 2nd ed. Libraries Unlimited, 2012. 285p. ISBN 9781598847864.
From University of New Mexico business librarian Susan Awe, this comprehensive resource presents knowledgeable overviews of key areas critical to starting a small-business start-up, followed by dozens of topic-related, annotated, print and online resources. An invaluable resource for those new to entrepreneurship, or to those already in business but needing some expert assistance.

**Bates, Mary Ellen. *Building & Running a Successful Research Business: A Guide for the Independent Information Professional,* 2nd ed. Information Today, 2010. 512p. ISBN 0910965854.
The must-read for those considering becoming an independent information professional. Bates walks readers through the entire range of issues related to starting, running, and growing the business, then provides a day-in-the-life scenario to give readers a detailed, realistic view of what the independent choice is likely to entail. Of value not only to those focusing on research businesses, but also to those considering any other type of independent information work.

**Beckwith, Harry. *Selling the Invisible: A Field Guide to Modern Marketing.* Business Plus, 1997. 272p. ISBN 0446520942.
A classic title on marketing services, although much has changed in what tools companies have at their disposal to communicate with potential clients. Beckwith has more recently published *You, Inc.: The Art of Selling Yourself,* based on the idea that (especially relevant to independent information professionals) clients of service companies are buying your brand and credibility as an indicator of the value of the professional services you provide.

**Blank, Steven Gary. *Four Steps to the Epiphany.* Cafepress.com, 2010. 275p. ISBN 0976470705.

Blank asserts that most start-ups have it backward: they come up with an idea for a product, sink a fortune into developing it, and then push their sales and marketing staff to convince the market to purchase that product. Instead, according to the author, companies should invest in market- and customer-development efforts before creating their product, to ensure that what they are creating is what people will find valuable. Common sense that is highly *uncommon* among most entrepreneurs, and an excellent read for anyone contemplating starting their own business.

de Stricker, Ulla. *Is Consulting for You? A Primer for Information Professionals.* ALA Editions, 2008. 101p. ISBN 0838909477.

This slim volume covers, in the author's words, "my experience in an effort to assist those considering a move into consulting. Covering the basics of setting up shop as well as typical project events and realities, I offer answers to questions I have often been asked: So what is it really like to be a consultant? What does it take? Is my personality suited?" de Stricker is well-known (and respected) among information professionals in Canada and the United States for her writings and seminars.

Edwards, Sarah and Paul Edwards. *The Secrets of Self-Employment: Surviving and Thriving on the Ups and Downs of Being Your Own Boss.* Putnam/Tarcher, 1996. 400p. ISBN 0874778379.

Sarah and Paul Edwards have been prolific authors of excellent books on working independently since the 1980s, and more than a decade later, even many of their earliest books still offer valuable insights. The authors are always enthusiastic, optimistic, and supportive, but also quite practical. This book was, of course, written before the arrival of many of the business and communications technologies we now take for granted, but like their other titles (*Getting Business to Come to You, Finding Your Perfect Work, On Your Own But Not Alone: The Small Business Guide to Collaborating with Others,* etc., all published by Tarcher) is nevertheless a useful and engaging resource for working as an independent.

**Fishman, Steven. *Working for Yourself: Law & Taxes for Independent Contractors, Freelancers & Consultants,* 8th ed. NOLO Press, 2011. 378p. ISBN 1413313310.

Fishman provides easily understood (and followed) advice for all manner of legal and tax issues related to working as an independent. His related NOLO Press title, *Deduct It! Lower Your Small Business Taxes,* 7th ed., points out that although if you're self-employed you get hit with a double-whammy on taxes, you're able to deduct many more business-expense items than most of us realize.

Halvorson, Kristina. *Content Strategy for the Web.* New Riders Press, 2009. 192p. ISBN 0321620062.

Halvorson, who's also the author of the popular Brain Traffic blog (www.braintraffic.com), has written perhaps the best overview of what content strategy is, its role in both web development and organizational strategy, and how to function effectively as a content strategist. An important resource for those independents considering content strategy and development as their business focus.

**Handley, Ann and C.C. Chapman. *Content Rules: How to Create Killer Blogs, Podcasts, Videos, Ebooks, Webinars (and More) That Engage Customers and Ignite Your Business.* Wiley, 2010. ISBN 0470648287.
Handley and Chapman's book has two aspects of value to information entrepreneurs. First, all of the types of content she discusses are excellent tools for marketing and promoting your business. Second, many of these can produce revenue streams as paid products in addition to your service offerings. Case studies provide further examples of the book's key concepts.

**Jantsch, John. *Duct Tape Marketing: The World's Most Practical Small Business Marketing Guide.* Thomas Nelson, 2011. 304p. ISBN 1595554653.
Jantsch, known as the Duct Tape Marketing Guy to his legions of blog and e-newsletter readers, here lays out the basics of small business marketing for those with little experience in this area. His previous work, *The Referral Engine: Teaching Your Business to Market Itself,* guides readers through the process of getting all-important word-of-mouth referrals from existing clients, the most valuable and cheapest type of marketing there is.

**Levinson, Jay Conrad. *Guerrilla Marketing: Easy and Inexpensive Strategies for Making Big Profits from Your Small Business,* 4th ed. Houghton Mifflin, 2007. 384p. ISBN 0618785914.
Levinson published the first edition of *Guerrilla Marketing* in 1984, and has been updating his concept of inexpensive marketing tactics for small businesses ever since. His basic premise: "Traditional marketing has always maintained that to market properly, you must invest money. *Guerrilla Marketing* maintains that if you want to invest money you can—*but you don't have to if you are willing to invest time, energy, imagination, and information.*" Also of interest from Levinson— *Guerrilla Marketing for Consultants: Breakthrough Tactics for Winning Profitable Clients,* although this work is focused more on large firms than on small, independent start-ups.

**Lewis, Laurie. *What to Charge: Pricing Strategies for Freelancers and Consultants,* 2nd ed. Outskirts Press, 2011. 186p. ISBN 143276764X.
A practical, realistic guide to effective pricing strategies. Topics include methods of pricing, task-based logs for record-keeping, identifying typical fees, gathering the information necessary to set an appropriate fee, negotiating, and how to raise fees, among others. Especially valuable to those new to freelance, contract, or consulting work.

**Phelps, Marcy. *Research on Main Street: Using the Web to Find Local Business and Market Information.* CyberAge Books, 2011. 254p. ISBN 9780910965880.
A key aspect of local business development is understanding the business and market information available to help local companies succeed.

Research on Main Street provides an overview of those resources, indicates how they are most effectively used, and presents case studies to demonstrate how local research information can be used to help local businesses, employment levels, and communities grow. In addition, the book can be used as a helpful guide for out-of-state companies exploring new geographic markets and business locations.

Start Your Own Business: The Only Start-Up Book You'll Ever Need, 5th ed. Entrepreneur Press, 2010. 704p. ISBN 1599183870.
The fifth edition of *Start Your Own Business* continues the strengths of previous editions. Under the broad topics of thinking about becoming an entrepreneur and what business you might start, planning, funding, preparing, buying (equipment for your business), marketing, and finances ("Profits"), it covers the basics in detail—rounded out with a list of business and government resources and a glossary. Although intended more for those planning to establish businesses that will include employees, this book nevertheless provides solid guidance for your own start-up.

**Weiss, Alan. *Value-Based Fees: How to Charge—and Get—What You're Worth,* 2nd ed. Pfeiffer, 2008. 288p. ISBN 0470275847.
Weiss's books (*Million Dollar Consulting, How to Establish a Unique Brand in the Consulting Profession, Getting Started in Consulting,* 2nd ed., etc.) are the go-to sources for independents wrestling with the trickiest issues of consulting. *Value-Based Fees* provides both conceptual frameworks for pricing decisions and the tactics for establishing and sticking with those fees. Since establishing fees (and confidently stating them) is often a challenge for independent information professionals, Weiss's guidance here is especially valuable.

Online Resources

About.com: Entrepreneurs
http://entrepreneurs.about.com/
An extremely content-rich resource with current articles on all aspects of entrepreneurship. See especially its articles on using social media, search engine optimization (SEO), and other cutting-edge approaches to marketing.

Adding Value—The Business of Independent Information Professionals
www.asist.org/Bulletin/Oct-10/Bulletin_OctNov10_Final.pdf
The October/November 2010 issue of the *Bulletin of the American Society for Information Science and Technology,* this special section is devoted to seventeen articles written by well-known leaders among independent information professionals. A terrific, wide-ranging overview of what independents do, and the value they provide their clients.

**Elance.com
www.elance.com
One of many websites that exist to broker freelance, contract, or project work, usually in specific skill areas. Elance, for example, focuses

on programmers, designers, writers, marketers, admins, consultants, and finance people. Similar sites are MediaBistro.com, Freelance Writing.com, Freelance Switch's Monster List of Freelance Job Sites— 2009 Update (http://freelanceswitch.com/finding/the-monster-list-of-freelance-job-sites-2009-update/), and Sologig.com's primarily IT and web-development jobs. Don't forget to also check the major general job sites and LIS job sites, including the words freelance, contract, project, or consulting in your job search.

Frequently Asked Questions about Information Brokering
www.marketingbase.com/faqs.html
From well-known information entrepreneur, teacher, and business coach Amelia Kassel, the site provides a quick overview of the most pressing questions for those contemplating becoming an information broker. Topics include the market for info brokers, skills, and attitudes needed, typical services offered, and working as a part-time info broker, among others.

The Independent Info Pro Business (a.k.a. Information Brokering)
www.batesinfo.com/info-brokering.html
Mary Ellen Bates is one of the most respected independent information professionals, and this resource aggregates links to key resources she has compiled on life as an information broker. At the website see also her archived tips of the month, which provide an ongoing heads-up about new search tools, research tips, and emerging issues of interest to independent information professionals, as well as her Librarian of Fortune blog (www.batesinfo.com/Writing/Writing/LOFblog.html).

**LAC Group
http://lac-group.com
One of the largest and best-known companies offering LIS project work of all types and durations, LAC (formerly Library Associates) offers a wide range of short-term and long-term contracts as well as permanent placements.

**Should You Be an Entrepreneur? Take This Test
http://blogs.hbr.org/cs/2010/02/should_you_be_an_entrepreneur.html
Harvard Business Review blog written by Daniel Isenberg, Harvard Professor of Management Practice, and an expert on entrepreneurship. His premise is that "there is a gut level 'fit' for people who are potential entrepreneurs," and his 2-minute, 20-question Isenberg Entrepreneur Test will help you determine what your gut's trying to tell you.

**Simply Hired
www.simplyhired.com
Aggregates more than 5 million job postings from across the web. Search by keyword and location, or browse by categories such as biotech/science, legal/paralegal, computer/technology, health care/nursing, part-time/temporary, and entry level/internships, among others.

For project work, use keywords such as freelance, contract, project, and similar terms.

SmartBrief on Entrepreneurs

www.smartbrief.com/news/entrepreneurs

One of the very useful SmartBrief products, this daily e-mail newsletter brings together best-in-class articles on entrepreneurship from around the web. It's a quick read and often delivers valuable insights, as well as leading you to entrepreneurship resources and thought leaders you may want to explore in more depth.

"Value-Added Deliverables: Rungs on the Info Pro's Ladder to Success"

www.infotoday.com/searcher/nov02/kassel.htm

From the November/December 2002 issue of *Searcher* magazine, 10 years later this article by industry leader Amelia Kassel is still an excellent introduction to this important topic. The focus is on making sure that what you're delivering is not data, but the analysis and synthesis that together translate into decision support.

What Is an Independent Information Professional?

www.aiip.org/WhatIsAnIndependentInfoPro

A highly useful collection of articles related to becoming an independent information professional. The article aggregation has been designed to help you understand more about the profession and how to get started in it. (See also the Just Getting Started section.) Members also have access to a broad range of additional business resources and insights through the AIIP discussion list.

Training and Coaching

Business Coaching for Info-Entrepreneurs

www.batesinfo.com/Coaching/CoachingMenu.html

Bates is well-known as an engaging and informative conference presenter, a highly successful information entrepreneur, and the author of the second edition of the popular and authoritative *Building and Running a Successful Research Business: A Guide for the Independent Information Professiona*. She also provides one-on-one business coaching for individuals who are either just starting their business or are wanting to grow an existing business to a new level.

Information Broker Mentor Program

www.marketingbase.com/mentor.html

From well-known and highly respected teacher and business coach Amelia Kassel, this one-on-one mentoring program covers the basics for getting started as an information broker (including how to use the key business research databases), coaches you through the start-up phase, helps you map out marketing strategies, and in general increases your odds of turning your business dreams into reality.

11
Transition Points: Finding Opportunity in Change

Chapter Highlights

- Taking a Career Time-out

- Relocating Your Career

- Moving into a New LIS Career Opportunity or Industry

- When Your Career Change Is a Layoff

- Retiring—or Not

- Exploring New Directions

Careers, like lives, are made up of many transition points—some of which can be anticipated, others sought out. But one of the great things about an LIS career is that with a bit of thoughtful strategizing and research, pretty much all of those transitions can be managed in a way that helps you create the career you aspire to.

The key to making the most of these transitions: assume that change is your friend. In fact, as you move through your career, you'll find that change, though often disruptive, can also be the source of wonderful new opportunities for you. Whether the change is driven by your employer, new commitments in your personal life, or simply changes in your individual career aspirations, it's up to you to determine (and drive) the outcomes of those changes in your career.

Taking a Career Time-out

Perhaps you've decided to stay home to spend more time with your young children for several years. Or your elderly parents are beginning to need more attention from you and it's compromising your ability to work full-time. Or you've had a major health setback, and recovery is likely to sideline you for a substantial period of time.

A career time-out doesn't necessarily have to mean career derailment. By staying professionally engaged and connected, you'll be able to keep doors open for you when you're ready to return. Happily, there are a number of terrific articles on how to handle these types of career challenges; one of the best sources is the Career Q&A with the Library Career People from LISjobs.com. See for example, "How Do I Get Back into the Workforce after an Illness, and Being a Stay-At-Home Parent," "How Do I Get My Career Back On Track after Staying Home for Two Years to Raise a Family," and "How Do I Go about Re-Entering the Workforce (Part-Time) After Taking Five Years Off," all timeless pieces with good advice. Another resource (with a strong corporate focus) is *Back on the Career Track: A Guide for Stay-at-Home Moms Who Want to Return to Work* by Carol Fishman Cohen and Vivian Steir Rabin. Although as the title makes clear, the specific life circumstance they address is moms who have chosen to take a career time-out, their "seven steps to relaunch success" can be equally valuable for dads in the same situation, or others who have stepped out of their careers for other reasons.

Regardless of your reasons for stepping away from your career, there are some basic steps that will keep you professionally viable.

Stay Professionally Visible

Attend conferences if you can (especially local/regional ones) and the meetings of the local chapters of your professional associations. Serve on virtual committees if possible to keep up your national visibility.

Maintain Your Professional Memberships

These are your key to maintaining your network, staying current with issues and emerging trends in your field, and finding potential volunteer opportunities that will signal your ongoing career engagement.

Do Occasional Projects If You Can

Are you a timing-out researcher? Cataloger? Information architect? Whatever your information skill, consider undertaking occasional research (fee-based or volunteer) projects. This offers multiple benefits: you'll be able to point to professional-level work when speaking with an interviewer, you'll keep your confidence level up, and you'll be continuing to build your professional network and career brand.

Stay Current with Industry Trends and Issues

Set aside a regular time to read about what's going on in your field. Whether print or online, there are dozens of resources available to help you stay abreast of your professional discipline and maintain your understanding of changes that impact how you will work.

Take Courses to Maintain the Currency of Your Existing Skills or Expand Your Value with New Skills

Check out the resources identified in Chapter 5, "Professional Development," for the easiest (and least expensive) ways to accomplish this, then make sure you add the information about your coursework to your LinkedIn profile.

Your goal is to devote just a small, but consistent, amount of time to keeping your career active so that when you *do* decide to return to the workplace, you won't have lost all that professional equity you'd built up before you stepped out.

Relocating Your Career

Planning to uproot yourself—and your career—and move to a new community? In Quintessentials Careers' "New City, New Job: How to Conduct a Long Distance Job Search," authors Katharine and Randall Hansen make the point that if you're contemplating a move to an unfamiliar city, it's important to "learn as much as you can about the city to which you wish to relocate, if for no other reason than to make sure that's where you really want to be." Clearly, part of that determination is whether or not you're likely to be able to find a job there.

Steps you can take to lay the groundwork for finding a new position in your target destination well before you land in town include the following.

Start Establishing Local Connections

There are a number of ways to start making local connections. For example, join the state library association (for the relevant state association's contact information, see ALA's State and Regional Chapters page, which also includes listings for all state library associations) as well as the local chapter of your professional associations (check the associations' websites for regional chapter information). Check out their membership lists to see whether there are individuals who may be in positions helpful to your job search. These will provide the beginnings of your local network. Also, if your MLIS program has an alumni group, check for any fellow graduates from you program in your target community.

Explore Potential Opportunities through Your Online Networks

Consider especially how LinkedIn can help you locate connections for your anticipated move (see LinkedIn's "Job Seekers" guide for in-depth information on how to make the most of this tool) in both your own network and those of your connections. Also consider your Facebook and Twitter feeds as sources of job leads and related information for your target location. Let everyone in your network know about your career relocation plans in case they have contacts they can connect you with.

See Who's Hiring—and for What

Again, LinkedIn provides a fairly easy way to identify and explore companies in your target location, see what potentially interesting jobs they may have open, and then sign up to follow developments at these companies. Create a target list of all potential employers, keeping in mind that you probably want to think as broadly as possible (traditional and nontraditional) when considering potential LIS jobs. But also check the state library and association job lists for your target locations, and set up alerts if possible.

Do Some Informational Interviews

In "What is an Informational Interview and How it Can Help Your Career," About.com career guide Alison Doyle makes the point that "skillfully used, an informational interview is one of the most valuable sources of occupational information." They become even more valuable when you are trying to gather information from afar. These can be with people you've met (even if virtually) through your work establishing local connections, via your online networking efforts, or directly with the hiring managers of organizations that interest you. Your goal may be to unearth information about the local job market, major local industries or employers, or specific job opportunities—but regardless of your specific purposes, informational interviews are one of the most effective ways to get up to speed quickly.

Consider Applying for Jobs before You Arrive

If you find a job opening of interest, why not go ahead and apply for it? Let potential employers know when you'll be available, and that you're willing to come for an interview on your own nickel (if the job is worth it). Even if you don't get the job, you will have started your job-hunting process. Also, if you arrive in your new location without a job in hand, seriously consider the benefits of doing LIS temp or contract work as a way of meeting local people in the profession, getting to know the local employers, and starting to build your professional visibility.

Moving into a New LIS Career Opportunity or Industry

Two types of career transition include a career change (recareering) or a career extension. A career change means starting over from scratch in a career unrelated to the one you've been engaged in previously—think going from neurosurgeon to organic peach farmer. You've got to learn new skills, understand a new operating universe or profession, and essentially build your brand, connections, and professional reputation again from scratch.

A career extension, however, is a much likelier scenario for many of us given the, ah, iffy economy—an economy as devastating for librarians as it has been for auto workers, journalists, and mortgage brokers. A career extension involves identifying your current career strengths—what you know, who you know, what you are known for—and extending that professional equity into a related field where those strengths will still be recognized and respected.

Although there are, of course, considerations specific to each industry (and for our purposes here, I consider academia to be an industry), there are some basic principles that can be applied across all industries and over a lifetime of career changes. These principles fall into the areas of

- identifying transferable business skills,
- developing an in-depth understanding of your target industry, and
- building professional connections/bridges to potential employers/opportunities.

Identifying Transferable Skills

The basis of career extension is transferable skills—those skills you possess that can be equally valuable in environments, organizations, or situations other than traditional or special librarianship. The closer those environments, organizations, and/or situations are to your home base (i.e., traditional or special librarianship), the more likely that your strengths will be valued, and that you will be compensated commensurately. Essentially, in a career change, you're starting from scratch and paying dues all over again; in a career extension, you're making a lateral move that keeps you at least somewhere in the same spot in terms of recognized expertise.

How to get started identifying your transferable skills? A good introduction is "Transferable Skills: Bringing Your Skills to a New Career," an About. com Career Planning article that, in addition to its overview of transferable skills, also provides a transferable skills worksheet and examples of transferable skills. For an LIS-specific approach, however, consider "Attention New Librarians and Career Changers: Identifying and Conveying Transferable Skills," an ALA-APA *Library Worklife* article by Julie Todaro, as well as the articles that come up on a search for transferable skills on the *Career Q&A with the Library Career People* site. And for those who thrive on Richard Bolles's eclectic approach to career design, check out Chapter IV, "Inventory of What You Have to Offer the World," of *What Color is Your Parachute: A Practical Manual for Job-Hunters and Career-Changers* for ways to approach this.

Getting ready for a career transition usually entails first identifying your marketable, transferable skills—which include your LIS-specific skills (e.g., metadata specialist, tech services manager, reference librarian), your business skills (supervisory experience, budgeting expertise, project management experience), and your professional strengths (leadership skills, strong interpersonal communications, innovative thinker, etc.).

So start by looking at your resume and seeing what you want to highlight for a potential new employer/position. And if you don't feel you have any transferable skills, now is the time to start working on them by asking for new assignments, volunteering for cool projects, and/or picking up some classes in key business skills. Another alternative is to get some coaching from friendly coworkers who have skills that you lack.

Developing an In-depth Understanding of Your Target Industry

This involves understanding

- what aspect of a new industry you want to work in (for example, in the health care industry, do you want to work for a hospital library, pharmaceutical company, nonprofit health care organization, etc.);
- what type of work you want to do within your target area, and where the job openings are/might be;
- the key information resources for your target area—print and online, mainstream (e.g., *New England Journal of Medicine, CableWorld, Chronicle of Higher Education*) and alternative (key blogs, etc), government and association;
- what the type of work you'd like to be doing requires in terms of skills/expertise; and
- what professional organizations exist for the type of work you'd like to do (for example, the Medical Libraries Association, Society of Competitive Intelligence, Art Libraries Society of North America).

Your goal in doing this will be to both understand what the opportunities may look like (and how your current skill set aligns with potential job openings) and how you will quickly develop the professional knowledge base you need to hit the ground running in a new position. This means understanding the industry, its issues, opportunities, and threats; understanding the company and its market/constituency; and understanding what skills you'll need to bring to potential jobs.

Where to find industry information? As noted in Chapter 3, some of the best resources are the *Plunkett's* publications, *Hoover's* database, annual trend and forecast issues for the major trade publications, the Bureau of Labor Statistics' *Industries at a Glance* overviews, and the relevant professional associations (findable through either an online search on your key terms or, if you have access to them, Gage/Cengage's comprehensive tools, *Encyclopedia of Associations* [print version] or the associations component of the online resource, *Gale Directory Library.*)

Building Professional Bridges to Potential Opportunities

After many years in one industry, you undoubtedly have tons of connections among other LIS colleagues in that industry—now your goal is to develop a similar set of connections in your new industry (or the part of it within which you want to work).

For example, for a switch to the health care industry, this could involve volunteering for work in a hospital library, joining MLA, networking with the medical/health care librarians in your local SLA chapter, and so on. These contacts will not only be able to help you identify where the jobs are but also coach you on expectations/requirements for various types of jobs, and possibly pass along insider tips about various employers and company environments.

After having completed the above three steps, you're then ready to check to see how your skills line up with the job requirements of various positions, and identify what, if any, further education/training you'll need to be competitive.

Following through with the health care industry example, that may mean taking a course in bioinformatics, or studying medical terminology and the MeSH system, or learning how to search PubMed effectively. Assume that you'll likely need to pick up at least *some* industry-related knowledge before you start applying for your new jobs—the more you have, the more confidence potential employers will have in your ability to transition into a new industry (i.e., theirs!).

Making the Leap

Consider these the basics for undertaking a major career transition. Yep, it takes some work, but it can be a very wise investment of your time if your current employer is in an industry beginning to contract. Similarly, if an early career opportunity took you in one direction and now you're ready to switch to a potentially more rewarding path, doing just this basic due diligence will raise the odds of making that leap successfully.

When Your Career Change Is a Layoff

Transitions are a lot easier to deal with positively when you're the one in charge of that change, but what if you're laid off? Although all those options outlined above are still in play, it may take some time before you're emotionally ready to pursue or embrace them. A great resource to help you deal with the emotional and practical aspects of being laid off is Martha I. Finney's *Rebound: A Proven Plan for Starting Over After Job Loss,* which acknowledges and addresses the reality of emotions such as bewilderment, a crisis in self-worth, and a sense of alienation and isolation, then moves on to specific strategies for moving forward.

Another useful resource, written specifically for LIS professionals, is Oliver Cutshaw's pragmatic, straight-from-the-heart guide, *Recovery, Reframing and Renewal: Surviving an Information Science Career Crisis in a Time of Change.* Formerly a librarian in the Conservation Services Department of Harvard University's Widener Library, Cutshaw left that job due to family issues and moved to California, where he then experienced a career crisis when he was unable to get a similar job in his new location. Although Cutshaw didn't experience a layoff, his subsequent job-hunting challenges entailed a similar sense of loss when he found himself forced to reframe his professional assumptions and renew his career in a new direction.

Although job-hunting strategies and tactics are covered in more detail in Chapter 3, it helps to know that the emotional blowback from a layoff is both real and pretty much universal. In fact, notes Dawn Rosenberg McKay in "Job Loss: How to Cope," job loss "can have a profound effect on your emotional well being. Most people experience a typical cycle. This cycle includes denial, anger, frustration, and eventually adaptation." To help you move beyond the loss and into the positive frame of mind you'll need to jumpstart your job search, consider the insights of a resource like Michael Froehls's *The Gift of Job Loss—A Practical Guide to Realizing the Most Rewarding Time of Your Life,* which focuses on using a job loss as a time for reflection and renewal. Another supportive resource is *Career Comeback: Eight Steps to Getting Back on Your Feet When You're Fired, Laid Off, or Your Business Venture has Failed—And Finding More Job Satisfaction Than Ever Before,* by Bradley Richardson, which suggests techniques for recovering from the shock of being laid off, learning whatever lessons you can, and finding solid emotional ground for restarting your career.

In the meantime, keep in mind that this is the time it's really, really important to be good to yourself. Soon you'll be doing the challenging work necessary for finding your next job, but for now, let yourself experience the full range of negative emotions you'll need to process while also spending time and energy doing things you enjoy. Go to the movies, read that book you've been putting off, hang out with friends who support you and make you laugh (and graciously let them pay for the pizza). Know that getting laid off is just one blip in your career (some of us, in fact, have gone through it multiple times), and learning how to deal with it in a way that's best for you will help you build your professional independence.

Retiring—Or Not

So, is the profession *really* going to be seeing a wave of retirements in the coming years? Well, since this prediction has been kicking around for roughly 20 years, it's likely that by now, retirement may actually be in the futures of some LIS professionals. The question is, what will that retirement look like? What will it look like for the retirees, and what will it look like for the profession?

Some trends are becoming clearer. One is the tendency for LIS professionals to continue to stay connected to their organizations and colleagues.

Leading LIS associations are establishing retired-member groups that enable their members to stay connected as well as providing opportunities for them to continue to contribute. Some of the association responses include ALA's *Retired Members Round Table,* SLA's *Encore—Retired Members Caucus,* the *US Military Librarians-Retired* and *US Navy Librarians-Retired* groups, and the *Medical Library Association's Retired Librarians Special Interest Group.* Retired members may end up in mentoring roles, taking on some of the associations' more time-consuming volunteer roles, or simply enjoying the friendship of colleagues.

Other professionals are considering redeploying their skills into second careers based on the knowledge and professional equity they've built up over the years. This may be the time to start that small consulting business, set up to do independent project work, or start sharing your skills as adjunct faculty for one of the LIS programs (or perhaps a local community college). Alternatively, you may consider moving into a part-time role at your current employer, which has the benefit of allowing them to continue to benefit from your knowledge and experience while also opening up a position for a new (and probably less highly paid) employee. Others are considering following entirely new dreams. (Happily, our information skills give us a substantial advantage when it comes to exploring new options.)

The great news here is that the entire concept of retirement is in flux—which means you can pretty much make it up as you go along. Naturally, publishers have recognized this as a terrific market opportunity, so you have a wealth of helpful resources to jumpstart your thinking about possibilities.

For exploring your own approach to structuring your retirement career options, consider David Corbett's *Portfolio Life: The New Path to Work, Purpose, and Passion after 50.* His basic premise:

> The central idea behind [a life portfolio] is to step back and—using a step-by-step process—create a balanced combination of five elements: (1) working in the form you want, (2) learning and self-development, (3) making time for personal pursuits and recreation, (4) enjoying family and friends, and (5) giving back to society. The combination of elements, or portfolio, is meant to reflect who you are and what you care about. (2)

Another good resource is Marc Freedman's *Encore: Finding Work that Matters in the Second Half of Life,* which focuses more on the contribution one can make via second-half work choices than on the income one can earn. (Needless to say, this is a message that will resonate most strongly with those not struggling financially postretirement.) Those who've enjoyed dipping into the various editions of the *What Color is Your Parachute* books over the course of their career will also want to check out John Nelson and Richard Bolles's contribution to retirement and careers, the second edition of *What Color is Your Parachute? For Retirement: Planning a Prosperous, Healthy, and Happy Future.*

What if you're one of the more, ah, seasoned professionals in your organization, however, but retirement is still a ways off for you? Then you'll want to make sure that you're making every effort to be a positive, high-value contributor. Consider the following attitudes and actions to keep you on track.

Understand the Strategic Benefit of Change

Okay, by now you know that change equals opportunity. But often the older we get, the more we feel like we're ready to slow down the rate of change a bit, thank you very much. The comfort of familiarity may seem to be a lot more appealing to you than it used to be. In that case, try instead to focus on creating that familiarity and stability in other areas of your life so you can more easily embrace change in your career.

Know That Your Initial Reaction's Likely to Be No, Then Put It Aside and Move on to Yes

It's pretty much human nature to resist change, and this tendency tends to rise in sync with our age. So similar to the idea "feel the fear but do it anyway," how about going with "know you'll be ticked off, then get over it and get moving." That way you don't waste time or energy on trying to fight your initial responses, and can instead focus on improving your subsequent actions.

Seek Out Opportunities to Learn and Use New Technologies

As part of the generation that didn't grow up with technology, every new communication or IT tech seems to speak a foreign language for many of us. Letting ourselves avoid using these tools means that we won't understand what they can do. As a result, we won't be able to contribute ideas, strategies, or solutions, and what fun would that be?

Look for Mentors in All the Right Places

That's probably going to be your younger staffers, or people in other departments, or possibly someone you heard speak at a recent conference. When most of us were younger and just starting out, our mentors were people older and more experienced than us. Now that we're the older and more experienced team members, we shouldn't hesitate to seek out anyone who knows about the stuff we want to learn more about: technology, social media, popular culture, social entrepreneurship, organic gardening, and so on. Depending on where you are in your career, these mentors may be 10, 20, or 30 years your junior. Feels a bit strange, but it can also be a lot of fun!

Keep a Sense of Humor

Okay, we've all probably socially humiliated ourselves on LinkedIn and Twitter a number of times as we've attempted to master these tools, and we're probably going to do it several more times (at least) in the foreseeable future. We can either be mortified (which will cause us to avoid trying again) or entertain our colleagues with stories of our social faux pas and keep at it. A sense of humor is a great tool for keeping both humiliation and our egos at bay.

Avoid Being Known as Ms./Mr. Cranky

The other great thing about hanging on to your sense of humor is that it allows you to avoid being known as The Cranky One. The reality is that it gets really easy to move into this persona as you get older and more set in your ways. But it's important to be positive and optimistic if you want people to look forward to working with you instead of dismissing you as a negative and obstructionist old geezer.

Stay Connected to Your Passionate Curiosity

In *The Corner Office: Indispensable and Unexpected Lessons from CEOs on How to Lead and Succeed,* author Adam Bryant makes the point that all the CEOs he interviewed had what he would describe as passionate curiosity. Although few of us are seeking to be the CEOs of our organizations, that doesn't mean that we can't bring a passionate curiosity to our jobs regardless of how long we've been in the workforce. Passionate curiosity and the energy and engagement that come with it are key to continuing to add value to your organization.

Will these attitudes and actions enable us to continue to enjoy our careers, contribute at a high level, and remain gainfully employed over the next however-many years of our careers? No guarantees. But it's pretty certain that if we *don't* actively seek to avoid the pitfalls of aging into obsolescence, our value will diminish like yesterday's hot stock.

Exploring New Directions

Not only can an LIS career allow you to create your own path, it can also enable you to pretty much endlessly take that career onto new paths as your life circumstances dictate. Many of the resources noted in previous chapters can help you learn more about different LIS career paths or roles (for example, management or leadership), but it's also a good idea to explore a bit *internally* as well when you're considering career transitions.

For example, what is your definition of success? Is it a higher salary, increasing levels of responsibility, the respect and recognition of your peers? Or perhaps it's the freedom to pursue whatever projects you find personally rewarding, or the ability to have substantial impact on peoples' lives. Maybe it's creating a career path that will enable you to remain professionally active (and revenue-producing) well past the traditional retirement age. Happily, there is a wealth of helpful resources to help you explore your best career, or career trajectory. One of the classic works with more of a spiritual approach is Gregg Levoy's *Callings: Finding and Following an Authentic Life* (favorite quote: "Whenever I assumed an angle of repose and attempted to quiet my mind, or understand how it worked, I immediately noticed how much it behaved like a roomful of toddlers.") Levoy frames the concept of an authentic career (i.e., one reflective of your true values and passions) within the challenges of not only recognizing that path, but also accepting the changes that it may require you to make.

Zen and the Art of Making a Living: A Practical Guide to Creative Career Design by Laurence G. Boldt, on the other hand, focuses on practical assessments, dozens of checklists, and detailed overviews of various approaches to one's life's work (corporate, entrepreneurship, freelance, nonprofit, etc.). One of the most interesting aspects of this title (besides its wealth of killer quotes) is that although it's a very wild-ranging exploration of potential life work paths, it's also highly relevant to the types of opportunities found among LIS careers.

Another excellent resource is *Get a Life, Not a Job: Do What You Love and Let Your Talents Work for You.* Author Paula Caligiuri lays out in her introduction a description that could easily apply to LIS professionals and the wide range of career options open to them:

> People who enjoy what they do for a living tend to own their careers in the sense that they themselves have planned, developed, and shifted their focus to create the stimulating, secure, and balanced work situations they desire. They craft the career acts they like the best, over time. They also have tailored for themselves a sense of financial security by knowing that if one aspect of their career is losing steam (or interest) other career acts can provide a safety net. (p. 5)

If you're an LIS professional—or contemplating becoming one—you'll find that it's a field whose potential career acts are to a great degree limited only by your willingness to create or go after them. They may be in the traditional areas of school, public, or academic librarianship or in any of the hundreds of other LIS-related career paths. You might decide to move from one type of traditional library, for example, an academic library, into another traditional but different library environment—perhaps a public library. You might decide to move from a corporate library job into an information role with a nonprofit. Or you might decide to take a traditional skill such as cataloging and expand your expertise into one of the emerging fields such as digital asset management. Or perhaps you'll at some point consider a path with more flexibility, for example, independent work, to enable you to fulfill a career goal or simply better deal with your personal circumstances.

Alternatively, if you enjoy multitasking, one of your potential new career options might actually be to pursue several directions at the same time. You might want to move from a full-time to a part-time position, write a book on a topic of interest to you, do some contract projects on the side, and/or perhaps do some adjunct teaching for the local MLIS program. These are all activities that you could sequence, or do one after the other, over the course of your career, *or* you could combine them into a blended career, where you had multiple income streams based on your multiple interests and skill sets.

Most of our careers follow paths of opportunity, especially starting out; but one of the joys of a long LIS career is that as you build professional equity, you start being able to create your own opportunities. Understanding your own definition of success will help guide you to the right choices—the ones that help you create your best career, and your best life.

Resources

Starred titles are mentioned in the chapter.

Associations

**Encore—Retired Members Caucus / SLA
http://encore.sla.org/
Encore's goal is to engage SLA members who are thinking about retirement, going through retirement, or who have retired to share their knowledge in order "to guide each other and continue providing leadership to SLA." See especially the Encore Mind Map put together by the DC SLA Encore Group.

Placement and Executive Search Firms / SLA
www.sla.org/content/resources/inforesour/reftool/placement.cfm
A list of two dozen North American and UK recruiting firms with descriptions of their key focus areas.

**Retired Librarians Special Interest Group / Medical Library Association
http://retiredlib.mlanet.org/
Intent is to be a "continuing resource for the next generation of medical librarians, and maintain ties with . . . colleagues formed over decades of managing medical libraries."

**Retired Members Round Table (RMRT) / ALA
www.ala.org/ala/membership/whoisala/retired/index.cfm
RMRT was created to provide a community, forum, and means for continued professional engagement for retired or soon-to-retire ALA members. Focus is on "maintaining networking relationships among persons either retired or in late career stages, on continuing professional and personal development focused on the unique interests of those persons, and on utilizing the unique skills and knowledge of long-time members for mentoring and membership development."

**State and Regional Chapters / ALA
www.ala.org/ala/mgrps/affiliates/chapters/state/stateregional.cfm
A listing and description of both state ALA chapters and state library associations, with contact information for each.

**U.S. Military Librarians Retired
www.facebook.com/home.php?#/pages/ Washington-DC/United-States-Military-Librarians-Retired/105040833894
Gathering spot for retired U.S. military librarians, where retired members can share photos, updates, and information.

**U.S. Navy Librarians Retired
www.facebook.com/pages/edit/?id=121903220420#/pages/Washington-DC/US-Navy-General-Library-Program/121903220420
Gathering spot for retired U.S. Navy librarians, where, similar to the Military Librarians group, retired members can share photos, updates, and information.

Print Resources

Beck, Martha. *Finding Your Own North Star: Claiming the Life You Were Meant to Live.* Three Rivers Press, 2001. 380p. ISBN 9780812932188.
A life coach, Beck went through her own struggle to find her path, and her guidance is informed by the lessons she learned as well as the insights she has gained from her clients. A key resource for identifying, describing, and nurturing your dreams, whether personal or professional.

**Boldt, Lawrence G. *Zen and the Art of Making a Living: A Practical Guide to Creative Career Design.* Penguin, 2009. 608p. ISBN 014311459X.
In addition to its wealth of really cool quotes, *Zen* provides a fascinating journey for readers through the art of life's work, the quest for life's work, the game of life's work, the battle for life's work, and the school of life's work. Packed with checklists, guidelines, graphics, and other supplementary materials that turn this book into a true career exploration at a deeply personal level.

**Bolles, Richard. *What Color is Your Parachute: A Practical Manual for Job-Hunters and Career-Changers.* Ten Speed Press, 2011. 384p. ISBN 1607740109.
The 40th edition of the classic work on job and career exploration, with sections on attitudes, advanced job-hunting techniques, job-creation techniques, self-inventory, and additional career-guidance pink pages. Creative, engaging, and insightful.

**Bryant, Adam. *The Corner Office: Indispensable and Unexpected Lessons from CEOs on How to Lead and Succeed.* 272p. Times Books, 2011. 272p. ISBN 0805093060.
Bryant (who writes the Corner Office column for the Sunday *New York Times* Business section) interviewed more than 75 business CEOs and executives from businesses large, small, and in between to create a collection of best-in-class advice on organizational leadership. The interviews are engagingly written, conversational, and packed with lessons learned. Notes Bryant: "The qualities these executives share: Passionate curiosity. Battle-hardened confidence. Team smarts. A simple mindset. Fearlessness."

**Caligiuri, Paula. *Get a Life, Not a Job: Do What You Love and Let Your Talents Work for You.* FT Press, 2010. 208p. ISBN 0137058497.
The author's main premise is that only by creating and structuring your work engagements to support the type of lifestyle you'd like to have will you have a truly fulfilling life. She encourages readers to explore what

motivates them, helps them develop the skills they need to pursue their paths, and provides practical coaching on how to integrate your best work with your best life.

**Cohen, Carol Fishman and Vivian Steir Rabin. *Back on the Career Track: A Guide for Stay-at-Home Moms Who Want to Return to Work.* CreateSpace, 2008. 320p. ISBN 1463785925.
Built around the concept of career relaunch, *Back on the Career Track* lays out the seven steps to relaunching your career, followed by stories of moms who have successfully restarted their careers. Includes resources, recommended books, and sample resumes of relaunchers.

**Corbett, David D. *Portfolio Life: The New Path to Work, Purpose, and Passion after 50.* Jossey-Bass, 2006. 208p. ISBN 078798356X.
Corbett's portfolio life integrates two concepts—(1) you can create a life uniquely tailored to your values and passions and (2) this is most easily accomplished during your retirement years. He strongly emphasizes the role lifelong learning plays in your ability to create your own portfolio life.

**Cutshaw, Oliver. *Recovery, Reframing and Renewal: Surviving an Information Science Career Crisis in a Time of Change.* Chandos Publishing, 2011. 200p. ISBN 184334632X.
How do you restart your LIS career after a major disruption? Cutshaw experienced this challenge first-hand, and his book reflects very pragmatic been there, done that advice about how to recover your emotional equilibrium, reframe your thinking about your skills and what you can do with them, and then create a new or renewed LIS career path. An encouraging and helpful book for those questioning their career options.

**Finney, Martha I. *Rebound: A Proven Plan for Starting Over After Job Loss.* FT Press, 2009. 187p. ISBN 0137021143.
Although this book would indicate the audience is those who've already lost their jobs, in fact it leads off with tactics to prepare for a job loss, followed by what to do if/when you've lost your job. Solid advice for those who are too traumatized by the prospect (or actuality) of job loss to think through these steps for themselves.

**Freedman, Marc. *Encore: Finding Work that Matters in the Second Half of Life.* PublicAffairs, 2008. 272p. ISBN 1586486349.
Encore makes the case for changing the concept of retirement from one of no work to one of less, but more rewarding, work. Freedman himself is strongly focused on civic ventures, but his basic premise can be applied across a multitude of work environments, including self-employment, part-time LIS work, or careers blending multiple paths. Although Freedman emphasizes the emotional rewards of doing meaningful work, that doesn't necessarily preclude financial rewards as well.

**Froehls, Michael. *The Gift of Job Loss—A Practical Guide to Realizing the Most Rewarding Time of Your Life.* Peitho Publishing, 2011. 194p. ISBN 0983119201.

One of the challenges of being in between jobs is that it would be a great time to pursue some of those things you've put off doing if only you weren't so crazed about finding a new job! Froehls recognizes this issue, but suggests that you can still use your unemployed time both enjoyably and strategically to develop new skills, new connections, and a broader sense of your opportunities. Although most of us would be uncomfortable spending savings for things like travel during a period of unemployment (as Froehls did), he still provides many good (and inexpensive) ways to make the best use of this time.

Helgesen, Sally. *Thriving in 24/7: Six Strategies for Taming the New World of Work.* Free Press, 2001. 258p. ISBN 0684873036.
Helgesen first gained fame with her landmark book *The Female Advantage: Women's Ways of Leadership* (1995; see Resources, Chapter 9). In this book, she looks at the 24/7 impact of work on everyone's lives and suggests ways to create more realistic and positive approaches to our jobs. See especially Chapter 5, on creating your own work (even if you stay in your job).

Kay, Andrea. *Life's a Bitch and then You Change Careers: 9 Steps to Get Out of Your Funk & On to Your Future.* Stewart, Tabori & Chang, 2005. 272p. ISBN 1584794879.
Terrible title, but solid information on how to lay the groundwork for making a career change at any point in your life. Starts with self-assessment then moves on to researching options, getting any necessary training, networking in all the right places, doing informational interviews (to determine if the new option is really right for you), and making the change. Practical and actionable.

**Levoy, Gregg. *Callings: Finding and Following an Authentic Life.* Three Rivers Press, 1998. 352p. ISBN 0609803700.
Levoy wrote this book before the world's economies and workplaces turned upside down, so his central premise doesn't take into consideration that these days, many people are simply grateful to have *any* job, let alone one that resonates with a personal calling. Nevertheless, if and when you do contemplate making a job or career change, the author's encouragement and guidance will provide a unique spiritual framework for considering those changes.

Miller, Caroline Adams and Michael B. Frisch. *Creating Your Best Life: The Ultimate Life List Guide.* Sterling, 2011. 288p. ISBN 1402779984.
The scope of *Creating Your Best Life* is broader than just your career. However, the process of discovery (including checklists, questionnaires, and useful exercises) described in the book will help you apply similar concepts to your career exploration (while also providing valuable life insights).

Mitchell, Pamela. *The 10 Laws of Career Reinvention: Essential Survival Skills for Any Economy.* Prentice Hall, 2011. 272p. ISBN 0735204535.
Leading off with Seneca's quote, "Every new beginning comes from some other beginning's end," *Career Reinvention* addresses making *big*

career changes—like moving from one role in one industry into another, different role in an entirely different industry. Mitchell's key concept is that "the people who will thrive in this new world order are those who can repeatedly and successfully transform themselves: *Reinventors.*" She then supplies 10 key laws that will help you successfully make such a transition.

Moses, Barbara. *What Next? The Complete Guide to Taking Control of Your Working Life.* DK Adult, 2003. 336p. ISBN 0789493551.
The five chapters in this exercise-rich guide—"Know Yourself," "Find Your Perfect Path," "Find Great Work," "Overcome Career Challenges," "Boost Your Career Intelligence"—provide a mini-course in how to re-think your career. The Dorling-Kindersley book reflects the stunning graphics the publisher is known for; they're used here to provide an easily followed, visually engaging how-to guide.

**Nelson, John E. and Richard S. Bolles. *What Color is Your Parachute? For Retirement: Planning a Prosperous, Healthy, and Happy Future,* 2nd ed. Ten Speed Press, 2010. ISBN 078798356X.
If you like the *Parachute* approach, you'll find this related work offers the same upbeat, creative approach to structuring a retirement that reflects your goals and aspirations. The book's scope is much broader than career information only, but retirement work options are woven throughout.

**Richardson, Bradley. *Career Comeback: Eight Steps To Getting Back On Your Feet When You're Fired, Laid Off, Or Your Business Ventures Has Failed—And Finding More Job Satisfaction Than Ever Before.* Broadway, 2004. 336p. ISBN 0767915577.
Bradley, who has endured his own career setbacks but now works for the *Wall Street Journal,* focuses on the emotional as well as tactical aspects of recovering from a job loss, anticipated job loss, or business failure. Some of his steps include finding solid ground, finding out what happened, finding out what others need from you, and finding your support system. These all precede finding your new job, which is followed by Richardson's last step, finding your stride and getting back on track. An encouraging, supportive resource.

Online

**"Attention New Librarians and Career Changers: Identifying and Conveying Transferable Skills"
http://ala-apa.org/newsletter/2005/04/17/attention-new-librarians-and-career-changers/
An ALA-APA *Library Worklife* article by Julie Todaro, this is an excellent, very comprehensive overview of the concept of transferable skills as well as those most common/applicable to LIS professionals. Even though this was written years ago, Todaro's key points and concepts are still highly relevant.

**Career Q&A with the Library Career People
www.lisjobs.com/CareerQA_blog/
A monthly career question-and-answer session with two exceptionally knowledgeable LIS professionals, Tiffany Allen (Director of Library HR, University of North Carolina, Chapel Hill University Library) and Susanne Markgren (Digital Services Librarian, Purchase College, State University of New York). Terrific, down-to-earth advice; see also the wealth of archived responses browsable by category (e.g., burnout, getting started, job seeking).

**Encyclopedia of Associations
[online access varies]
Available as the associations component of the Gale Directory Library online resource, a database licensed by many public and academic libraries, or through the DIALOG and LexisNexis database services, or as a multivolume print directory. Entries include name, contact information, history and mission, membership numbers, estimated budget, presence of a library, publications, events, and type of organization for each association covered. An invaluable resource for researching potential association/nonprofit employer or professional groups of interest.

**Hoover's Online
www.hoovers.com/
Hoover's company and industry information is primarily available by subscription through academic and/or large public libraries, since its primary market is large companies doing market or competitive research. If available to you, Hoover's can be a good source for descriptions of key companies in a given industry, as well as for overviews, analysis, and forecasts for those industries themselves.

**"How Do I Get Back Into the Workforce after an Illness, and Being a Stay-At-Home Parent?"
www.lisjobs.com/CareerQA_blog/?p=58
Strategies for getting back into the LIS workforce after a personal time-out.

**"How Do I Get My Career Back on Track after Staying Home for Two Years to Raise a Family?"
www.lisjobs.com/CareerQA_blog/?p=32
More tactics for getting back into the workforce after time spent outside the profession.

**"How Do I Go about Re-Entering the Workforce (Part-Time) after Taking Five Years Off?"
www.lisjobs.com/CareerQA_blog/?p=56
The focus here is on what types of libraries or companies would be most receptive to a reentering professional, and whether they might be receptive to a part-time work proposal.

**Industries at a Glance
www.bls.gov/iag/
This Bureau of Labor Statistics (BLS) resource provides "a 'snapshot' of national data obtained from different BLS surveys and programs" as

well as additional industry detail, including state and regional data, when available. Searchable by alphabetical industry index or by industry numerical order (North American Industry Classification System/ NAICS). A good place to start gathering information about industries of potential interest for employment purposes.

**Job Loss: How to Cope

http://careerplanning.about.com/od/jobloss/a/job_loss.htm
By Dawn Rosenberg McKay, About.com guide for Career Planning, this is a collection of articles about all the things to think about if you get laid off or anticipate it happening. Lots of practical information about unemployment compensation, COBRA policies, etc.

**Job Seekers Guide

http://learn.linkedin.com/job-seekers/
LinkedIn's online tutorial for job seekers. Addresses how to complete your profile, seek connections, search the LinkedIn job listings, message your contacts, and build visibility for your expertise.

"A Librarian Without a Library: Staying Professionally Active While Unemployed"

http://liscareer.com/shontz_activeunemployment.htm
Author and LIS career specialist/librarian Priscilla K. Shontz, creator of the LISCareer.com site, talks about her own experience stepping out of the workforce and strategies for maintaining professional engagement and visibility.

LIScareer.com: Career Strategies for Librarians

http://liscareer.com
Hundreds of articles written by LIS practitioners on a wide range of career topics, including career exploration, job-searching, and work/life balance, many of which touch on topics related to career transitions.

"Mind the Gap: 8 Ways to Handle Gaps between Jobs"

http://blog.rezscore.com/2011/09/mind-the-gap-8-ways-to-handle-gaps-between-jobs
Transition points often result in periods of unemployment. If your plans involve moving from one employer to another with an interim phase of unemployment, this article will help you frame that interim period in a positive way.

"Making the Move"

www.wetfeet.com/advice-tools/job-search/making-the-move
The five factors you'll want to consider when evaluating a possible career relocation decision. By Wetfeet writer Liz Seasholtz.

"Making the Shift: Using Transferable Skills to Change Career Paths"

http://liscareer.com/taylor_transferable.htm
A terrific overview from LIS practitioner Deborah Taylor on using transferable skills (which she helps you identify) to create career path options.

"Move Along: Relocation for Librarians"
http://liscareer.com/gertz_relocation.htm
A thorough overview of relocation considerations where, instead of envisioning a sequence of linear steps, readers are encouraged to think about the job hunt "as a holistic and integrated process by which actions taken at any time will move you closer to your ultimate goal." From Christine Gertz, Library and Information Specialist at Career and Placement Services, University of Alberta.

"Moving Onward and Upward in the Wake of Adversity"
http://lisjobs.com/career_trends/?p=453
An upbeat but realistic take on dealing effectively with the often chaotic transitions of the contemporary workplace—including layoffs, promotions, transfers, relocations, budget cuts, and every other imaginable transition point. From Pam North, Library Manager of the Sherwood Public Library (Sherwood, OH), the advice in this article is wise and actionable.

**"New City, New Job: How to Conduct a Long-Distance Job Search"
www.quintcareers.com/long-distance_job-search.html
Eighteen smart strategies for laying the groundwork to land a job in your new locale, from Quintessential Career experts Katharine and Randall Hansen.

Placement Services and Recruitment Firms: Library Job Postings on the Internet
www.libraryjobpostings.org/placement.htm
Listing of U.S.-based agencies and offices of recruiting firms plus international (non-U.S.) agencies.

**Plunkett Research
www.plunkettresearch.com
Like the Hoover's information, Plunkett's data is now primarily available as an online database via academic or large public libraries. Although Plunkett does publish print industry guides, their cost is generally prohibitive for the average job-seeker, so best bet is to check your local libraries to see if any of them include Plunkett among their online resources. If so, check out their industry overviews, company write-ups, and trends and forecast information.

Relocating: The Beginning of a Great Adventure
http://liscareer.com/dickinson_relocation.htm
A thorough and practical guide for picking up your LIS career and relocating to a new location, written by Thad Dickinson, who's relocated numerous times and generously shares his lessons learned.

Retirement and Second Careers
www.cla.ca/Content/NavigationMenu/Resources/Feliciter/PastIssues/2009/Vol55No5/default.htm
A special issue of *Feliciter,* the Canadian Library Association's bimonthly professional publication, whose articles focus on what to consider

regarding retirement, career continuation options postretirement, and creative ways LIS professionals are approaching their retirement lives.

**Transferable Skills

www.lisjobs.com/CareerQA_blog/?s=transferable+skills

From Career Q&A with the Library Career People, this collection of questions and answers about using transferable skills to open up additional LIS career opportunities offers terrific insights in how to make the most of your own transferable skills.

**"Transferable Skills: Bringing Your Skills to a New Career"

http://careerplanning.about.com/od/careerchoicechan/a/transferable. htm

An About.com article written by Dawn Rosenberg McKay, this piece from her *Career Planning* guide covers what transferable skills are, how to identify your own transferable skills, and understanding how you can most effectively use and sell your transferable skills to a prospective employer. See also the many related articles on transferable skills linked from Ms. McKay's.

Wetfeet.com: Careers & Industries

www.wetfeet.com/careers-industries

With a mission of equipping "job seekers . . . with the advice, research, and inspiration you need to plan and achieve a successful career," WetFeet provides a wealth of articles, blog posts, insider tips, employee profiles, and industry overviews to help you accomplish that goal. WetFeet is in the business of selling career overviews (e.g., "Careers in Marketing"), but they are generally current and very reasonably priced. While Wetfeet doesn't offer a guide on the library profession, it does offer insights into non-LIS career paths that may have relevance to those considering a career change into a new industry or out of the LIS profession.

**"What is an Informational Interview and How it Can Help Your Career"

http://jobsearch.about.com/cs/infointerviews/a/infointerview.htm

An About.com article written by Alison Doyle, this article from her *Job Searching* guide discusses what an informational interview is, how to conduct one, what questions to ask, and follow-up etiquette. See also the related articles on informational interviews linked from Ms. Doyle's.

Appendix
ALA, CLA, and SLA Groups

ALA Groups

Committees
www.ala.org/ala/mgrps/committees/index.cfm
Like many large and complex organizations, ALA pursues its mandates through a number of committees and subcommittees, divisions, round tables, and several other types of groups. The purpose of each committee is defined when it is established. Current committees are: Council Committees, Division Committees, Joint Committees, Round Table Committees (for example, the New Members Round Table), and Special Committees.

Council
www.ala.org/ala/aboutala/governance/council/index.cfm
Governing body of the ALA, the Council is the group that "delegates to the divisions of the association authority to plan and carry out programs and activities with policy established by Council. Only personal members of ALA are allowed to serve on council.

Regional Chapters
www.ala.org/ala/mgrps/affiliates/chapters/state/stateregional.cfm
Reflecting its national mandate, ALA has affiliate relationships with state library associations (chapters) in all 50 states, the District of Columbia, Guam, the U.S. Virgin Islands, and regional library associations in the Mountain Plains, New England, Pacific Northwest, and Southeastern regions. According to ALA, the purpose of each regional chapter is to "promote general library service and librarianship within its geographic area, provide geographic representation to the Council of the American Library Association, and cooperate in the promotion of general and joint enterprises with the American Library Association and other library groups."

Student Chapters
www.ala.org/ala/mgrps/affiliates/chapters/student/studentchapters1.cfm
ALA student chapters are a great way for those in MLIS programs to practice their professional skills and start building their national professional network and visibility. Because, as ALA notes, "each Student Chapter has its own character and purpose," they offer a unique opportunity for individual impact.

Divisions

ALA's 11 divisions reflect broad areas of popular interest within the organization. Each division is based on either a type of library (for example, school libraries) or a type of function within libraries (e.g., technical services, leadership and management). The divisions have a strong education and best-practices role, as evidenced by their active publications programs (journals, books, newsletters, etc.); continuing education offerings for division members and non-members; awarding of grants and scholarships; and involvement with institutes and conferences.

American Association of School Librarians (AASL)
www.ala.org/ala/mgrps/divs/aasl/index.cfm
Association for Library Collections and Technical Services (ALCTS)
www.ala.org/ala/mgrps/divs/alcts/index.cfm
Association for Library Service to Children (ALSC)
www.ala.org/ala/mgrps/divs/alsc/index.cfm
Association of College & Research Libraries (ACRL)
www.ala.org/ala/mgrps/divs/acrl/index.cfm
Association of Library Trustees, Advocates, Friends & Foundations (ALTAFF)
www.ala.org/ala/mgrps/divs/altaff/index.cfm
Association of Specialized & Cooperative Library Agencies (ASCLA)
www.ala.org/ala/mgrps/divs/ascla/ascla.cfm
Library and Information Technology Association (LITA)
www.ala.org/ala/mgrps/divs/lita/index.cfm
Library Leadership & Management Association (LLAMA)
www.ala.org/ala/mgrps/divs/llama/index.cfm
Public Library Association (PLA)
www.ala.org/ala/mgrps/divs/pla/index.cfm
Reference & User Services Association (RUSA)
www.ala.org/ala/mgrps/divs/rusa/index.cfm
Young Adult Library Services Association (YALSA)
www.ala.org/ala/mgrps/divs/yalsa/yalsa.cfm

Round Tables

Round Tables have a more narrow focus and mandate than do the Divisions. Depending on the goals of the group, however, they may charge member dues, develop their own programs and publications, and affiliate with other related groups.

Ethnic and Multicultural Information Exchange (EMIERT)
    http://ala.org/ala/mgrps/rts/emiert/index.cfm
Exhibits (ERT)
    http://ala.org/ala/mgrps/rts/ert/index.cfm
Federal and Armed Forces Libraries (FAFLRT)
    http://ala.org/ala/mgrps/rts/faflrt/index.cfm
Games & Gaming
    http://connect.ala.org/gamert
Gay, Lesbian, Bisexual, Transgender (GLBTRT)
    http://ala.org/ala/mgrps/rts/glbtrt/index.cfm
Government Documents (GODORT)
    http://ala.org/ala/mgrps/rts/godort/index.cfm
Intellectual Freedom (IFRT)
    http://ala.org/ala/mgrps/rts/ifrt/index.cfm
International Relations (IRRT)
    http://ala.org/ala/mgrps/rts/irrt/index.cfm
Learning Round Table (LearnRT)—formerly CLENERT
    http://ala.org/ala/mgrps/rts/clenert/index.cfm
Library History (LHRT)
    http://ala.org/ala/mgrps/rts/lhrt/index.cfm
Library Instruction (LIRT)
    http://ala.org/ala/mgrps/rts/lirt/index.cfm
Library Research (LRRT)
    http://ala.org/ala/mgrps/rts/lrrt/index.cfm
Library Support Staff Interests (LSSIRT)
    http://ala.org/ala/mgrps/rts/lssirt/index.cfm
Map and Geography (MAGERT)
    http://ala.org/ala/mgrps/rts/magert/index.cfm
New Members (NMRT)
    http://ala.org/ala/mgrps/rts/nmrt/index.cfm
Retired Members Round Table (RMRT)
    http://ala.org/ala/mgrps/rts/rmrt/index.cfm
Social Responsibilities (SRRT)
    http://ala.org/ala/mgrps/rts/srrt/index.cfm
Staff Organizations (SORT)
    http://ala.org/ala/mgrps/rts/sort/index.cfm
Video (VRT)
    http://ala.org/ala/mgrps/rts/vrt/index.cfm

Membership Initiative Groups

ALA Membership Initiative Groups (MIGs) are established when a group of members identifies a common concern or interest about librarianship that falls outside the delegated responsibility of a single division, round table, or unit, and wishes to establish a short-term mechanism to address this concern or interest.

Games and Gaming in Libraries
    Staff liaison, Jenny Levine, jlevine@ala.org.
Information Commons
    Staff liaison, Mary W. Ghikas, mghikas@ala.org.
Libraries Fostering Civic Engagement
    Staff liaison, Mary W. Ghikas, mghikas@ala.org.
Virtual Communities and Libraries
    Staff liaison, Tina Coleman, ccoleman@ala.org.

Canadian Library Association

Networks

Established by and for CLA members, networks provide an area for focus on member-identified needs within the broad national library and information community. Per CLA, networks may be based on (among other topics) a type of library activity; a type of material; a type of library or library patron; a geographic location; a social, political or educational issue; or a category of worker in the information sector.

Accessible Collections and Services Network
    www.cla.ca/Content/NavigationMenu/CLAatWork/Networks1/Acces
    sible_Collections_and_Services_Network.pdf
Canadian Libraries Are Serving Children
    www.cla.ca/Content/NavigationMenu/CLAatWork/Networks1/CLASC_
    Network_ToR_final_sep11.pdf
Canadian Libraries Are Serving Youth
    http://clasy.wordpress.com/
CLA Ottawa
    www.cla.ca/Content/NavigationMenu/CLAatWork/Networks1/CLA_
    Ottawa_Network_ToR_approved_27jun11.pdf
Community-Led Library Service
    www.cla.ca/Content/NavigationMenu/CLAatWork/Networks1/CLLSN_
    ToR_final_aug11.pdf
Evidence-Based Library and Information Practice
    www.cla.ca/Content/NavigationMenu/CLAatWork/Networks1/EBLIPN_
    TOR_final_sep11.pdf
Government Information
    www.cla.ca/Content/NavigationMenu/CLAatWork/Networks1/Govern
    ment_Information_Network_proposal.pdf
Government Library and Information Management Professionals
    www.cla.ca/Content/NavigationMenu/CLAatWork/Networks1/GLIMP_
    Network_ToR_final_aug11.pdf
Human Resources
    www.cla.ca/Content/NavigationMenu/CLAatWork/Networks1/HRN_
    ToR_final_sep11.pdf

Information Services for Business
    www.cla.ca/Content/NavigationMenu/CLAatWork/Networks1/Infor
    mation_Services_for_Business_Network_ToR_approved_27jun11.
    pdf
Library History
    www.cla.ca/Content/NavigationMenu/CLAatWork/Networks1/LHN_
    ToR_final_sep11.pdf
Library Technicians and Assistants
    www.cla.ca/Content/NavigationMenu/CLAatWork/Networks1/Library_
    Technicians_and_Assistants_Network_ToR_approved_27jun11.pdf
Moderators
    www.cla.ca/Content/NavigationMenu/CLAatWork/Networks1/Modera
    tor_Network_ToR_final_sep11.pdf
Montreal
    www.cla.ca/Content/NavigationMenu/CLAatWork/Networks1/Mon
    treal_Network_ToR_final_sep11.pdf
Southern Alberta Information
    www.cla.ca/Content/NavigationMenu/CLAatWork/Networks1/South
    ern_Alberta_Information_Network_proposal.pdf
Technical Services
    www.cla.ca/Content/NavigationMenu/CLAatWork/Networks1/Techni
    cal_Services_Network_ToR_final_aug11.pdf
Toronto Special Libraries & Information Services
    www.cla.ca/Content/NavigationMenu/CLAatWork/Networks1/TSLIS_
    Network_ToR_final_sep11.pdf
Trustee
    www.cla.ca/Content/NavigationMenu/CLAatWork/Networks1/Trustee_
    Network_ToR_approved_27jun11.pdf
Voices for School Libraries
    www.cla.ca/Content/NavigationMenu/CLAatWork/Networks1/Voices_
    for_School_Libraries_Network_ToR_approved_27jun11.pdf

SLA Groups

Chapters

www.sla.org/content/community/units/chapters/index.cfm
The 56 regional SLA chapters "elect officers, issue bulletins or meeting announcements, hold three to nine program meetings during a year, and initiate special projects." Many of the regional chapters are very active, and offer a great way to build your professional network.

Divisions

www.sla.org/content/community/units/divs/index.cfm
SLA divisions represent a wide range of subject interests, fields, or types of information-handling techniques. Divisions elect their own officers and publish bulletins or newsletters, as well as conducting professional programs during ALA's annual conferences. Members choose one division to join at no charge as part of their ALA membership.

Academic
    http://wiki.sla.org/display/SLAAD/Home
Advertising & Marketing
    http://admarketing.sla.org/
Biomedical & Life Sciences (DBIO)
    http://www.sla.org/division/dbio/
Business and Finance
    http://bf.sla.org
Chemistry
    http://chemistry.sla.org
Competitive Intelligence
    http://www.sla.org/division/dci/cihome.htm
Education
    http://www.sla.org/division/ded/index.html
Engineering
    http://www.sla.org/division/deng/index.html
Environment & Resource Management
    http://wiki.sla.org/display/SLADERM
Food, Agriculture & Nutrition
    http://www.sla.org/division/dfan/
Government Information
    http://govinfo.sla.org/
Information Technology
    http://units.sla.org/division/dite/
Insurance & Employee Benefits
    http://www.sla.org/division/dieb/index.htm
Knowledge Management
    http://wiki.sla.org/display/SLAKM/
Leadership & Management
    http://lmd.sla.org
Legal
    http://units.sla.org/division/dleg
Military Librarians
    http://military.sla.org/
Museums, Arts, & Humanities
    http://mah.sla.org/
News
    http://www.ibiblio.org/slanews/
Petroleum & Energy Resources
    http://sites.google.com/site/sladper/Home
Pharmaceutical & Health Technology
    http://www.sla.org/division/dpht/
Physics—Astronomy—Mathematics
    http://pam.sla.org
Science—Technology
    http://scitech.sla.org
Social Science
    http://socialscience.sla.org

Solo Librarians
    http://solo.sla.org
Taxonomy
    http://wiki.sla.org/display/SLATAX
Transportation
    http://wiki.sla.org/display/SLATAX

Caucuses

The handful of SLA caucuses enable members who share a common interest not covered by any other SLA chapter, division, or committee to connect, share information, and learn from each other.

Architecture, Building Engineering, Construction & Design
    http://units.sla.org/caucus/kabc/index.html
Archival & Preservation
    http://www.sla.org/caucus/kapc/
Association Information Services
    No website; list address: SLA-KAIS@lists.sla.org
Baseball
    http://baseball.sla.org/
Encore—Retired Members
    http://encore.sla.org/
Gay & Lesbian Issues
    http://www.sla.org/caucus/kglic/
Information Futurists
    http://www.sla.org/caucus/kinf/
International Information Exchange
    http://www.sla.org/caucus/kiie/
Natural History
    http://www.lib.washington.edu/sla/
User Experience
    SLA-KUX@sla.lyris.net

Index

About the Author

G. KIM DORITY is the founder and president of Dority & Associates, an information consulting and content development company. She has led multiple large-scale information projects for clients while also teaching a course in alternative LIS career paths for the University of Denver's MLIS program. She writes and presents extensively on LIS career topics and authors the Infonista.com blog. Her previous publications include *Rethinking Information Work: A Career Guide for Librarians and Other Information Professionals* (Libraries Unlimited, 2006).